T0214505

# Communications in Computer and Information Science 936

*Commenced Publication in 2007*
Founding and Former Series Editors:
Phoebe Chen, Alfredo Cuzzocrea, Xiaoyong Du, Orhun Kara, Ting Liu,
Dominik Ślęzak, and Xiaokang Yang

## Editorial Board

More information about this series at http://www.springer.com/series/7899

Lemonia Ragia · Robert Laurini
Jorge Gustavo Rocha (Eds.)

# Geographical Information Systems Theory, Applications and Management

Third International Conference, GISTAM 2017
Porto, Portugal, April 27–28, 2017
Revised Selected Papers

 Springer

*Editors*
Lemonia Ragia
Technical University of Crete
Marousi, Athens, Greece

Robert Laurini
Knowledge Systems Institute
Skokie, IL, USA

Jorge Gustavo Rocha
Departamento de Informática
Universidade do Minho
Braga, Portugal

ISSN 1865-0929 ISSN 1865-0937 (electronic)
Communications in Computer and Information Science
ISBN 978-3-030-06009-1 ISBN 978-3-030-06010-7 (eBook)
https://doi.org/10.1007/978-3-030-06010-7

Library of Congress Control Number: 2018964271

This Springer imprint is published by the registered company Springer Nature Switzerland AG
The registered company address is: Gewerbestrasse 11, 6330 Cham, Switzerland

# Preface

The present book includes extended and revised versions of a set of selected papers from the Third International Conference on Geographical Information Systems Theory, Applications and Management (GISTAM 2017), held in Porto, Portugal, during April 27–28.

GISTAM 2017 received 70 paper submissions from 34 countries, of which 24% were included in this book. The papers were selected by the event chairs and their selection is based on a number of criteria that include the classifications and comments provided by the Program Committee members, the session chairs' assessment, and also the program chairs' global view of all papers included in the technical program. The authors of selected papers were then invited to submit a revised and extended version of their papers having at least 30% innovative material.

The International Conference on Geographical Information Systems Theory, Applications and Management aims at creating a meeting point of researchers and practitioners to address new challenges in geo-spatial data sensing, observation, representation, processing, visualization, sharing and managing, in all aspects concerning both information communication and technologies (ICT) as well as management information systems and knowledge-based systems. The conference welcomes original papers of either practical or theoretical nature, presenting research or applications, of specialized or interdisciplinary nature, addressing any aspect of geographic information systems and technologies.

The papers selected to be included in this book contribute to the understanding of relevant trends of current research on geographical information systems theory, applications, and management, including: urban and regional planning, water information systems, geospatial information and technologies, spatio-temporal database management, decision support systems, energy information systems, and GPS and location detection.

We would like to thank all the authors for their contributions and also the reviewers who helped ensure the quality of this publication.

April 2017

Lemonia Ragia
Robert Laurini
Jorge Gustavo Rocha

# Organization

## Conference Chair

Lemonia Ragia — Technical University of Crete, Greece

## Program Chair

Jorge Gustavo Rocha — University of Minho, Portugal

## Honorary Chair

Robert Laurinia — Knowledge Systems Institute, USA

## Program Committee

| | |
|---|---|
| Pedro Arnau | Universitat Politècnica de Catalunya, Spain |
| Jan Blachowski | Wroclaw University of Science and Technology, Poland |
| Arnold K. Bregt | Wageningen University and Research Centre, The Netherlands |
| Alexander Brenning | Friedrich Schiller University, Germany |
| Manuel Campagnolo | Instituto Superior de Agronomia, Portugal |
| Jocelyn Chanussot | Grenoble Institute of Technology Institut Polytechnique de Grenoble, France |
| Filiberto Chiabrando | Politecnico di Torino- DIATI, Italy |
| Keith Clarke | University of California, Santa Barbara, USA |
| Antonio Corral | University of Almeria, Spain |
| Joep Crompvoets | KU Leuven, Belgium |
| Paolo Dabove | Politecnico di Torino, Italy |
| Anastasios Doulamis | National Technical University of Athens, Greece |
| Arianna D'Ulizia | IRPPS - CNR, Italy |
| Ana Paula Falcão | Instituto Superior Técnico, Portugal |
| Ana Fonseca | Laboratório Nacional de Engenharia Civil, Portugal |
| Cidália Maria Parreira da Costa Fonte | Coimbra University, Portugal |
| Jinzhu Gao | University of the Pacific, USA |
| Lianru Gao | Chinese Academy of Sciences, China |
| Andrea Garzelli | University of Siena, Italy |
| Gilles Gesquière | Liris, France |
| Luis Gomez-Chova | Universitat de València, Spain |
| Cédric Grueau | Polytechnic Institute of Setúbal/IPS, Portugal |
| Hans W. Guesgen | Massey University, New Zealand |
| Bob Haining | University of Cambridge, UK |

| | |
|---|---|
| Stephen Hirtle | University of Pittsburgh, USA |
| Wen-Chen Hu | University of North Dakota, USA |
| Haosheng Huang | University of Zurich, Switzerland |
| Simon Jirka | 52 North, Germany |
| Wolfgang Kainz | University of Vienna, Austria |
| Harry D. Kambezidis | National Observatory of Athens, Greece |
| Andreas Koch | University of Salzburg, Austria |
| Barbara Koch | University of Freiburg, Germany |
| Artur Krawczyk | AGH University of Science and Technology, Poland |
| Marc van Kreveld | Utrecht University, The Netherlands |
| Roberto Lattuada | myHealthbox, Italy |
| Robert Laurini | Knowledge Systems Institute, USA |
| Songnian Li | Ryerson University, Canada |
| Tianhong Li | Peking University, China |
| Christophe Lienert | Canton of Aargau, Department of Construction, Traffic and Environment, Switzerland |
| Vladimir V. Lukin | Kharkov Aviation Institute, Ukraine |
| Yannis Manolopoulos | Aristotle University, Greece |
| Teresa Sá Marques | Universidade de Porto, Portugal |
| Gavin McArdle | University College Dublin, Ireland |
| Janet Mersey | University of Guelph, Canada |
| Anand Nayyar | KCL Institute of Management and Technology, India |
| Simonetta Paloscia | IFAC, National Research Council, Italy |
| Dimos N. Pantazis | TEI of Athens, Greece |
| Nikos Pelekis | University of Piraeus, Greece |
| Marco Piras | Politecnico di Torino, Italy |
| Dimitris Potoglou | Cardiff University, UK |
| Lemonia Ragia | Technical University of Crete, Greece |
| Guoyu Ren | National Climate Center, China |
| Armanda Rodrigues | Faculdade de Ciências e Tecnologia, Universidade Nova de Lisboa, Portugal |
| Markus Schneider | University of Florida, USA |
| Sylvie Servigne | INSA Lyon, France |
| Yosio Edemir Shimabukuro | Instituto Nacional de Pesquisas Espaciais, Brazil |
| Francesco Soldovieri | Consiglio Nazionale delle Ricerche, Italy |
| Uwe Stilla | Technische Universität München, Germany |
| Rui Sun | Beijing Normal University, China |
| José António Tenedório | Universidade NOVA de Lisboa/CICS.NOVA, Portugal |
| Ana Cláudia Moreira Teodoro | Oporto University, Portugal |
| Fabio Giulio Tonolo | ITHACA - Information Technology for Humanitarian Assistance, Cooperation and Action, Politecnico di Torino, Italy |
| Miguel Torres-Ruiz | Instituto Politécnico Nacional, Mexico City, Mexico |
| Goce Trajcevski | Northwestern University, USA |

| Theodoros Tzouramanis | University of the Aegean, Greece |
| Michael Vassilakopoulos | University of Thessaly, Greece |
| Jan Oliver Wallgrün | The Pennsylvania State University, USA |
| Jean-Pierre Pierre Wigneron | Institut National de la Recherche Agronomique INRA, France |
| May Yuan | University of Texas at Dallas, USA |

## Invited Speakers

| George Vosselman | University of Twente, The Netherlands |
| Jorge Miguel Alberto de Miranda | University of Lisbon, Portugal |
| Yannis Ioannidis | Athena Research and Innovation Center and University of Athens, Greece |

# Contents

# GIS Systems on the Pipelines Thermographic Aerial Inspection

Sergiy Sadovnychiy[(✉)], Edgar A. Canul, Juan M. López,
Andriy Sadovnychyy, and Marco A. Hernandez

Instituto Mexicano Del Petróleo, Ciudad de México 07730, Mexico
ssadovny@imp.mx

**Abstract.** This article is about the implementation of Geographical Information System (GIS) with Thermographic technologies for oil and gas pipelines aerial inspection. Since every pipeline under pressure is prone to present leaks, several methods have been investigated and implemented for leakage detection among them, thermographic methods play an outstanding role. Since every leak in the pipeline modifies its temperature environment, whatever the state (solid, liquid or gas), it is feasible to detect this change through a video infrared camera. This is the core principle for thermographic leakage detection however, when applied to aerial surveillance several issues such as: interpretation of the IR scenes, accuracy on tracking the route of the pipeline and locating events, accurate quantitative thermal measurement or estimation, among others; make difficult the detection process. In this work it is presented a system to cope with the mentioned problems. Equipment, software and some inspection results using this system are presented.

**Keywords:** GIS · GPS · Oil · Gas · Pipeline · Inspection · Infrared
Thermal · Analysis

## 1  Introduction

The pipeline network is subjected to deterioration caused by many factors among the most prominent are physical phenomena and human activities. Therefore, reliable inspection is primordial to detect damage yielding in leaks on the pipeline. With this on- time information it is possible to take actions to fix these findings before they scale up to important risks for the facilities and environment.

Distributing the product as liquid petroleum, gas or basic petrochemicals is maybe one of the most important aspects in the petroleum industry, as such, if no suitable methods are applied in the leak detection over pipelines there could be small and imperceptible damages such as inner corrosion, bumps to the facilities caused by thirds, interference from natural environment, etc., which in sum will constitute a very high risk in which is matter of time to bring disastrous consequences. Environment pollution is the most important damage since contamination to water bodies and mantles, damage to flora and fauna, air quality disturbance among others; are not always reversible.

The customary procedures for inspection show deficiencies and inconveniences mainly for pedestrian inspection since it is inaccurate, slow and dangerous for the

© Springer Nature Switzerland AG 2019
L. Ragia et al. (Eds.): GISTAM 2017, CCIS 936, pp. 1–18, 2019.
https://doi.org/10.1007/978-3-030-06010-7_1

person who performs the inspection. Even when aerial inspection is executed there are still drawbacks where the accuracy in follow the path and leak valuation are the fundamental fails.

In the last years technologies such geographical information systems, remote detection, thermography, image processing and the like have been consolidated and now constitute a great resource to increase accuracy, reliance, speed and coverage in the incidents detection.

With the aid of these technologies, we have developed methods based on the anomaly's thermal trace such as excavations, machinery function, landslides, leakage, buildings and exposed pipelines, among others. The use of a thermal spectra IR camera and a global positioning device (GPS) greatly improves the accuracy on localizing the failure and evaluating its seriousness. The convergence of these technologies have resulted in an integral system with sophisticated techniques and methods yet easy to implement for potential danger, leakage and illegal tapping detection on transport pipelines.

The system presented in this work is able to detect surface temperature with resolution close to or better than $0.1°K$. It can provide the following data: thermal mapping areas of the pipeline to be measured, control of land texture above the pipeline, gas leakage in pipelines, estimation of soil erosion related with the subsurface process and heat leakage information from subsurface layer.

## 2  System Description

The overall system is constituted of four basic modules: the in-office equipment for analysis, evaluation and report generation, the airborne equipment of data registration and pre-processing, the airborne equipment for pipeline tracking and the operator airborne equipment for recording the pipeline path in infrared and video range. The former is an application software implemented on a workstation used to process the incoming data from the rest of the modules. A scheme of the processing system is presented in Fig. 1. It can be seen that the Global Positioning System capabilities are present in every part of the processing system, only thermal analysis module disregards this technology. It has been a great complement to improve precision and quality of the inspection and detection methods.

### 2.1  Recording Video Equipment

It was designed a specific-purpose mechanical frame in order to mount the two cameras, one for the infrared (IR) and the other one for the high definition (HD) recordings. It's of fundamental importance the orientation and zoom settings of both cameras in order to make their scenes to match. Additionally a gyroscope is installed in the bottom of the frame to achieve a better stability control on the position when recording. It is also connected a laptop for storing the recording of the IR camera and GPS data for latter processing. Figure 2 shows the details of this frame.

For thermal anomalies detection caused by gas or oil leakages, a foundational component of the system is an infrared camera [1], its use is based on three basic physical principles.

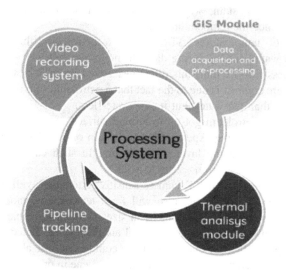

**Fig. 1.** System architecture for pipeline processing software.

**Fig. 2.** Airborne recording equipment.

For the first principle, the supposed theory that according to Joule-Thomson effect, the liquid that escapes out of a pressured pipe through a crack reaches a gas phase and cools the environment temperature (surface over the pipeline) generating a thermal contrast around the pipe segment which can be sensed by the IR equipment. For gas pipes similar arguments follows.

For second principle, an IR camera can produce images at two bands: the absorption and ethane bands, this latter almost transparent.

For the third principle the foundation is the phenomenon of thermal contrast of superficial petroleum stains which leaked from the pipeline. Since the petroleum temperature in the pipeline is usually near to environment ground temperature. Thus, the superficial temperature of leaked petroleum on ground or water surface is determined by the heat exchange with its environment. Factors such as geometrical parameters of petroleum stain, wind, intensity of vaporization and solar radiation among others influence the temperature change.

A difference of temperatures $\Delta T$ between a petroleum film (film thickness $h < 0.1$ mm) and water surface during daylight hours can get to $0 \div 5°K$. For thick films (film thickness $h > 0.1$ mm) this difference grows up to $3 \div 8°K$, as shown in [2]. This temperature contrast is due to the fact that a petroleum film is heated up by the Sun radiation more than the water, but it evaporates less.

In the case where petroleum got up to ground surface, the temperature difference would be a little bit less at the expense of vaporization of petroleum and therefore, at the expense of cooling the top layer of petroleum. In such case, the difference of temperatures will be greater (from $-2$ up to $+7°K$).

As already mentioned the $0.1°K$ camera sensitivity together with the three above mentioned principles of leak appearance will form temperature anomalies with the sufficient temperature contrast and geometrical sizes suitable for camera detection.

Now, since not always the detected thermal anomalies are related to leakages but also caused atmospheric thermal anomalies, there could exist false alarms, so that a HD camera is employed for comparison with the infrared scene in order to count with more information over a specific anomaly.

## 2.2    Data Acquisition

The position data from the system is gotten from a GPS receiver. With equipment the operator can identify the site of some finding with more accuracy. The data is, thus, stored on hard disk on a computer (see Fig. 2).

The leakage detection method presented in this chapter relies on the analysis of thermal anomalies and comparison of IR and HD video images together with coordinate determination. Detection and location of pipeline leaks is possible mainly thanks to the pre-processing of the mentioned data.

In the time when inspection flight is being performed, a GPS device acquires the global position of the system simultaneously. Coordinates, timestamp and speed are stored in the National Marine Electronics Association (NMEA 0183) format at the basis of 2 s sampling to the on-board computer for later analysis.

The GPS device computes and updates its position using up to 12 satellites at rate of 1 s. The position accuracy is less than 15 m and velocity accuracy less than 0.05 m/s. The parameters to establish the communication interface are the NMEA data format and the baud rate is automatically set to 4800, since it cannot be changed in the device the data is acquired every 2 s.

## 2.3   Pipeline Tracking

It's common that, during the flight, the pilot or the personnel in charge are not completely certain about the pipeline path. Sometimes changes in the terrain or simply the guide person doesn't precisely remember the pipe trajectory. Under such circumstances the tracking flight can be repetitive and erratic trying to locate the exact path, as consequence the analysis and processing turns difficult. To cope with this problem and to improve accuracy on pipeline tracking, a flight planner and pipeline tracker have been developed. The former module counts with a GPS and an on-board computer to store the position data and to provide it to an own-design software application which with the help of a geographical information system application displays the correct position respect to a preloaded pipeline path. This allows to get an almost perfect pipeline tracking because reference trajectory is completely known, it is possible now to dispense the exact knowledge of the path by the guide person. If the airship gets too far from the pipeline path it will raise an alarm on the software application to inform such condition. It can be specified a maximum distance as a tolerance around the pipeline. Figure 3 present two different pipeline paths tracking as a comparison between the tracking with and without the use of the tracking module. An average distance of 150 m was stipulated for the case with module tracking.

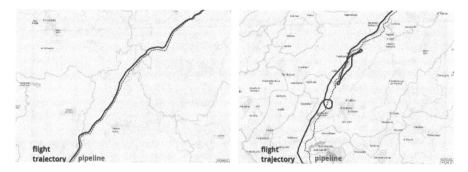

**Fig. 3.**   Flight (left) with pipeline tracking and (right) without pipeline tracking.

The flight-planning module is also based on GIS and is used to prepare the flight plan for the inspection. This module is employed to load and render the pipeline path, perform geodesic length measurements, estimate the time or velocity for the flight, build the flight route, get the coordinates elevation over the sea level to construct a topographic profile of the pipe and establish a proper height control of the airship when inspection is being performed. Complementary tools such as batch and individual coordinate conversion between NMEA format and WGS84 and Web Mercator geographic references are also provided. When there are repeated points or the geographic sequence is not correct there are optimization algorithms for the pipeline coordinates. Compatibility with third application software is possible with the data generation in formats such as comma separated values (*csv*), key-hole mark-up language (*kml*), Esri Shape (*shp*) and GPS exchange format (*gpx*) is possible. In Fig. 4 it is presented the graphical user interface of this module.

## 2.4    Processing System

At the conclusion of the inspection flight it's necessary to analyze the collected information in order to temperature anomalies, conditions which present possible damage, leakage and illegal tapping on the pipeline.

A processing software application was designed for the determination of potential leaks on the inspected pipeline. The comparison of IR and HD terrain video images around the same instant is the basis of the inspection task. Synchronization between the video screenshots and GPS coordinates is a key function that allows the exact location knowledge so that it can be showed on the map viewer.

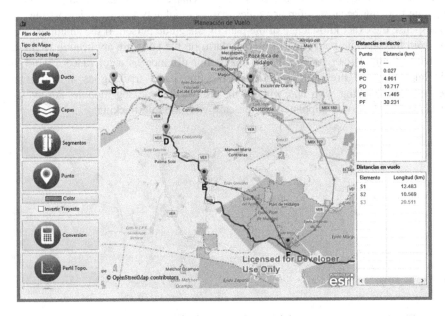

**Fig. 4.**  Flight planning module.

Java 8 was the language of program development in conjunction with the following APIs for the core functions:

- *vlcj* [3] and *ffmpeg* [4] used in video recordings visualization and control, snapshots extraction, segments extraction, filtering implementation.
- *ArcGis* [5] SDK for Java development was used for the geographical information system (GIS) implementation. Visualization, distance estimation and mark annotations on the pipeline and flight paths are the most important features.
- *JAK* [8] and *GeoKarambola* [9] for *gpx* and *kml* files compatibility.
- *Google Elevation* [6] for getting terrain elevation for each coordinate of the pipeline trace.
- *JasperReports* [11] for report implementation.

- *Eclipse SWT* [7] for native operating system compatibility of the graphical user interface.
- *OpenCV* [10] for the processing images and temperature estimation algorithms.

Figure 5 presents the design of the software application.

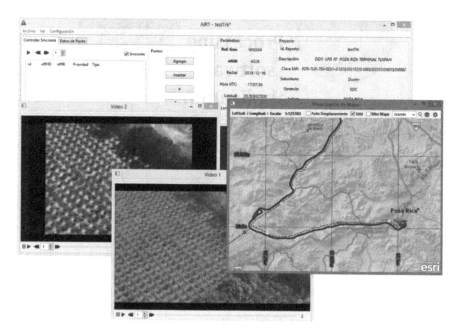

**Fig. 5.** Thermal analysis application software.

Five core functional modules (see Fig. 6) composes the processing software application. The pre-processing is in charge of preparing the data [2] for synchronization purposes.

**Synchronization.** The timestamp and route coordinates are bound to the simultaneous video films reproduction so that the geographic positions for each specific instant on the video recordings is available. This mechanism allows the scene identification over the map viewer every second. The GPS coordinates are recorded in the waypoint format which is practically supported by all program variations of GPS. To check the consistency of the coordinates on the basis of 1 s sampling rate, the pre-processing module is employed.

For each GPS sampled and interpolated point there is an elevation information request to Google's servers through its Google Elevation API. The retrieved elevation is in meters with reference on the sea level. The resulting dataset from the pre-processing module is presented in comma separated values.

Since video scenes and map visualization have to match for the same instant the synchronization is implemented based on HD video reproduction such that position

**Fig. 6.** Processing application core modules.

rendering in map visualization is adjusted through data navigation collected from GPS. IR video is adjusted with HD video based on the elapsed time. If a phase lag occur it is possible to adjust IR video manual and independently to match with HD video specific scene. Figure 7 shows a scheme of the synchronization system.

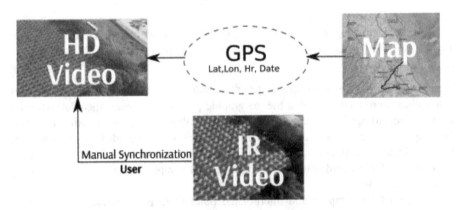

**Fig. 7.** HD video scene is the reference for the synchronization system.

Video control module. It deals mainly with the task of simultaneous playing of HD and IR video recordings. The video API can directly handle the reproduction of the common .mp4 and .mts video formats so that compression is not necessary. The storage demand can constrained to 32 GB.

The operator performs the comparison of the images through visual observation. When he/she detects some anomaly a mechanism for fixing the coordinates of this object in the report is available. The common functions of a video player are accessible for work: rewind - forwards, pause, full screen output etc. When the image quality is poor it's possible to use video filters adjustment in both videos reproduction (Fig. 8).

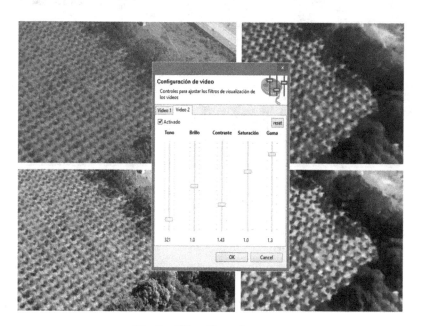

**Fig. 8.** Video filter adjustment.

**GIS Module.** This module is ubiquitous since it is present almost in all the system although it is evident only through the map viewer. The pipeline and flight trajectories vector layers are loaded, for the corresponding visualization, through this module. Timestamp and coordinates is input data from the pre-processing for every second, thus, videos reproduction is linked to the map viewer to update the marker position according points and load several detail layers which can be prepared with QGIS or ArcGIS. *Kml* files for Google Earth generation is also possible. There are implemented algorithms for pipelines length estimation and offsets compensation, in order to match the absolute distance of a reported point with the nominal distances in the pipes. In Fig. 9 one can see the map viewer which is the principal element using this module.

ArcGIS API, by default, employs by default a Projected Coordinate System (PCS) named Web Mercator Auxiliary Sphere also known by its well-known ID 3857 or EPSG-3857. Unfortunately the coordinates derived from a GPS device are returned in a Geographic Coordinate System (GCS) named WGS84 with well-known ID 4326

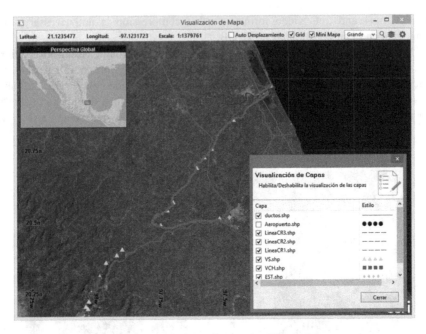

**Fig. 9.** Graphical interface to the GIS module.

or EPSG-4326 so that for visualization purposes a conversion must be done. It is performed through Eqs. (1)–(4)

$$a = lat * 0.017453292519943295 \tag{1}$$

$$b = lon * 0.017453292519943295 \tag{2}$$

$$x = 6378137b \tag{3}$$

$$y = 3189068.5 * \ln\left((1 + \sin a)/(1 - \sin a)\right) \tag{4}$$

In some cases an additional conversion (UTM to WGS84) is required. The conversion is simple yet tedious so that the details are omitted. The interested reader can review [12–14].

## 2.5   Temperature Estimation

The IR camera used in this system can provide radiometric information just for photos but not on video recording therefore, thermal measurements are not available. Under this scenario temperature estimation is needed in order to know the temperature of a pixel in the image. This section presents the algorithm implementation details that complement the section presented in [15].

The only image information available for the system are RGB channels for each pixel in the image and temperature limits showed in the lateral color scale, so that the above estimation has to be done through linear interpolation among the pixel values and temperature limits. When the color palette, converted to grayscale, is linear grayscale; such as Iron palette (a very common palette in the thermographic area), the estimation is quite easy (see Fig. 10).

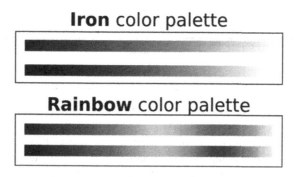

**Fig. 10.** Employed color palettes and their corresponding grayscale palettes. (Color figure online)

In this case the color image is converted into a grayscale image resulting in an image where each pixel has just one value which together with temperature limits it is possible to estimate a temperature value for each pixel value. There are several conversion algorithms if a more precise control channel ponderation is required [16]. To perform the conversion from gray value to temperature a simple linear equation is employed

$$t = \Delta m \left( p - p_{min} \right) + t_{min} \tag{5}$$

where $t$ is the estimated temperature, $p$ is the gray value at the selected pixel, $\Delta m$ is the slope of the line which passes through points $(p_{min}, t_{min})$, $(p_{max}, t_{max})$, which in turn are the upper and lower limit values of temperature and gray values in the image.

Observing the Rainbow palette it's a fact that no all color palettes have a linear equivalent grayscale (Fig. 12) when converted. In this case it's not possible to apply a direct linear interpolation estimation.

Two approaches could be used to get a temperature estimation under this scenario. One consists on using a channel of the color palette as a linear gray scale equivalent. As can be seen in Fig. 11 only red channel keeps a linear behavior along the temperature range.

But the above linearity is concentrated in the middle of the range leaving the extremes constants. This is not a good alternative for temperature estimation due to the non-homogeneous nature. Also, the data on the other channels is discarded losing information that count when the direct mapping[1] is performed.

---

[1] The procedure or function used to transform the measured temperature, in the recording phase, into color.

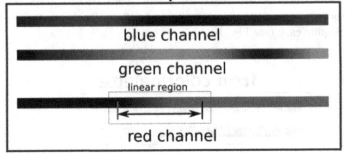

**Fig. 11.** Linearity on individual channels.

Another approach, which has been used in this work, takes into account all channels (r, g and b pixel components) according to the following procedure.

Firstly, the *rainbow* color palette has to be extracted from an image radiometric meta-data in order to have the exact color levels that constitute it. There are 118 color levels (r, g, b, combinations) which define a trajectory on the $RGB \subset \mathbb{R}^3$ color space as shown in Fig. 12.

The temperature range must be distributed along this path with the temperature limits in the extremes. Homogeneous distribution is established with constant increments of temperatures defined as

$$\Delta t = \frac{t_{max} - t_{min}}{118} \tag{6}$$

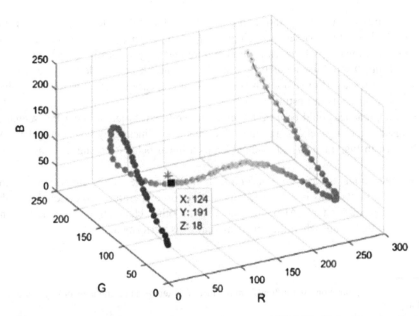

**Fig. 12.** Rainbow palette trajectory on the color space RGB [15]. (Color Figure online)

Every selected image pixel $p_s$, on ideal case, will match with a point $p_i$ over this trajectory (a rainbow palette color level) and the length over this path will be the temperature assigned to it. In the real case it is not so since the image is a screenshot from a coded video, without radiometric meta-data, also the direct mapping could have generated intermediate color levels which doesn't match with a point in the trajectory on Fig. 12.

Then, for any point on $RGB \subset \mathbb{R}^3$ color space not contained in the path, there always exists a unique point in the path determined by the minimum Euclidean distance such that:

$$p_i = \{p_t : min_t \|p_s - p_t\|\} \tag{7}$$

where $p_t$ is any point on the rainbow color level set which define the path in Fig. 15. Equation (7) tells that no matter the point in the IR image, it can always be approximated by some point in the rainbow palette color level set, Fig. 13 illustrate this principle. Of course, it is expected that the selected point $p_s$ be sufficiently near (approximated to the path showed in Fig. 12).

But it is not as simple as just picking such point because in practice almost none image pixel matches exactly with an element on this set, it would be to reduce an infinity amount of possible points into just 118 so that we proceed as follows.

Once $p_i$ has been identified through Eq. (7) it's necessary to estimate the temperature by mean of linear interpolation which cannot be done in a joint manner, it must be done over each independent channel. But arise some situations where even independent channel linear interpolation is not easy. For example, consider Table 1 which explicitly shows the point channel values in Fig. 13. The selected point $p_s = (125, 200, 20)$

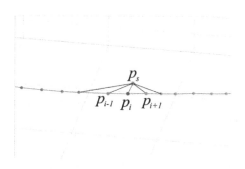

**Fig. 13.** Minimum Euclidean distance for selecting a point in the color levels set. (Color Figure online)

**Table 1.** Selected and adjacent points.

| ID | Number | Red | Green | Blue | Temperature |
|----|--------|-----|-------|------|-------------|
|  | 48 | 97 | 183 | 31 | 38.734184 |
| $p_{i-1}$ | 49 | 113 | 188 | 22 | 39.105125 |
| $p_i$ | 50 | 124 | 191 | 18 | 39.476067 |
| $p_{i+1}$ | 51 | 134 | 195 | 13 | 39.847008 |
|  | 52 | 142 | 198 | 8 | 40.21795 |

As can be seen the red value lies in the upper interval $(p_i, pi_{+1})$, the green value is not present in any interval at all and the blue value lies in de lower interval $(p_{i-1}, p_i)$. According to the previous example three different scenarios could arise for each independent channel interpolation. To cope with these cases it is used an algorithm displayed in Fig. 14.

---

***Algorithm***. RGB channels interpolation for temperature estimation.

Be $p=(r,g,b)$ any point in RGB color space with its corresponding assigned temperatur $T$

---

1. Determine $(p_i)$ according to equation (7).

2. **For each** selected point component $p_s=(r_s,g_s,b_s)$ verify the interval in which lies the channel value. Consider the case of the $r_s$ component.

   a) **If** $r_s$ lies on previous/next interval $(r_{i-1}, r_i)/(r_i, r_{i+1})$ temperature estimation is done with $T_{i-1},T_i/ T_i, T_{i+1}$

   b) **If** $r_s$ matches with $r_{i-1}, r_i$ or $r_{i+1}$ the estimated temperature will be the corresponding temperature $T_{i-1}$, $T_i$ or $T_{i+1}$.

   c) **Otherwise** discard $r_s$ without generating estimated temperature

3. Estimated temperature $T_s$ for $p_s$ will be the arithmetic average of estimated temperatures gotten son step 2 (3 an most, one per channel).

---

**Fig. 14.** Algorithm for temperature estimation.

**Remarks**

1. In the case that no partial estimated temperature is generated at step 2 the final estimated temperature $T_s$ will be that of $p_i$, that is $T_i$

2. The lesser the temperature range $(t_{max} - t_{min})$ is the greater the estimation precision will be.

3. An alternative to increase the precision of the estimation is to add more points (color levels) to the rainbow palette through simple linear 3D interpolation among the adjacent pairs already present in the set.

4. Since radiometric meta-data is unavailable, there is no way to compare/validate the estimated temperature with the real measured temperature. Don't forget that this estimation relies only in the reported temperature limits and rainbow color palette data.

5. Finally, this algorithm can be applied with any color palette provided that temperature limits are known, even if it is one with a linear grayscale equivalent such as iron color palette. Therefore it is suitable when image conversion is to be avoided

In Fig. 15 the graphical interface of the above estimation tool is shown. Temperature upper and lower bounds are needed to execute the estimation algorithm therefore it's vital that these parameters are displayed when recording.

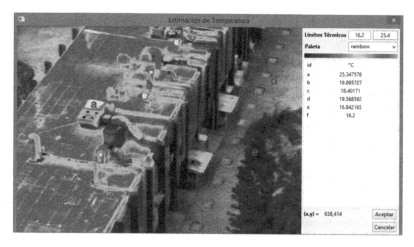

**Fig. 15.** Temperature estimation of an IR image.

**Heat Map Implementation.** Is a tridimensional generated surface obtained from an IR image where the height coordinate represents the estimated temperature estimated for each pixel [17]. This visualization tool is useful when representing the IR video snapshot for having a better visualization. This function permits to count with a 3D visual representation which can be zoomed, translated and rotated in a manner such that the user can have several perspectives thus facilitating detection points which otherwise couldn't be appreciated [15]. In Fig. 16 it is shown an IR screenshot and its corresponding heat map respectively.

**Fig. 16.** (Left) screenshot of a thermal record specific instant. (Right) heat map of the screenshot.

It can be used any color palette, standard and even user-defined color palette (see Fig. 16). In the case of the above example, Tessellation/Surface is the display mode but it can be any, wire framed or scatter points for example. This displaying function can be performed with several tools: Matlab, OpenGL and Point Cloud Data are some examples.

### 2.6   Reporting

There exist a considerable amount of information for each reported find (nature of the finding, the priority, a detailed description, HD, IR and Map screenshots, video fragments, timestamp, coordinates and temperature estimation points).

If, for every inspection task, 50 to 100 finding points are generated, there is a lot of information which needs to be persisted and organized in order to have a consistent report. To cope with this requirement it has been designed a module dedicated to reporting services.

With this it is possible to organize and accommodate all the data points' information in a visually appealing report to be consulted by the interested parts. HTML and PDF, are the default formats in which the reports are generated. Additionally, the reported points are stored in .csv and .kml files for being visualized as layers in any commercial GIS software.

## 3   Test Results

The system presented in this work was tested with a real aerial inspection over a pipeline. The pipeline segment in which the inspection took place was unknown (for the inspection team). The only condition of flying above the pipeline was required.

The pipeline segment was 100 km and the inspection flight speed 120 km/h average with an elevation of 400 m [15].

Fourteen findings were reported after processing the inspection generated data. Several factors were registered from landslides, degradation by water and excavation for maintenance functions to emersion of a tube in marshland.

Nine thermal anomalies were detected. One month after aerial inspection the ground verification was allowed just for 4 places, the brightest thermal abnormalities ones were chosen. GPS coordinates and images of anomalies contributed to rapidly locate these points.

In Fig. 17 are show the HD and IR images of one of these reported points. In this case HD image displays no relevant information but in the IR spectra one can clearly see the thermal contrast over the ROW.

a)

b)

**Fig. 17.** A finding reported in the test inspection of the system. (a) HD video screenshot. (b) IR video screenshot.

## 4   Conclusions

As can be seen, the GIS system is ubiquitous in the processing module being the map rendering for positioning the most remarkable. This technology improves a lot the inspection task for gas and oil pipelines. The designed remote inspection system considerably lightens the work of operator and raises the service quality and integrity. Accuracy and speed in locating points over the right of way in the verification phase are greatly improved. Persistence and reporting the inspection are convenient way for future references and comparisons on specific pipelines segments.

# References

1. Sadovnychiy, S., Ramírez, A., López, M., Solís, N.: Pipeline leakage remote detection system. J. WSEAS Trans. Syst. **5**(3), 1988–1992 (2004)
2. Sadovnychiy, S., Bulgakov, I., Subramaniam, V.: Pipeline right-of-way remote inspection system. J. WSEAS Trans. Circ. Syst. **4**(3), 805–809 (2004)
3. Caprica Software Limited. http://capricasoftware.co.uk/. Accessed 7 Dec 2016
4. FFmpeg.org. https://ffmpeg.org/. Accessed 7 Dec 2016
5. ArcGIS for Developers. https://developers.arcgis.com/java/. Accessed 7 Dec 2016
6. Google Maps Elevation API. https://developers.google.com/maps/documentation/elevation/intro?hl=es-419. Accessed 7 Dec 2016
7. Eclipse SWT: The Standard Widget Toolkit. https://www.eclipse.org/swt/. Accessed 7 Dec 2016
8. Micromata Labs. Java API for KML. https://labs.micromata.de/projects/jak.htmlAccessed 7 Dec 2016
9. GeoKarambola, https://plus.google.com/u/0/communities/110606810455751902142Accessed 7 Dec 2016
10. OpenCV. http://opencv.org/. Accessed 7 Dec 2016
11. Jasper Reports Library. http://community.jaspersoft.com/project/jasperreports-library. Accessed 7 Dec 2016
12. Snyder, J.P.: Map projections - a working manual. In: U. S. Geological Survey Professional Paper. vol. 1395, p. 383. U. S. Government Printing Office, Washington (1987)
13. Department of the Army, DMATM 8358.2 The Universal Grids: Universal Transverse Mercator (UTM) and Universal Polar Stereographic (UPS). U. S. Army Technical Manual, USA (1989)
14. Karney, C.F.F.: Transverse mercator with an accuracy of a few nanometers **85**(8), 475–485 (2011)
15. Sadovnychiy, S., Canul, E., Lopez, J., Sadovnychyy, A., Hernandez, M.: Geographical information system applications for pipeline right of way aerial surveillance. In: Proceedings of the 3rd International Conference on Geographical Information Systems Theory Applications and Management, pp. 26–34 (2017)
16. Parker, J.: Algorithms for Image Processing and Computer Vision. Wiley, Hoboken (2011)
17. Lo, R.C.H., Lo, W.C.Y.: OpenGL Data Visualization Cookbook. Packt, Birmingham (2015)

# Sentinel-1 for Object-Based Delineation of Built-Up Land Within Urban Areas

Arthur Lehner[1,2(✉)], Vahid Naeimi[3], and Klaus Steinnocher[1]

[1] Center for Energy, AIT – Austrian Institute of Technology, Vienna, Austria
arthur.lehner@ait.ac.at
[2] Department of Geoinformatics - Z_GIS, University of Salzburg,
Salzburg, Austria
[3] Department of Geodesy and Geoinformation,
Research Group Remote Sensing E120.1, Vienna University of Technology,
Vienna, Austria

**Abstract.** This work deals with the delineation of built-up land within urban areas from Sentinel-1 data using object-based image analysis. The produced layers allow differentiation between built-up and non-built-up area. Additionally a layer is produced, presenting different types of built-up densities. The results are visually compared with a standardized product of the Copernicus earth observation program, the Copernicus High Resolution Layer Imperviousness Degree. For evaluation of the accuracy, the European Settlement Map 2016 was chosen as a reference data set. Results from the built-up density analysis are visually compared with reference layer generated from open government data. The results reveal the suitability of Sentinel-1 data for the delineation of built-up land within urban areas. The quality of the produced layers (built-up land map and built-up density map) is comparable to standardized products that are based on data from optical sensors e.g. Copernicus High Resolution Layer Imperviousness Degree, European Settlement Map 2016 or high resolution building density maps respectively. The accuracy of the built-up land map (BULM) is equal (78.2%) to the one of the settlement layer produced by use of the ISODATA cluster algorithm [1].

**Keywords:** Remote · Sensing · Sentinel-1 · OBIA · Built-up
Copernicus

## 1 Introduction

Based on Earth Observation systems, land monitoring within Europe and the European Union is fundamental regarding its scientific, cultural and environmental impacts. With the agreement in 1985 to produce the first CORINE [2] land cover (CLC), the foundation for a European land monitoring program was laid. The program maintains a number of databases including an inventory of land cover\land use (LCLU), produced operationally for most areas of Europe on a 6 to 10 year cycle [3]. The CLC program later was incorporated in the European earth observation program "Copernicus". Copernicus, previously known as GMES (Global Monitoring for Environment and Security), represents the European Programme for the formation of a European capacity for Earth Observation.

© Springer Nature Switzerland AG 2019
L. Ragia et al. (Eds.): GISTAM 2017, CCIS 936, pp. 19–35, 2019.
https://doi.org/10.1007/978-3-030-06010-7_2

Pan-European High Resolution Layers (HRLs) are complementary to LCLU mapping such as in the CORINE land cover (CLC) datasets and provide information on specific land cover characteristics. Through a combination of automatic processing and interactive rule based classification, the HRLs are generated from 20 m resolution satellite imagery [4]. Out of five layer themes, the imperviousness layer presents the degree of sealed soil as it captures the spatial distribution of artificially sealed areas, including the level of sealing of the soil per area unit. The layer represents a base map for various fields of research [5–7]. Different applications using the Copernicus Imperviousness Layer [8, 9] reveal its fundamentality and its usability.

In addition, the European Settlement Map (ESM) 2016 represents the percentage of built-up area coverage per spatial unit using SPOT5 and SPOT6 satellite imagery from the year 2012 [10]. The ESM is a map expressing the proportion of the pixel area covered by buildings. The ESM was produced in 2013/2014 [11] and its follow-up product is being developed. In addition to these developments, the European commission recently announced the provision of an information layer on built-up presence. This information layer will be derived from Sentinel-1 image collections (2016) and resolution will be about 20 m. These data has not been available yet and could not be considered for a visual comparison nor an accuracy assessment in this study.

The European Space agency ESA aimed to satisfy the need of the Copernicus program by launching the Sentinel mission in 2014. Sentinel-1 is the first of five missions that ESA developed for the Copernicus initiative [1]. Sentinel-1 is a constellation of two satellites (Sentinel-1A, Sentinel-1B), operating day and night performing C-band synthetic aperture radar imaging, enabling them to acquire imagery regardless of weather conditions or light conditions [12].

This work presents the delineation of built-up land within urban areas from Sentinel-1 data using object-based image analysis. The derived layers differentiate between built-up and non-built up area as well as between densely built-up and sparsely built-up areas. These layers are compared with current remote sensing derived map products such Copernicus high-resolution layer 'Imperviousness Degree' and the European Settlement Map (ESM) 2016 as well as with local maps produced by the municipality of Vienna. The application of object-based image analysis allows for extraction of different types of information and improves the overall results. In contrast to CLC data that are confined for Europe, satellites of the Sentinel mission collect data globally [1]. Therefore, it is possible to establish a global settlement layer. This work is based on the findings of a previous study using different stacks of Sentinel-1 composite images for automatic derivation of settlement layers [1].

## 2  Data

In our study we use Sentinel-1 image data (see Fig. 1), collected from 3 months of the year 2016, the Copernicus HRL imperviousness for the year 2012 and European Settlement Map 2016. A Sentinel-2A scene (date of acquisition: 02.07.2016) is used for visual interpretation of the results. Additionally we use a building density map of the city of Vienna generated from freely available data for the visual comparison of our built-up density map (BUDM).

## 2.1 Sentinel-1 Data

The Sentinel program is the most comprehensive and ambitious European Earth Observation program. The Sentinel satellites provide unique operational sensing capabilities across the whole measurement spectrum, covering a broad range of applications. Thanks to their advanced sensing concepts and outstanding spatio-temporal sampling characteristics, the Sentinel satellites will collect more data than any earth observation program before [13]. The first of the Sentinel satellite series, Sentinel-1A was launched on 3 April 2014. Seninel-1 (S-1) is a Synthetic Aperture Radar (SAR) mission for ocean and land monitoring. S-1 is the continuity mission to the SAR instruments flown on board of ERS and ENVISAT. The S-1 mission is implemented through a constellation of two satellites. The S-1B was launched on 25 April 2016. The S-1 data over the land masses are mainly acquired in Interferometric Wide swath (IW) mode. The S-1 Level-1 Ground Range Detected (GRD) products, which are suitable for the most of the land applications, consist of focused SAR data that has been detected, multi-looked and projected to ground range using an Earth ellipsoid model such as WGS84. The IW GRD products are provided in two High (20 m × 22 m) and Medium (88 m × 87 m) spatial resolutions resampled to 10 m and 40 m pixel spacing grids respectively [14].

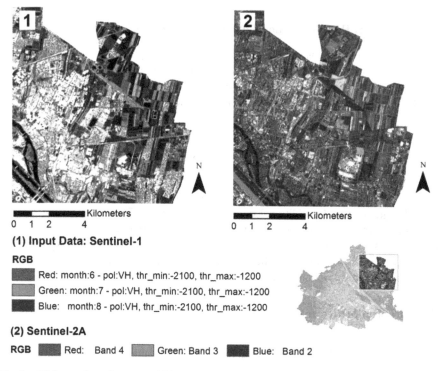

**Fig. 1.** (1) Input data: three monthly composites of S-1 IW GRD high resolution product, VH polarization, during the summer period (June, July, and August) from the year 2016; (2) Sentinel-2A "true color" image, R (4) G (3) B (2). (Color figure online)

Despite all corrections from Level-0 up to Level 1 data, the GRD data still need to be processed further before generating level-2 products. The S-1 Level-1 GRD data used in this study were pre-processed using the TU Wien SAR Geophysical Retrieval Toolbox (SGRT) [15]. The pre-processing workflow include calibration, noise removal, georeferencing and terrain correction using a Digital Elevation Model (DEM), shadow mask generation, data conversions, and data resampling and tiling to a regular grid using an appropriate cartographic map projection. For the calibration, georeferencing and the terrain correction, the ESA's Sentinel-1 toolbox (S1TBX) is employed. The S1TBX operators are called via SGRT to perform the georeferencing using the S-1 precise orbit files provided externally by ESA. In this study the S1TBX Range Doppler algorithm and SRTM digital elevation data are used for terrain correction of the SAR scenes. After some further preprocessing steps like thermal noise removal, data format conversion and shadow mask generation the geocoded SAR scenes are resampled to the TU Wien Equi7 Grid. The TU Wien Equi7 Grid is designed to minimize the oversampling rate of the high resolution satellite data globally, while keeping its structure simple [16]. After the pre-processing step, the S-1 backscatter time series were used to generate composites of monthly mean of backscatter for each polarization separately over the test site. In this study we used three monthly composites of S-1 IW GRD high resolution product, VH polarization, during the summer period (June, July, and August) from the year 2016 as input for the classification.

## 2.2 Copernicus High Resolution Layer Imperviousness Degree

The HRL imperviousness is produced using an automatic algorithm based on calibrated NDVI. Similar to other HRLs of the Copernicus program, the imperviousness HRL is derived from 20 m resolution optical satellite imagery. The layer has 20 m geometric resolution and provides 101 classes of imperviousness while:

- 0: all non-impervious areas
- 1–100: imperviousness values
- 254: unclassifiable (no satellite image available, or clouds, shadows, or snow)
- 255: outside area [17].

It is produced in a three years cycle and covers all 28 EU members (including United Kingdom) and 11 additional countries (see Fig. 2). The imperviousness layer contains two products: a 2012 status layer (degree of imperviousness 2012), as well as an imperviousness density change layer (2009–2012), based on the existing imperviousness product for 2009 [17]. In the presented study, we do not consider the imperviousness density change layer.

## 2.3 European Settlement Map 2016

The European Settlement Map is a spatial raster dataset with 10 m resolution; an aggregated version with 100 m resolution is also available. The ESM is mapping human settlements in Europe based on SPOT5 and SPOT6 satellite imagery from the year 2012. Similar to the Copernicus HRL it covers all 28 EU members (including United Kingdom) and 11 additional countries. For the ESM a 95% accuracy for the built-up class is stated [10]. Based on the accuracy and its other properties, the ESM was chosen as reference data for the accuracy assessment of the built-up land map (BULM).

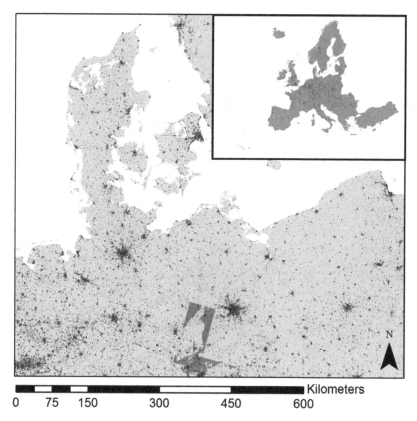

**Fig. 2.** Coverage of the Copernicus HRL imperviousness degree, red = impervious surface, grey = no satellite image available, source: [1]. (Color Figure online)

## 2.4   Building Density Map Vienna

The only publicly available building density map for the city of Vienna dates back to the year 2010 [18]. Therefore, we decided to produce an updated version of it, using open government data (OGD) provided by the city of Vienna and data products from a previous project. These input data consist of a modified version of the "real land use map" of the year 2008/09 (German: Realnutzungskartierung) and a district layer for the city of Vienna as .shp-file. The updated version (2014) of the "real land use map" was developed within the ProbateS project. The objective of the PRoBateS project was amongst others to analyze both existing room for action and potential for energy-related measures in spatial planning and building law [19]. Additionally, we use an adapted version [19] of the "building model" layer (German: Baukörpermodell) as input data. This layer contains information about building heights, building volumes and building areas and excludes buildings with a building area lower than 25 m². The information of the "building model" layer and the "real land use map" are combined and a building density map for the city of Vienna is produced. In our case the building density for the year 2014 reached from 0 to 15.9 (see Fig. 3). The respective values of the building density map Vienna provide information about the relation between the gross floor space of a building and the total area of a particular plot of land. For the visual comparison, the building density map (7 numeric classes) is reclassified according to the classification of the produced built-up density map using S-1 data (3 classes with labels: non-built-up, sparsely built-up and densely built-up) and serves as a reference layer within this study.

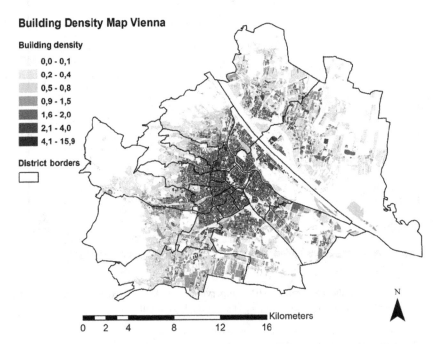

**Fig. 3.** Reference layer: high resolution building density map Vienna for the year 2014, Vienna, Austria.

## 2.5    Study Area

The chosen test site is the city of Vienna (coordinates: 48°12′N 16°22′E), the capital of Austria. The terrain ranges from hilly in the west to flat in the east of the city. In the west, forest areas are predominate and agricultural areas are mainly found in the east and southeast. The urban spectrum ranges from single-family houses to high-rise buildings, covers green houses and industrial areas [1].

# 3  Methodology

The objective of this study is to produce information layers using Sentinel-1 image data regarding built-up structure. The chosen method is Object-based Image Analysis (OBIA). Instead of only using the intensity values of individual pixels, a set of pixels is grouped to an image object. The most common approach used for building (image) objects is image segmentation [20]. Depending on the segmentation process and segmentation parameters, resulting image objects vary in color, shape, size and other intrinsic properties. The introduction of such objects also allows for analysis of the relationships between them: horizontally within one image layer and vertically through different super-imposed layers. Objects have (topological and non-topological) neighborhood relationships and hierarchical relationships, such as "is-part-of" or "consists-of" [21]. In addition to S-1 backscattering intensity value, built-up and non-built-up land can be further differentiated based on the mentioned characteristics of image objects and their relationships with each other. The research in this manuscript strives for overcoming misclassifications that occurred in previous studies [1] where classification only depended on single pixel values. Parameters such as "distance" to existing built-up areas are introduced as well as neighborhood relationships and texture analysis using the Gray-Level Co-Occurrence Matrix (GLCM).

The initial point of all object-based image analysis is the image segmentation. In our case, we start with a multiresolution segmentation [22, 23]. After the segmentation process, the whole image is partitioned by image objects; all image objects of such partition are called an image object level [24]. We create the image object level "Level1". The parameters used for all the used algorithms can be found in the appendix since all processing steps are part of a ruleset. A ruleset contains a set of conditions or rules and is based on the expert knowledge of the user. In the next step, a Multiresolution Segmentation Region Grow algorithm is applied [22]. This algorithm applies an optimization procedure which locally minimizes the average heterogeneity of image objects for a given resolution [22]. The existing image object level "Level1" (see Fig. 4) is overwritten. Further we select the core candidates of built-up area that are later used as an initial nucleus for further classifications. We use the classification algorithm "assign class" in order to classify the areas that are most likely to be built-up area. This algorithm assigns all objects of the image object domain to the class specified by the Use Class parameter [22]. The areas that have highest probability to be built-up land, are those with highest gray value in the image. This fact leads back to the specific backscattering behavior of different objects within the urban landscape such as built-up area, water or vegetation respectively [1].

Classified image objects are merged and in a next step another multiresolution segmentation is performed, equal in scale parameters (10) but different in terms of homogeneity criteria (shape: 0.1; compactness: 0.7) in order to keep the created image objects compact. The scale parameter is an abstract term that determines the maximum allowed heterogeneity for the resulting image objects. By modifying the value in the scale parameter value the size of image objects can be influenced [22]. As a result of the multiresolution segmentation process, a new image object level "Level2" is created (see Fig. 4). Although the creation of new image object levels is not obligatory for applying subsequent rules and conditions it is chosen for clarity purposes. The new object level does not contain any qualitative information from the previous level such as classification results. Therefore, by use of the "assign class" algorithm, image objects of "Level2" that share a relative area ($\geq 0.6$) with image objects previously classified as built-up land of the subjacent image object level "Level1" are classified as built-up land. To summarize, classification results are adopted from previous image object levels. The classified image objects of "Level2" represent a base for the following classifications. In the next step, unclassified image objects adjacent to objects classified as built-up land ("border to built-up $\geq 1$ px") are examined and classified as "built-up land" depending on the respective gray value ($\geq 230$) of the blue channel (month:8 - pol: VH). This process is itinerated two times with the same conditions and parameters. In a next step, the same algorithm is chosen while gray values ($\geq 240$) of all channels are considered as well as the texture features (GLCM Homogeneity [quick 8/11] [all directions] $\geq 0.2$) of the respective image objects. In our case, texture features are based upon the gray level co-occurrence matrix (GLCM) after Haralick which is a tabulation of how often different combinations of pixel gray levels occur in an image [22]. A GLCM value of 1 indicates high homogeneity of an image object whereas values below 0.1 indicate high heterogeneity respectively. Last-mentioned rule is itinerated once.

Considering the neighborhood of image objects as decision support for classification is one way of avoiding misclassifications that may occur by assigning classes to image objects purely based on their gray values. However, within the urban landscape different objects exist that represent natural obstacles to continuous and uninterrupted building activity such as forest, parks, rivers or other water areas. Thus, distant image objects to existent built-up land are also considered for the classification process.

By use of the "assign class" algorithm, image objects within a certain distance ($\geq 15$ px) are considered for classification as built-up land; again depending on the gray values of the respective channels (cf. appendix). This rule is applied 7 times while raising the distance, i.e. the field of observation (15 px–90 px), and while modifying the thresholds for the respective gray values of the image channels.

By evaluating the preliminary results and visual comparison with the Sentinel-2 image scene, parts of actual built-up area were still not classified as built-up land. Misclassifications occurred in areas with sparse building distribution such as areas where single family houses and allotment are predominant. In order to overcome these problems a new image object level "Level3" (see Fig. 4) is created by performing another multiresolution segmentation with a scale parameter of 65. Resulting image objects are bigger and more heterogenic than those on subjacent levels (Level1, Level2). By use of the "assign class" algorithm, image objects of "Level3" that share a relative area ($\geq 0.01$) with image objects previously classified as built-up land of the subjacent image object level "Level2" are classified as built-up land. As a result, also sparsely built-up areas can be classified as built-up land. This product is named built-up land map (BULM). It is quantitatively compared with the European Settlement Map 2016 (ESM) and the results of the accuracy assessment of a previous study [1].

Although sparse built-up land could be included in the classification, the class "built-up land" now also includes deliberately non-built-up land. In order to address this fact, a differentiation between densely built-up areas and sparsely built-up areas is made. A new image object level "Level4" is created by performing another

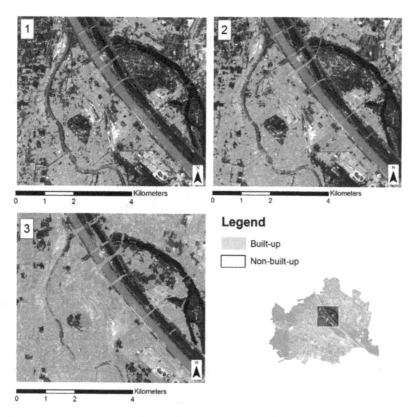

**Fig. 4.** Three image object levels: (1) "Level1", (2) "Level2", (3) "Level3", gradual use of image object properties for classification of built-up land and non-built-up land; background: Sentinel-2A "true color" image, R (4) G (3) B (2). (Color Figure online)

multiresolution segmentation based on image object level "Level2" with a scale parameter of 80. By use of the "assign class" algorithm, image objects of "Level4" that share a relative area ($\geq 0.6300001$) with image objects previously classified as built-up land of the subjacent image object level "Level2" are classified as densely built-up area. Image objects of "Level4" that share a smaller relative area ($\leq 0.63$) (less than two-thirds of built-up land) with image objects previously classified as built-up land of the subjacent image object level "Level2" are classified as sparsely built-up area. All remaining unclassified image objects are classified as "Non-built-up land". The resulting product is named built-up density map (BUDM). It is visually compared with the updated version (2014) of the Building Density Map Vienna. The reclassification of the reference layer was done according to the classes of the produced density map using S-1 data. The numeric values of the building density map Vienna provide information about the relation between the gross floor space of a building and the total area of a particular plot of land. Areas that showed a density of 0 were reclassified as "non-built-up", areas with densities higher than 0 up to a value of 1.6 were reclassified to "sparsely built-up" and the remaining areas were reclassified as "dense built-up".

The ESM layer is aggregated to a 20 m resolution. 500 points randomly distributed across the study area are used to assess the accuracy of the classes "built-up" and "non-built-up". The authors are conscious of the fact that the comparison of layers from different acquisition years can be seen critically. However, the areas that were chosen for this study did not face extensive changes over the last 10 years. Moreover, changes in the buildings type (e.g. loft/attic conversion) within the urban landscape do not affect the comparison.

## 4   Results

The objective of this research was to produce information layers using Sentinel-1 image data. Using a reduced amount of input data [cp. 1] and object-based image analysis methods, a differentiation between built-up and non-built-up land was successfully made and the overall accuracy of the resulting product is equal to the accuracy achieved in a previous study [1] (Table 1). Additionally a second information layer, differentiating between densely-, sparsely and non-built up area, was produced. The results of the object-based creation of a built-up land map (BULM) are quantitatively compared with the European Settlement Map 2016 [10] that was used as reference data. The overall accuracy (OA) of the final layer (BULM) is 78.2% (Table 1). We compared the results (Table 1) of the object-based approach with the ones achieved in a previous study [1] by application of the ISODATA cluster algorithm (S1-USC II). Additionally we quantitatively compared a preliminary product of the BULM, the image object level "Level2", with the ESM 2016 (Table 2). In Fig. 5, the produced layer BULM and the Copernicus HRL are visually compared.

**Table 1.**  Accuracy assessment (BULM & S1-USC II).

| BULM | | | | S1-USC II | | | |
|---|---|---|---|---|---|---|---|
| **Classification** | Non Built-up | Built-up | **Totals** | **Classification** | Non Built-up | Built-up | **Totals** |
| Non Built-up | 219 | 32 | 251 | Non Built-up | 272 | 69 | 341 |
| Built-up | 77 | 172 | 249 | Built-up | 40 | 119 | 159 |
| **Totals** | 296 | 204 | 500 | **Totals** | 312 | 188 | 500 |
| Producers Accuracy | 74.0% | 84.3% | **OA: 78.2%** | Producers Accuracy | 87,2% | 63,3% | **OA: 78,2%** |
| Users Accuracy | 87.3% | 69.1% | | Users Accuracy | 79,8% | 74,8% | |

**Table 2.** Accuracy assessment (preliminary product: BULM-Level2).

| BULM – image object level "Level 2" | | | |
|---|---|---|---|
| **Classification** | Non Built-up | Built-up | **Totals** |
| Non Built-up | 275 | 88 | 363 |
| Built-up | 25 | 112 | 137 |
| **Totals** | 300 | 200 | 500 |
| Producers Accuracy | 91.7% | 56.0% | **OA: 77.4%** |
| Users Accuracy | 75.8% | 81.8% | |

## 5   Discussion

The results from the object-based delineation of built-up land within urban areas reveal the possibility of mapping built-up areas and producing different information layers for urban areas. In the produced layer BULM, different non-built up classes like urban parks, forest, cemeteries and other spacious vegetated areas are grouped and can particularly be distinguished from built-up areas. Agricultural fields are also related more accurately to non-built up areas, independent from their degree of vegetation cover. Furthermore, water bodies are classified as non-built-up areas independent from its amount of algae, depth, water quality or ground conditions. The "separation" between built-up and non-built up areas is improved by use of the object related properties, use of neighborhood relationships and considering different features of image objects besides the mean gray value of a particular image channel.

In comparison to Copernicus HRL Imperviousness Degree, the produced layer BULM shows generally a finer representation of the urban inventory (see Fig. 5). Green and (pervious) open spaces are visually easier to distinguish from built-up areas such as buildings, bridges and railroads.

The shape of buildings appear sharper. The outlines of rivers and channels are more exact (see Fig. 6).

In comparison to European Settlement Map 2016, bridges crossing the Danube River are represented in the final produced layer BULM. Urban structures such as courtyards or street canyons are represented in greater detail within the ESM layer. This richness of detail leads back to fact that the ESM 2016 itself has a higher geometric resolution. The data set used for compiling the ESM 2016 has a higher geometric resolution (SPOT 5 and SPOT 6 data of 2.5 m pixel size) and includes use of ancillary datasets (e.g. OpenStreetMap) [11].

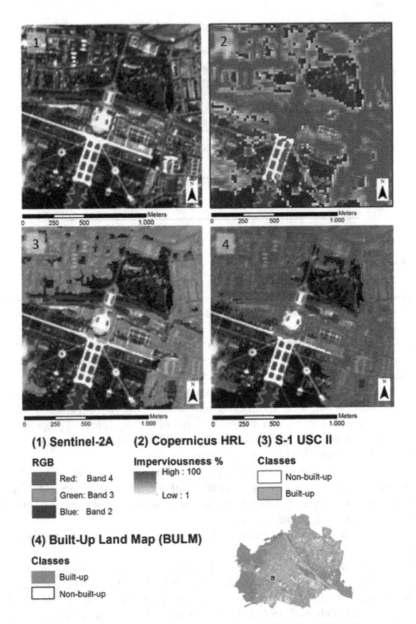

**Fig. 5.** Visual comparison of S-1 USC II [1], BULM and Copernicus HRL, Vienna, Austria): (1) and background: Sentinel-2A image, "true color" image, R (4) G (3) B (2); (2) Copernicus HRL, (3) S-1 USC II [1]; (4) BULM. (Color figure online)

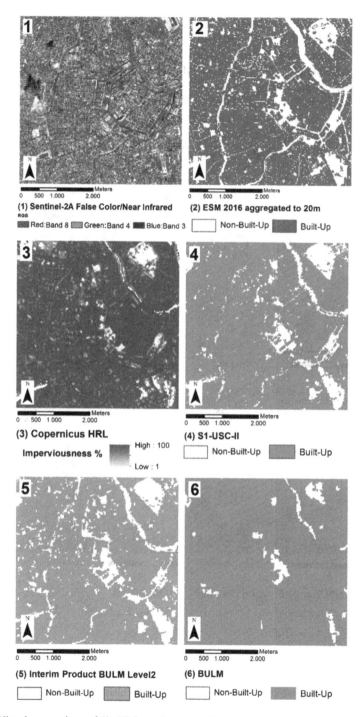

**Fig. 6.** Visual comparison of (1) "False color/near infrared" image from Sentinel-2A, (2) ESM 2016, (3) Copernicus HRL, (4) S-1 USC II [1], (5) interim product BULM Level2 and (6) BULM. (Color figure online)

Although the results are overall promising, some challenges remain regarding the accuracy of the classification. High pixel values that indicate built-up area are found within forest areas, mainly in steep slopes. We attribute this to the fact that the backscatter measured by S-1 sensor is influenced by the terrain. Such areas with complex topography could be masked using a digital elevation model.

By evaluation of the error matrix of the BULM and the S1-USC-II layer, we find an overestimation of built-up land for the product BULM. In our case, this overestimation led to a coarser representation (see Fig. 6) of urban structures such as courtyards or street canyons when compared to results (S1-USC-II) of the previous study [1].We

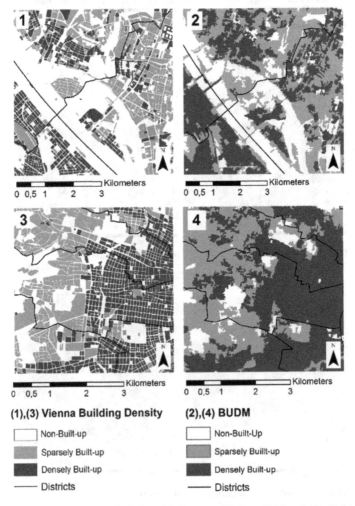

**Fig. 7.** Comparison of the (1, 3) building density map Vienna, 2014 and (2, 4) the produced building density map BUDM, Vienna, Austria.

refer that to fact of creating of too large image objects for the subsequent assignment of classes. Moreover, the selection of a proper threshold for the classification of built-up land based on the classification of the previous image object-level "Level2" appears to be amendable. Within BULM-image object level "Level2" we find an underestimation of built-up land. The accuracy assessment for the interim layer "Level2" and the aforementioned findings reveal that gradual and finer assignment of classes by small steps allows for achieving better results. Both S1-USC-II and the interim product BULM-image object level "Level2" show an underestimation of built-up area.

The produced built-up density map (BUDM) shows generally acceptable correspondence compared to the reference layer, the building density map Vienna (see Fig. 7). Some urban artefacts such as bridges, roads or areas with special land use (parks and other recreational zones) remain within the BUDM. These areas were masked out within the reference layer. With its coarser resolution, the BUDM layer cannot catch up with the fine representation of the reference layer. However, it may serve as good instrument for giving a fast overview of the distribution of building densities of an urban area on a coarser scale.

## 6 Conclusions

This study could demonstrate the value of Sentinel-1 data for mapping built-up land. The preliminary results revealed that the object-based classification of S-1 stacked backscatter composites allows for differentiating between built-up and non-built-up land within the urban landscape. The quality of the produced information layer (BULM) is comparable to standardized products based on optical sensors e.g. Copernicus HRL Imperviousness Degree, or European Settlement Map 2016 respectively. The accuracy of the product BULM is equal to the settlement layer of a previous study [1]. This finding is of significance since it allows for differentiation between built-up and non-built-up land based on a reduced number of images and a reduced amount of data respectively. The density map BUDM contributes to the built-up land map (BULM) and shows the usability of Sentinel-1 data for relevant questions and tasks within an urban context.

The introduction of object-based methodologies where classification do not only depend on single pixel values but also on relation between objects helped to correct misclassifications. A refinement and possible extension of the presented ruleset may help to improve the classification results. Finally, a proposal for an operational use is the use of ancillary data (OSM, land use maps) in order to enhance the differentiation between built-up and non-built-up land.

# Appendix

## eCognition Developer 9.2 Ruleset:

- Segmentation Scale 5
  - 5 [shape:0.1 compct.:0.5] creating 'Level1'
- Segmentation Scale 10
  - at Level1: <- none: 10 [shape:0.1 compct.:0.5]
- Core Candidates Selection
  - with Mean Layer 1 >= 250 and Mean Layer 2 >= 250 and Mean Layer 3 >= 250 at Level1: Built-up
- Object Merging Built-Up
  - Built-up at Level1: merge region
- Segmentation for 2nd level
  - at Level1: 10 [shape:0.1 compct.:0.7] creating 'Level2'
- Take over classification from Level1
  - with Rel. area of sub objects Built-up (1) >= 0.6 at Level2: Built-up
- Neighbour Check
  - unclassified with Border to Built-up >= 1 Pxl and (Mean Layer 1 >= 230 ) at Level2: Built-up
- Neighbour Check 2nd
  - unclassified with Border to Built-up >= 1 Pxl and (Mean Layer 1 >= 230 ) at Level2: Built-up
- Neighbour Check 3rd
  - unclassified with Border to Built-up >= 1 Pxl and (Mean Layer 1 >= 230 ) at Level2: Built-up
- Neighbour Check 4th
  - unclassified with Border to Built-up >= 1 Pxl and (Mean Layer 1 >= 240 and GLCM Homogeneity (quick 8/11) (all dir.) >= 0.2 and Mean Layer 2 >= 240 and Mean Layer 3 >= 240 ) at Level2: Built-up
- Neighbour Check 5th
  - unclassified with Border to Built-up >= 1 Pxl and (Mean Layer 1 >= 240 and GLCM Homogeneity (quick 8/11) (all dir.) >= 0.2 and Mean Layer 2 >= 240 and Mean Layer 3 >= 240 ) at Level2: Built-up
- Environment Check 15px Distance 1st
  - unclassified with Distance to Built-up <= 15 Pxl and (Mean Layer 1 >= 245 and Mean Layer 2 >= 250 and Mean Layer 3 >= 250 ) at Level2: Built-up
- Environment Check 25px Distance 2nd
  - unclassified with Distance to Built-up <= 25 Pxl and (Mean Layer 1 >= 245 and Mean Layer 2 >= 245 and Mean Layer 3 >= 245 ) at Level2: Built-up
- Environment Check 15px Distance 3rd
  - unclassified with Distance to Built-up <= 15 Pxl and (Mean Layer 1 >= 245 and Mean Layer 2 >= 245 and Mean Layer 3 >= 245 ) at Level2: Built-up
- Environment Check 40px Distance 4th
  - unclassified with Distance to Built-up <= 40 Pxl and (Mean Layer 1 >= 245 and Mean Layer 2 >= 245 and Mean Layer 3 >= 245 ) at Level2: Built-up
- Environment Check 25px Distance 5th
  - unclassified with Distance to Built-up <= 25 Pxl and (Mean Layer 1 >= 235 and Mean Layer 2 >= 235 and Mean Layer 3 >= 235 ) at Level2: Built-up
- Environment Check 25px Distance 6th
  - unclassified with Distance to Built-up <= 25 Pxl and (Mean Layer 1 >= 235 and Mean Layer 2 >= 235 and Mean Layer 3 >= 235 ) at Level2: Built-up
- Environment Check 90px Distance 7th
  - unclassified with Distance to Built-up <= 90 Pxl and (Mean Layer 1 >= 235 and Mean Layer 2 >= 235 and Mean Layer 3 >= 235 ) at Level2: Built-up
- Segmentation for 3rd level
  - at Level2: 65 [shape:0.1 compct.:0.5] creating 'Level3'
- Built-Up Classification through adoption
  - unclassified with Rel. area of sub objects Built-up (1) >= 0.01 at Level3: Built-up
- Non-Built-Up classification
  - unclassified at Level3: Non-built-up
- Segmentation for 4th level
  - at Level2: 80 [shape:0.1 compct.:0.5] creating 'Level4'
- Differentation in density
  - with Rel. area of sub objects Built-up (1) >= 0.6300001 at Level4: Densely built-up
  - with Rel. area of sub objects Built-up (1) <= 0.63 and (Rel. area of sub objects Built-up (1) >= 1e-006 ) at Level4: Sparsely built-up
  - unclassified at Level4: Non-built-up

# References

1. Lehner, A., Naeimi, V., Steinnocher, K.: Sentinel-1 for urban areas - comparison between automatically derived settlement layers from sentinel-1 data and copernicus high resolution information layers. In: Ragia, L., Rocha, J.G., Laurini, R. (eds.) 2017 3rd International Conference on Geographical Information Systems Theory, Applications and Management, pp. 43–49. SCITEPRESS - Science and Technology Publications, Setubal (2017)
2. EEA: Corine Land Cover, p. 163. European Environment Agency (2000)
3. Ben-Asher, Z.: HELM-harmonised European land monitoring: findings and recommendations of the HELM project. Tel-Aviv, Israel (2013)
4. Sannier, C., Gallego, J., Dahmer, J., Smith, G., Dufourmont, H., Pennec, A.: Validation of Copernicus high resolution layer on imperviousness degree for 2006, 2009 and 2012. In: 12th International Symposium of Spatial Accuracy Assessment in Natural Resources and Environmental Sciences, Montpellier, France, 12th edn, pp. 5–8 (2016)
5. Ciobotaru, N., et al.: Mapping romanian wetlands – a geographical approach, p. 14, Tulcea, Romania (2016)

6. Lefebvre, A., Picand, P.-A., Sannier, C.: Mapping tree cover in European cities: comparison of classification algorithms for an operational production framework. In: 2015 Joint Urban Remote Sensing Event, pp. 1–4. IEEE (2015)
7. Mücher, C.A., Hennekens, S.M., Schaminee, J.H.J., Halada, L., Halabuk, A.: Modelling the spatial distribution of EUNIS forest habitats based on vegetation relevés and Copernicus HRL. European Topic Centre Biological Diversity (2015)
8. Hennig, E.I., Schwick, C., Soukup, T., Orlitová, E., Kienast, F., Jaeger, J.A.: Multi-scale analysis of urban sprawl in Europe: towards a European de-sprawling strategy. Land Use Policy **49**, 483–498 (2015)
9. Steinnocher, K., Köstl, M., Weichselbaum, J.: Grid-based population and land take trend indicators – new approaches introduced by the geoland2 core information service for spatial planning. In: NTTS Conference, Brussels (2011)
10. European Commission: ESM 2016 European Settlement Map (2016)
11. Florczyk, A.J.: A new European settlement map from optical remotely sensed data. IEEE J. Sele. Top. Appl. Earth Obs. Remote Sens. **9**(5), 1978–1992 (2016)
12. D'Aria, D., Piantanida, R., Valentino, A., Riva, D.: Freesar, an innovative SAR data processing framework. In: 2016 IEEE International Geoscience and Remote Sensing Symposium (IGARSS), pp. 1214–1216. IEEE (2016)
13. Attema, E., et al.: Sentinel-1-the radar mission for GMES operational land and sea services. ESA Bull. **131**, 10–17 (2007)
14. European Space Agency: Sentinel-1 User Handbook. ESA (2013)
15. Naeimi, V., Elefante, S., Cao, S., Wagner, W., Dostalova, A., Bauer-Marschallinger, B.: Geophysical parameters retrieval from sentinel-1 SAR data: a case study for high performance computing at EODC. In: 24th High Performance Computing Symposium, p. 10. Society for Computer Simulation International (2016)
16. Bauer-Marschallinger, B., Sabel, D., Wagner, W.: Optimisation of global grids for high-resolution remote sensing data. Comput. Geosci. **72**, 84–93 (2014)
17. Langanke, T.: GIO land (GMES/copernicus initial operations land) high resolution layers (HRLs) – summary of product specifications (2013)
18. MA 18 - Stadtentwicklung und Stadtplanung: Geo data city 14.1. BIS 25.3.2011. Geoinformation und Stadtentwicklung in Wien, Vienna (2011)
19. Madner, V., et al.: Potenziale im Raumordnungs- und Baurecht für energetisch nachhaltige Stadtstrukturen – ProBateS. Schriftenreihe 36, p. 142. BMVIT (2016)
20. Blaschke, T.: Object based image analysis for remote sensing. ISPRS J. Photogramm. Remote Sens. **65**(1), 2–16 (2010)
21. Blaschke, T., et al.: Geographic object-based image analysis–towards a new paradigm. ISPRS J. Photogramm. Remote Sens. **87**, 180–191 (2014)
22. Trimble Documentation: Trimble eCognition® developer version 9.2.1 reference book. Trimble Germany GmbH, Munich (2016)
23. Baatz, M., Schäpe, A.: Multiresolution segmentation: an optimization approach for high quality multi-scale image segmentation. In: XII Angewandte Geographische Informationsverarbeitung, pp. 12–23. Wichmann-Verlag, Heidelberg (2000)
24. Zhou, H., Wu, J., Zhang, J.: Digital Image Processing: Part II. Bookboon, London (2010)

# Improvement of Database Updating: Semi-automatic Urban Detection

Bénédicte Navaro[✉], Zakaria Sadeq, and Nicolas Saporiti

Geo212, 25 bis rue Jean Dolent, Paris, France
{benedicte.navaro, zakaria.sadeq,
nicolas.saporiti}@geo212.fr

**Abstract.** Some years ago, the main issue of regular spatial databases updating addressed the quantity and availability of the sources. Nowadays, the abundance of satellite images moved the problem to an analytic point of view. Satellite imagery actors are currently dealing with data storage and distribution of added-value products. In this context, we present a scalable semi-automatic tool for urban detection: it is qualified with different image sources, different databases (proprietary, open source, detailed, basic etc.). The aim is not to exhaustively map buildings from a satellite image, but to give an overview of the situation regarding urban areas. It is conceived to guide stakeholders and producers throughout the updating process. The workflow presented in this article is based on existing algorithms and software resources so the application could be tested quickly on various landscapes with different sensors, in a demanding industrial context. The process is generic and adaptable, with a phase of uncorrelation, chaining a Minimum Noise Fraction transformation with a textural analysis, a learning phase, processed from an existing database, and an automatic modelling of the detected objects. The results are quantified to assess the product's quality: 90% of the existing database is successfully recreated with less than 1% rate of potential big omissions. The method allows to detect destroyed buildings and has run in "real" updating operations, on Spot6 images (1.5 and 6 m resolution), Pleiades (1.5 and 2 m), Landsat-8 (15 m) and Sentinel-2 (10 m).

**Keywords:** Urban areas · Object detection · Spatial databases
Minimum noise fraction · Supervised learning · Geodesic dilation

## 1 Introduction

A tremendous amount of techniques in the change detection and database updating fields have already been explored. Lu [1] gives an overview of the most common techniques and qualify them in terms of characteristics, advantages, disadvantages and key factors. The heterogeneity of urban environments and the large number of mixed pixels inherent images often induced difficulty in urban land use/cover classification based on spectral signature [2]. Recently, in the image change detection field, much attention shifted to advanced classification algorithms like neuronal network, object-oriented and knowledge-based classification approaches [3]. This study aims at updating an existing database of urban GIS objects with recent satellite imagery. The concept is that, having assumed that the number of wrongly detected GIS objects and

© Springer Nature Switzerland AG 2019
L. Ragia et al. (Eds.): GISTAM 2017, CCIS 936, pp. 36–56, 2019.
https://doi.org/10.1007/978-3-030-06010-7_3

the number of changes in the real world are substantially less than the number of all GIS objects of the data set, training areas can be derived from existing GIS data [4].

As this study is realized in an industrial context and aims at a generic and adaptable process, it is focused on a simple chain processing, based on existing algorithms. The easiest way to configure these algorithms is to use the ones implemented in software like ENVI and ArcGIS, available in the company. These tools are not mandatory as the image processing algorithms and statistical measures they use, are well-known by the community and can easily be reproduced in any computing languages. The choice of a radiometric analysis is made due to the simplicity of its implementation. The first phase chains a Minimum Noise Fraction transformation and a textural analysis resulting in two images: a relevant component from the MNF transformation and a grey scale image corresponding to the previous component's variance. The pixels' values in the two resulting images are combined with a selection of relevant objects in the database to establish a threshold. This learning phase finishes with the morphological reconstruction of the detected objects using a geodesic dilation with the existing database as a mask.

## 2 Image Processing

In both detailed and qualified cases (cf. 6 Results and qualification) a multispectral Pleiades image (4 bands: blue, green, red and PIR) with a 2 m resolution, is processed. In the Dire Dawa case the image is from 2015/09/02, in the Bangui case the image is from 06/06/2014. The method aims at extracting a specific thematic (urban objects) from spectral information within a complex landscape mixing vegetation, water, anthropogenic features, soil etc. To reduce the dimensionality of the image and obtain a signal uncorrelated from the noise, a Minimum Noise Fraction forward transform is processed. The MNF transformation as modified from [5] and implemented in ENVI, is a linear transformation that consists of the following separate principal components analysis rotations [6, 7]:

- The first rotation uses the principal components of the noise covariance matrix to un-correlate and rescale the noise in the data (a process known as noise whitening), resulting in transformed data in which the noise has unit variance and no band-to-band correlation.
- The second rotation uses the principal components derived from the original image data after they have been noise-whitened by the first rotation and rescaled by the noise standard deviation.

The result of the MNF first rotation is a two part data set, one part associated with large eigenvalues and coherent eigen images, and a complementary part with near unity eigenvalues and noise dominated images. The information is compressed in different bands in which the redundancy of the information is eliminated. In our case, the majority of the information is contained in the first 3 bands.

Then, the analysis of the spatial variation of a component's grey scale levels is processed: the variance measures the dispersion of the values around the mean. The solution implemented in ENVI uses a co-occurrence matrix to calculate texture values.

This matrix is a function of both the angular relationship and distance between two neighboring pixels. It shows the number of occurrences of the relationship between a pixel and its specified neighbor. Haralick [8] refers to this as a "gray-tone spatial-dependence matrix". The texture analysis is done, in our case, on the second band of MNF components (Fig. 1).

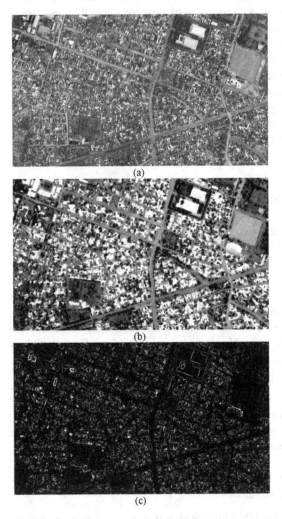

**Fig. 1.** Image processing results: (a) Pleiades 2m image of Dire Dawa (Ethiopia), (b) MNF band 2, (c) Variance of MNF band 2 [9].

The chosen MNF component (band 2) and the variance image are considered to be the resulting images of the image processing phase. The learning phase is applied on these two images.

# 3   Learning Process

In order to calculate the threshold that will discriminate urban objects in the resulting images (Fig. 1), the mean of the pixels' values that are located in areas labelled as "urban" amongst the available database, is calculated.

## 3.1   Labelling Objects as "Urban Areas"

The selection of anthropogenic objects in the database can be different regarding the type of the available database. The positive learning in an outdated database is justified by the rare disappearance of urban objects. In the case of this study, the buildings are represented individually so the selection of a sample can easily be done in the whole existing "building" layer. In other cases a simple SQL request can sort the data by attributes and randomly create fragments within the selection. The choice of urban areas results from a human consideration as it depends on the attributes the user considers as "urban". For example, urban places with a lot of vegetation should not be inventoried (like cemetery), nor punctual objects that are too thin to be representative of the local area (like pylon or water tanks). The choice of representative objects in the database is, then, flexible, and can be updated when changing area, if a new type of relevant anthropogenic object appears. Nevertheless, the list of these attributes has to be made just once for a data model.

## 3.2   Thresholding

In order to establish a threshold, the mean of the pixels' values located in fragments of buildings, is calculated on both images resulting from the image processing (Fig. 2).

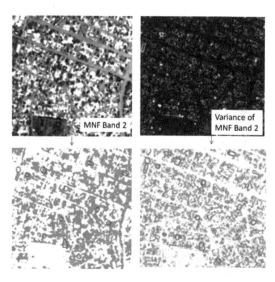

**Fig. 2.** Thresholding results based on the fragments (red areas) in Dire Dawa, Ethiopia [9]. (Color figure online)

The final result consists in the intersection of the two thresholded images and is presented in Fig. 3 over the original footprint of the buildings (grey polygons).

**Fig. 3.** Urban detections in a Pleiades image (2 m) over Dire Dawa (Ethiopia) [9]. (Color figure online)

Figure 3 shows the multiple detections of anthropogenic objects inside the city and the differences with the database. These detections are still blobs with undetermined shapes, so for them to get the shape of the buildings, a step of reconstruction is necessary.

## 4 Morphological Reconstruction

The geodesic dilation enables the reconstruction of the buildings' shapes. This is the dilation of an image constrained by another image (Fig. 4). The first image is the assembly to dilate (marker) by a structuring element, which is a 3 pixels square (this is a size one dilation). The second image limits the expansion of the dilation: it is the mask.

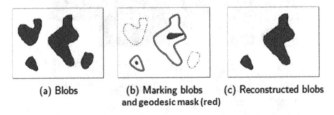

(a) Blobs        (b) Marking blobs        (c) Reconstructed blobs
                 and geodesic mask (red)

**Fig. 4.** Blob extraction by marking and reconstruction [9, 10].

In the example of Fig. 4, even if the marking blob only represents a small part of the mask it is, thus, reconstructed.

In this study, the anthropogenic detections are the blobs to reshape (red elements in Fig. 5). Blobs intersecting the existing database are the markers to be dilated (blue elements in Fig. 5), and the database itself is the mask (yellow polygons in Fig. 5).

**Fig. 5.** Geodesic dilation of the MNF detections [9]. (Color figure online)

This reconstruction allows obtaining maximum benefit from the MNF method, able to detect small and isolated buildings. A certain number of iterations lead to the reconstruction of the buildings existing in the database and detected by the MNF method (Fig. 6).

**Fig. 6.** Evolution of the geodesic reconstruction (iteration from 1 to 185) [9].

As the database used as a mask is outdated, detections corresponding to new buildings are out of the database: not all of the detections become markers. So, this morphological reconstruction must be completed by another step of reshaping. The anthropogenic detections that have not been reconstructed are reshaped.

## 5   Automatic Reshaping

The automatic reshaping method is the one imbedded in the ArcGIS solution: Minimum Bounding Geometry [11].

The first step of the reshaping is the selection of the MNF detections that have not been reconstructed. This step is a simple GIS combination of merging and intersection that enables to analyse, for each MNF detection, if it is "well represented" by the reconstruction. If the detection is covered by the reconstruction polygon at a minimum of a 60% rate, it is, thus, considered as well represented in the reconstruction. If not, the part of the detection that is not covered at all by the reconstruction is isolated and reshaped, as shown in Fig. 7.

Figure 7 illustrates the reshaping of a detection that is not correctly represented in the reconstruction step. Indeed, the blue circle shows an extended building visible on the image that is not in the existing database. The detection of this building is reshaped, as are the isolated surrounding ones. Notice that detections on the left side of the image are not reshaped because they are considered as "well represented" by the step of reconstruction (yellow polygons). Polygons smaller than 5 m² are cleared from the results, considered as not significant.

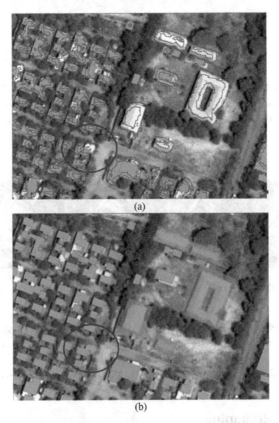

(a)

(b)

**Fig. 7.** Result of the reshaping (green polygons) from the MNF detections (red blobs) after the reconstruction step (yellow polygons) [9]. (Color figure online)

## 6 Results and Qualification

The compilation of the 3 steps (MNF detection, morphological reconstruction and automatic reshaping) leads to a global detection of buildings whether they already exist in the database, or are new buildings (respectively yellow and green polygons in Fig. 8).

The process enables to delete buildings present in the database that do not exist anymore and to complete the database with new buildings whether they are simple extensions of buildings or obvious urban expansion (green polygons in Fig. 8).

**Fig. 8.** Building detections in Dire Dawa [9]. (Color figure online)

### 6.1 Quantification with Individual Buildings Composed Database

**Dire Dawa Case.** Out of the 58,473 buildings present in the database, 52,528 have been reconstructed which represent 89% of the original database (90% in surface) (Fig. 9).

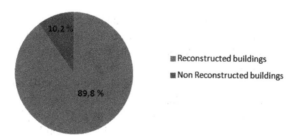

**Fig. 9.** Result of morphological reconstruction [9].

Out of the 5,945 non-reconstructed objects, 93% of them are small buildings with a surface smaller than 100 m$^2$. In the 7% of potential omissions of big buildings, the analysis of every and each building reveals (Fig. 10) that nearly 75% is a real omission, but in 17.5% of the cases, the buildings that have not been reconstructed have actually been destroyed.

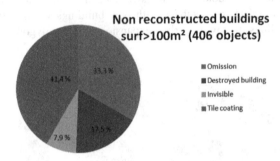

**Fig. 10.** Analysis of the non-reconstructed buildings which surface is over 100 m$^2$ [9].

In terms of percentage, 11% of the initial database was not reconstructed (potential omission) (Table 1), but significant omissions only represent 0.52%.

**Table 1.** Error Type II considering the reconstructed objects in Dire Dawa [9].

| | Total objects (reconstructed) | Total objects (in database) | Total potential omission (Error Type II) | Total potential omission (Error Type II) (%) | Important omission (buildings > 100 m$^2$) (Error Type II) | Important omission (buildings > 100 m$^2$) (Error Type II) (%) |
|---|---|---|---|---|---|---|
| Building reconstructed | 52528 | 58473 | 5945 | 11 | 303 | 0,52 |

Figure 11 highlights buildings present in the database (red polygons) that are not reconstructed because they do not exist anymore in the recent satellite image.

Detecting destroyed buildings allows to rapidly point outdated objects to producers in the context of rapid mapping.

One can notice that a large amount of omissions is due to a tile coating of houses. Indeed, this type of coating has a similar signal to vegetation and is not representative of the majority of houses. The learning process, as it uses a sample of buildings, is based on the major type of coating which is not tile. This problem is inherent to a radiometry based analysis in a complex landscape. An optional improvement step can be performed using additional data (cf. 7 Improvement step).

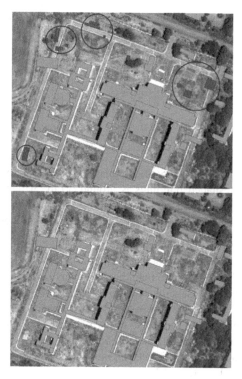

**Fig. 11.** Non-reconstruction of destroyed buildings (red polygons) [9]. (Color figure online)

An updated version of the database not being available, it is complicated to estimate type I errors concerning false positives. This would imply to check each of the reconstructed and reshaped polygons to validate their existence. This work has been done on a 100 polygons sample to estimate the quantity of false positives. Each polygon is checked and qualified as:

- positive: the corresponding building is clearly seen on the image. The shape of the polygon matches the reality or makes a relevant envelope around the buildings.
- false positive: no corresponding building on the image.
- not identifiable: the polygon does not really match the outline of the corresponding building. In this case it is possible that the building is not the detected element, but the detection is still relevant to point out anthropogenic features (cars and elements of the road are not comprised in these features). The results are presented in Table 2.

This analysis is made separately on the polygons resulting from the phase of reconstruction and the ones resulting from the phase of reshaping, in order to estimate which one of the phases produces more errors. Table 2 highlights the fact that the phase

**Table 2.** Error type I estimated on a sample of polygons [9].

|  | Total objects | Positive | False positive (Error Type I) | Not identifiable | Mean size of false positive (m$^2$) |
|---|---|---|---|---|---|
| Buildings reconstructed | 100 | 72 | 5 | 23 | 30 |
| Buildings reshaped | 100 | 59 | 23 | 18 | 14 |
| All buildings | 100 | 65 | 8 | 27 | 17 |

of reconstruction produces few errors of commission (5%). Moreover, the mean size or false positives in the reshaped buildings is around 30 m$^2$ which is a small surface. These results may be improved by changing the threshold of significant surfaces applied at the end of the reshaping phase (cf 5 Automatic Reshaping).

**Bangui Case.** In this case, the incoming data is the open source vector data OpenStreetMap. In 2013, because of the Central African conflict, the geographical community has strongly mobilized to map the city: many buildings were digitized. The images they used were Bing imageries and are filled in as from 2011 to 2013, which is only 1 year before the date of the processed Pleiades image.

The results over this city are similar to those obtained over Dire Dawa: 89% of the original database has been reconstructed (125,566 out of the 139,743 polygons present in the database). The non detected objects are in majority (88%) small buildings with a surface smaller than 100 m$^2$ (Fig. 12).

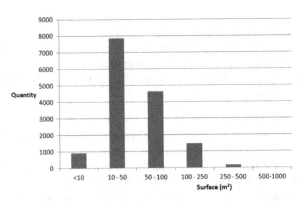

**Fig. 12.** Frequency distribution of non-reconstructed objects' surfaces in Bangui.

The number of objects with a size between 100 and 250 m$^2$ makes it difficult to verify all of them: only the non reconstructed objects with a size over 250 m$^2$ have been checked individually (Fig. 13).

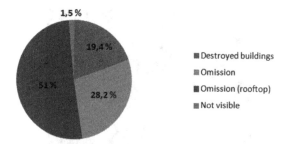

**Fig. 13.** Analysis of non-reconstructed objects with a surface over 250 m² (total of 206 objects).

Nearly 20% of the non-reconstructed objects are actually buildings that do not exist anymore. Nevertheless, the context of civil war in this area implies important and very fast changes in the landscape: Figure 14 puts this phenomenon in evidence showing changes occurring in Bangui within 6 months around the date of the processed Pleiades image.

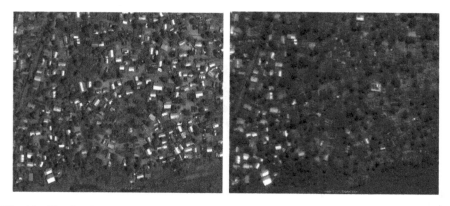

**Fig. 14.** Massive destructions south of Bangui airport between april 2014 (left) and august 2014 (right) (Google Earth images).

In this context, it is obvious that the potential omission rate announced (11%) is overestimated compared to the real omission rate. Considering the nature of the destructions, their estimation is investigated in polygons with a surface <100 m². A sample of 100 non-reconstructed polygons is randomly selected and verified (Fig. 15). It appears that 39% of the potential omissions correspond to disappeared buildings. Moreover, 16% of the selection corresponds to invisible buildings that are hidden by vegetation or that cannot be distinguished from its context in the satellite image. In the end, 29% of the polygons correspond to real omission. The remaining 16% correspond to a lack of detection linked to a problem of shift error between the image and the database (Fig. 16).

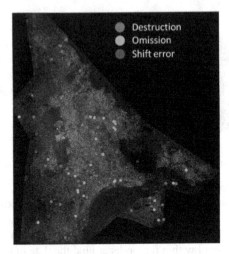

**Fig. 15.** Spatial distribution of confirmed destructions (red points), omissions (yellow points), and shift error (blue). (Color figure online)

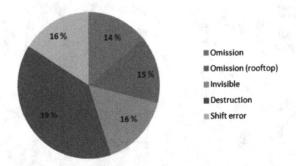

**Fig. 16.** Analysis of a sample of non-reconstructed objects with a surface under 100 m$^2$ (100 objects).

We observe, like in the Dire Dawa case, a lack of detection because of non reflective roof coatings: in Bangui lots of habitations are hardly distinguishable from the surrounding soil in a satellite image. Figure 17 illustrates objects that are not detected by the method because of their rooftops.

The statistics presented in Figs. 13 and 16 cannot be directly linked as they consider 2 classes of objects. In one hand, the omission rate is calculated around 79% for big buildings, on the other hand the omission rate is estimated at 29% for small buildings. Table 3 presents the global error type II for reconstructed objects and does not consider the estimated or calculated omission rate. Even in these conditions, the important potential omission rate is less than 1.5%.

**Fig. 17.** Example of invisible objects and omission linked to roof coating.

**Table 3.** Error Type II considering the reconstructed objects in Bangui.

|  | Total objects (reconstructed) | Total objects (in database) | Total potential omission (Error Type II) | Total potential omission (Error Type 11) (%) | Important potential omission (buildings > 100 m²) (Error Type II) | Important potential omission (buildings > 100 m²) (Error Type II) (%) |
|---|---|---|---|---|---|---|
| Building reconstructed | 125566 | 139743 | 15099 | 11 | 1695 | 1,21 |

The estimation of error type I (Table 4), reveals similar results than in the Dire Dawa case, meaning better results in the phase of reconstruction.

**Table 4.** Error type I in Bangui.

|  | Total objects | Positive | False positive (Error type I) | Not identifiable | Mean size of false positive (m²) |
|---|---|---|---|---|---|
| Buildings reconstructed | 100 | 78 | 6 | 16 | 74 |
| Buildings reshaped | 100 | 53 | 39 | 8 | 74 |

These results are easily explained considering the resolution of the satellite image and the spatial organization of the city: many buildings, with different types of roof coatings and sparse vegetation (Fig. 18).

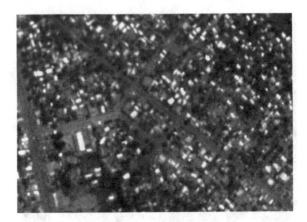

**Fig. 18.** Complex aspect and reflective answers of Bangui city.

In terms of database updating, the results are still satisfactory as they give relevant information on changes that occurred. Figure 19 shows detections of refugees' camps on the airport's site.

**Fig. 19.** Refugees habitations on the airport site.

Moreover, as the MNF method is just an indicator for database updating and has no motivation to become an exhaustive automatic mapping tool, we can accept to downgrade its precision to raise the surface of studied areas and free ourselves from financial limitations. Indeed, in both Dire Dawa and Bangui cases, the processed images are commercial imagery with a resolution better than 5 m, and for Dire Dawa, the database is not free of charges.

Sentinel-2 delivers images at 10 m resolution, free of charges in the context of the European Copernicus program.

The scale of the resulting detections (minimum 100 m$^2$ corresponding to a 10 × 10 m pixel) not being compatible with the scale of the database (buildings as small as few square meters), a simplified version of the MNF (no reconstruction nor reshaping phases) is implemented. A visual analysis reveals analogous results than the previous method (with reshaping and remodeling of detections) (Fig. 20).

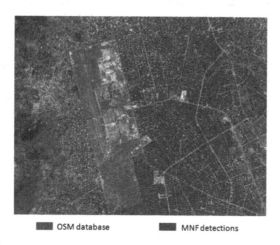

■■■ OSM database          ■■■ MNF detections

**Fig. 20.** Comparison between OSM outdated database (blue) and MNF detections (violet) processed on a Sentinel-2 image (2017-05-13). (Color figure online)

In Fig. 20 the detections quickly highlight the apparition of buildings in the northeast part of the airport (Fig. 21).

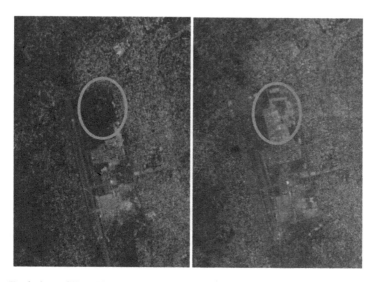

**Fig. 21.** Evolution of Bangui airport between august 2014 and february 2017 (Google Earth images).

## 6.2  Visual Qualification on Various Areas

The robustness of the MNF method has been tested with 3 different types of images (Spot6, Pleiades, Landsat), with 3 different spatial resolutions (1.5 m, 6 m, 15 m), with different landscapes (desert, dense urban area, mangrove, mine), on different swathes and with different levels of the database's obsolescence. Each one of the 11 tests were realized with the same settings: a unique list of representative urban objects for the learning phase (no "building" layer available, as in the Dire Dawa case), a variance calculated from the second band of the MNF result, and a size of fragment proportional to the pixel size. And each one of them led to an enriched analysis of the database's obsolescence. Most of all, the method has been tested in an operational context as an input data for the map producers.

In Saint-Louis (Senegal) the method spotted urban extensions, in Mali it detected a whole gold mine (Loulo) that was absent from the database (Fig. 22). In the following figures the red marks correspond to the indicator and the grey areas correspond to the objects in the database.

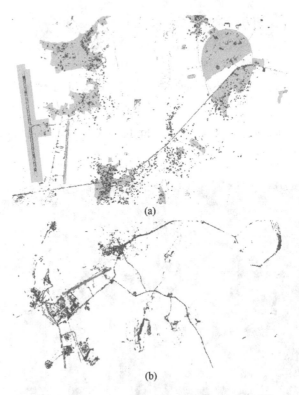

(a)

(b)

**Fig. 22.** Urban extensions in Saint-Louis, Senegal (a) and detection of the Loulo gold mine in Mali (b) [9]. (Color figure online)

At a different scale, in Dubai and Bamako new infrastructures and non-existing ones were highlighted by superimposing the indicator on the initial database (Fig. 23).

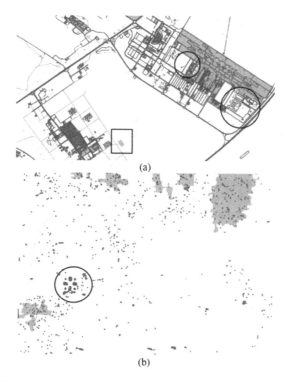

(a)

(b)

**Fig. 23.** New (circles) and obsolete (square) infrastructures in Dubaï (a) and Bamako (b) [9].

In addition of detecting the infrastructures, the process limits the false detections which are, in most of change detection methods, a limiting factor of use. In [12] the impervious surface was overestimated in the less-developed areas but was overestimated in the well-developed areas. In our case, if the false detections still exist, they are so few that they don't perturb the visual analysis of the indicator. Figure 24 illustrates the ability of the process to concentrate the detections in the urban area amongst a wide desertic study area.

Note that detections in (b) Fig. 24 correspond to small settlements.

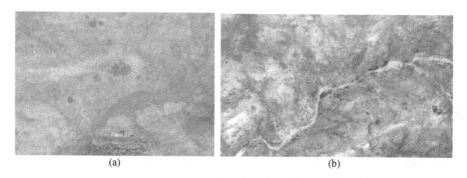

(a)                                            (b)

**Fig. 24.** Desertic areas with very few false detections in Abeche (a) and Forchana (b), Chad. [9].

## 7  Improvement Step

If the method gives good results, an improvement is always possible. A choice of useful band is done after the MNF transformation. It appears that the urban information is not represented in just one band. The detailed process can be performed on another band or with additional data.

Surface elevation models provide a useful additional information as it is independent of the radiometric aspect of the data. With such a model, the tile coating of the buildings, in the Dire Dawa example, and the fact that its spectral signal is very close to vegetation, is not a problem anymore. The introduction of a geometric primitive (and not radiometric) allows a more invariant detection of buildings. Nevertheless, we chose not to work initially with a surface elevation model as we focused on the satellite image. Derivating such a model from a stereo or tri-stereo satellite image is thus possible, but is not the focusing point of our work. In his thesis, Champion [13] proposes an innovative database updating based on the improvement of a Digital Terrain Model (DTM) derived from a Digital Elevation Model (DEM).

In the case of Dire Dawa, DEM and DTM data were available. The vegetation index (NDVI) is calculated on the image to improve the distinction between elevated objects corresponding to buildings and other ones corresponding to trees. The elevation data, masked from the vegetation, is then used in the reconstruction step. In the first reconstruction step, 156 buildings with a surface superior to 200 m$^2$ were missing. The improvement step allows to reconstruct 73% of the omissions and 70% of the tile coating buildings (Fig. 25).

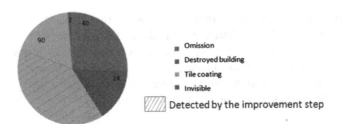

**Fig. 25.** Improvement due to elevation and NDVI data [9].

The major inconvenient to this step is that it adds commission errors to the results. Indeed, Fig. 25 shows the reconstruction of 33% of destroyed buildings.

## 8  Conclusion

This article presents a semi-automatic tool detecting urban areas. The tool does not aim at exhaustively map each and every buildings present in the satellite image, it is an indicator of location and amount of urban areas.

In the context of database updating it tends to answer the question "where and when" but furthermore gives a quantitative estimation of the number of new buildings to collect with an acceptable inaccuracy to manage the updating process. The scalability of the method allows different uses: the results can be presented in a map, to spot the necessity of the database update, it can be presented over the original image to help the producers to focus on important updating areas (especially destroyed buildings), or it can be used at the end of the production process as a quality control.

The evolution from "urban indicator for database updating" to "urban change detection tool" is reachable thanks to a pile of images with a good resolution. A strength of this method is to be source agnostic: it can be processed on a SPOT6 image at time A and on a Pleiades image at time B.

Even if it was not the initial context of this research, we have been able to isolate buildings in low density built-up areas. Thus, the process gives quantitative indicators for a "from scratch" production and allows, with low cost methods, figurative automatic reconstruction that could be provided within very short-time period.

The method, using radiometric primitives improvable with geometric primitives, is adaptable to the type of landscapes, images, scales, and has been recognized as useful by independent producers during a real updating process test, not only as a detection of anthropogenic areas process, but as a real decision support instrument.

## 9  Discussion

If this tool has proved its efficiency in a context of rapid mapping, it cannot be trusted as it is for an exhaustive automatic mapping tool. Indeed, a building that has changed its shape between the date of the database and the date of the image will probably be reconstructed as it was in the past.

If we were able to observe very few errors of commission (error type I) we didn't establish real statistics on a representative amount of elements. Moreover, in the statistics established on type II errors, some missing polygons were considered as omission but the field reality (the image) was obviously different than the representing database: in this case the qualification of omission is not really correct.

In this study, two types of databases were tested. The most advanced cases (Dire Dawa and Bangui) used databases in which the buildings were individually drawn. This allowed us doing the reconstruction and the derived statistics and declaring the method efficient. This is not possible with a database in which the buildings are not individually drawn. This is why a simple visual qualification is done on the other tested areas (Sect. 6.2). When using this type of database another type of statistics can be calculated to estimate the changes and the amount of work in the pre-production phase, but the quality assessment of the method by calculating the reconstruction rate is not possible. Another option would be to compare our detection to other urban products (mixing different types of data) like Global Urban Footprint or Landscan.

The cartographic representation of the results could help harmonize results obtained with different sources, like the count of urban areas (in $m^2$) in a pre-defined grid. Moreover, the size of the grid could be adapted to the scale of the study (city, province, state etc.).

# References

1. Lu, D., et al.: Change detection techniques. J. Remote Sens. **25**(12), 2365–2407 (2003)
2. Lu, D., Weng, Q.: Spectral mixture analysis of the urban landscapes in Indianapolis with Landsat ETM + imagery. Photogram. Eng. Remote Sens. **69**, 973–980 (2004)
3. Zhang, Q., Wang, J.: A rule-based urban land use inferring method for fine-resolution multispectral imagery. Can. J. Remote. Sens. **29**, 1–13 (2003)
4. Walter, V.: Automatic change detection in GIS databases based on classification of multispectral-data. In: ISPRS Archive, Amsterdam, vol. XXXIII Part B4 (2000)
5. Green, A.A., Berman, M., Switzer, P., Craig, M.D.: A transformation for ordering multispectral data in terms of image quality with implications for noise removal. IEEE Trans. Geosci. Remote Sens. (GRS) **26**(1), 65–74 (1988)
6. ENVI 4.2: User's Guide, vol. 2, chapt. 7 (2005)
7. Vermillion, S., Sader, S.: Use of the minimum noise fraction (MNF) transform to analyze airborne visible/infrared imaging spectrometer (AVIRIS) data of northern forest types. In: AVIRIS Workshop Bibliography (1999)
8. Haralick, R., Shanmugan, K., Dinstein, I.: Textural features for image classification. IEEE Trans. Syst. Man Cybern. **SMC-3**(6), 610–621 (1978)
9. Navaro, B., Sadeq, Z., Saporiti, N.: Urban indicator for database updating - a decision tool to help stakeholders and map producers. In: Proceedings of the 3rd International Conference on Geographical Information Systems Theory, Applications and Management, vol. 1: GISTAM, pp. 81–89 (2017). https://doi.org/10.5220/0006327600810089. ISBN 978-989-758-252-3
10. Van Droogenbroeck, M.: Computer Vision. Open Repository and Bibliography. Université de Liège (2015–2016)
11. ArcGIS for desktop Help. http://desktop.arcgis.com/en/arcmap/latest/tools/data-management-toolbox/minimum-bounding-geometry.htm. Accessed 23 Aug 2017
12. Lu, D., Weng, Q.: Use of impervious surface in urban land-use classification. Remote Sens. Environ. **102**(1), 146–160 (2006)
13. Champion, N.: Détection de changement 2D à partir d'imagerie satellitaire. Application à la mise à jour des bases de données géographiques, thesis (2011)

# Implications of Data Density and Length of Collection Period for Population Estimations Using Social Media Data

Samuel Lee Toepke$^{(\boxtimes)}$

Private Engineering Firm, Washington DC, USA
I.samueltoepke@gmail.com
http://www.samueltoepke.com

**Abstract.** When programmatically utilizing public APIs provided by social media services, it is possible to attain a large volume of volunteered geographic information. Geospatially enabled data from Twitter, Instagram, Panaramio, etc. can be used to create high-resolution estimations of human movements over time, with volume of the data being of critical importance. This investigation extends previous work, showing the effects of artificial data removal, and generated error; though using over twice as much collected data, attained using an enterprise cloud solution, over a span of thirteen months instead of five.

**Keywords:** Media · Enterprise systems · Cloud
Volunteered geographic data

## 1  Introduction

Population estimation of an urban area is of critical importance for resource planning, emergency response, land-use allocation, environmental protection, etc. Governing bodies have continued to rely on a combination of traditional practices to generate population data; namely through the use of census information, time-use surveys, land-use maps and geospatial data. These methods are time consuming, of low spatiotemporal precision, and costly to implement; though novel fusion of the aforementioned methods has been shown to increase utility [8].

In recent years, research involving the estimation of population density of an urban space, using social media services, has been rapidly gaining interest. A user of a social media service can generate geospatially enabled 'posts' while tagging an image, string of text, or other piece of information. Disaggregation of this data based on its latitude, longitude and temporal components generates insight into the population patterns of a given geographic space [28]. Population estimation is best visualized as a function of time and space; common representations include a dasymetric map [21] and/or an occupancy curve [29].

© Springer Nature Switzerland AG 2019
L. Ragia et al. (Eds.): GISTAM 2017, CCIS 936, pp. 57–69, 2019.
https://doi.org/10.1007/978-3-030-06010-7_4

Massive growth of connected technologies has created new opportunities for using volunteered social media data to supplement traditional population estimation methods. These technologies include:

- Social media services. Twitter, Facebook, Foursquare, Panaramio, etc. allow users to generate geospatially enabled data, and make that data publicly available [11].
- Pervasive computing devices. Modern smartphones and tablets are readily accessible, with a low financial barrier to entry. The majority are outfitted with a GPS sensor, touch-screen, battery, Internet connection, and a full sensor suite.
- Highly available Internet. A constant, inexpensive connection through cellular or Wi-Fi allows distribution of generated data to a wide audience.

Using an application programming interface (API) published by the social media service, it is feasible to use an enterprise software solution to regularly query these services, and receive/process crowd-sourced data [2]. Denser data often leads to a more complete population estimation; but constraints may limit the amount of data that can be attained/stored/processed for a given area.

This investigation focuses on running data-loss experiments on Twitter data obtained from the downtown areas of cities in the United States of America (USA). Data acquisition/processing is discussed, and the implications of data-loss are explored in several charts.

## 2   Background

The field of earth observation consists of using electronic resources to explore the planet. Aforementioned growth of use/accessibility of smart devices and social media services has enabled the 'citizens as sensors' [10] paradigm, allowing contributors to provide a wealth of crowd-sourced information to those who are interested [6]. This information can range from annotating satellite data using the OpenStreetMap project [15], to contributing to a wiki page, to reporting on unique geographic locations using text or imagery. Not only does the contributed information provide value, processing of the geospatial metadata can provide insight into the human population patterns and individual activities throughout the day [3].

The use of volunteered data is not without challenges. It is imperative to not treat the data as absolute; incorrect submissions can exist for any number of reasons, and objective comparison to truth is often difficult to affect [16]. This specific use case can have accuracy degraded by the use of illicit accounts to boost perceived population in certain locations and/or venues. Nonetheless, the data is still useful for this estimation, with follow-on work including comparison against an objective measure.

One of the benefits of crowd-sourced data is also one of its biggest drawbacks, the massive amount of data being produced, consumed, processed, and stored

[4, 22]. Effective knowledge extraction requires planning, provisioning, maintenance and retiring of computational, algorithmic and human resources. Policies on how to best manage this data directly affect the end result of processing, for each project. Constraints include cost, time, skillset of investigators, access to enterprise/human resources, etc. With the intention of exploring how algorithmic output can change based on data density, this investigation shows the implications of artificial data loss on Twitter data being used for population estimation.

Previously, only one city was the focus of investigation; recent code refactoring allows the rapid addition of new cities to query. Five major cities in the western U.S. were chosen for the following reasons:

- Each city has a densely populated downtown area.
- The west coast is directly at risk for coastal and seismic natural disasters. With a possible "Cascadia Rising" [7] level event in the future, population estimation for emergency first responders will be critical for cities like Portland and Seattle [17].
- A high level of tech-adoption, and voluntary use of social media services by the city's residents is beneficial to the investigation.

The cities are as follows:

- San Diego, California (CA); a coastal town in southern California with a large military presence, and many institutions of higher learning.
- San Francisco, CA; a metropolitan port city surrounded by water on three sides.
- San Jose, CA; the southern end of Silicon Valley.
- Portland, Oregon (OR); a counter-cultural and environmentally conscious city.
- Seattle, Washington (WA); home to many technology firms including Amazon and Microsoft.

The Tweets are retrieved/stored for the above cities, and processed as described in the following section.

## 3   Architecture

Geospatially enabled, crowd-sourced Twitter data is gathered using a modern enterprise implementation based on elastic cloud and web services. This solution is the next generation of the previous Twitter retrieving software [30]. While the previous code was a proof of concept, this implementation is modularly designed for rapid expansion to new cities of interest. This task is completed by adding another configuration file with the specifications for the city, mainly the latitude/longitude coordinates for each Twitter query.

Amazon Web Services (AWS) [26] is a suite of inexpensive cloud services that are available to the general public. AWS's cloud offerings have gained massive growth in the past few years, and have made a powerful platform available with a low barrier to entry [20].

The AWS technologies used are as follows:

– Lambda, runs as a scheduled task twice an hour that executes the source code, using a serverless, code-in-the-cloud paradigm.
– DynamoDB, is leveraged as a fully managed, NoSQL object store for the Twitter data.
– Elastic MapReduce (EMR), Data Pipeline, and S3 export the Twitter data to a text file for local processing.
– Identity and Access Management, CloudWatch and CodeCommit are used administratively.

The source code is written using Java Platform, Enterprise Edition [25]; and performs all web service, security, data storage and AWS integration tasks. The inherent scalability/elasticity in Lambda/DynamoDB allows the implementation to grow organically as new cities are added, and with no further infrastructure configuration from the developer. Architecture blueprint can be seen in Fig. 1.

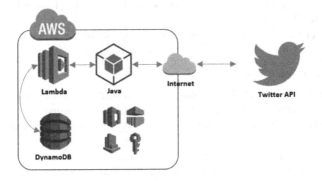

**Fig. 1.** AWS Twitter query/storage architecture [32].

To create the functionality of true geospatial queries, the Java Topology Suite (JTS) [19] is leveraged during Tweet processing. JTS is a lightweight library that enables spatial analysis methods, and is utilized heavily by open source Java geographic information system projects, e.g. GeoServer, GeoTools and uDig. In this case, the point-in-polygon [14] algorithm is used, which allows geographic searching without a full geospatial solution like PostgreSQL/PostGIS [27]. While the current Tweet collection code utilizes a quadrangle with horizontal/vertical edges, JTS allows querying of areas with arbitrary orientation and number of edge vertices, which is critical when analyzing individual structures.

Existing functionality that is not currently utilized includes the creation of a geohash [24] which is generated when each Tweet is placed in the data store. The geohash string is a lightweight description that allows efficient searching for geographic neighbors. A geohash of twelve characters is used, which maps to a cell space of $3.7\,cm * 1.9\,cm$ [9], and is more than adequate precision for this work. The geospatial resolution of each Tweet is dependent on the device submitting the data, and the combination of technologies leveraged e.g. global positioning, Wi-Fi, cellular triangulation, etc. While none of the aforementioned technologies have centimeter-level accuracy, the extra length of the geohash does not add undue complexity; and future-proofs the algorithm against increases in resolution.

Twitter and Instagram were both considered as sources of crowd-sourced data for reasons previously elucidated [30]. As of mid-2016, the Instagram API is constructed such that downloading freely available data for the purpose of research is no longer supported, further discussion can be found in [32]. There is a company [12] which sells historical and/or full-stream access to social media data, but the cost is out of scope for this work.

In [32], five months of data was captured; in this follow-on work over double the amount of data points will be used. The data is exported from DynamoDB using an EMR job when a snapshot is desired, and saved into a text file for local processing. Using Java, queries/experiments were run on the data to show the implications of a loss of data density. The experiments start with using 100% of the gleaned Tweets, then proceed to remove 5% for each further run, until the density is down to 0% of the original post quantity. Charts are generated using an open source tool named GNU Octave [13], and are discussed in the results/observations section. These experiments are run on both sets of data (5 months and 13 months), and a comparison is drawn between the results of the two collection periods.

## 4    Results/Observations

The data consists of geospatially enabled posts from the Twitter API occurring from two time periods. The first from 2016-06-08 03:01:35 (GMT) to 2016-11-05 03:57:03 (GMT), and the second from 2016-06-08 03:01:35 (GMT) to 2017-07-16 23:43:19 (GMT). The first set of data, spanning 5 months is utilized in [32]; the collection code continued to run, resulting in the new 13 month dataset. Publicly available web service APIs were used to download the data in a JavaScript Object Notation format.

Upon processing the Twitter data from the collection time periods, immediate observations can be made. The raw Tweet count for the different cities varies, with the most (Seattle, WA), having more than twice as many Tweets as the least (San Jose, CA), which can be seen in Table 1, and visualized in Fig. 2. A reason for the disparity is unknown, and could range from differing population density, to more/less user activity on social media services. Each city's Tweet count for the longer collection period is mostly proportional with the shorter collection period. During collection, the same geospatial distance is kept between the latitude/longitude boundary points for the different cities, with the collection area being placed over downtown as precisely as possible. The average query area for each city is approximately $3.2633612\,km\char`^2$. A map visualizing the boundary, and overlapping queries for the city of San Jose, CA can be see in Fig. 3.

On average, the cities show a dip towards the middle of the week, with Tweet count growing stronger at the end of the week, which can be seen in Fig. 4. Of

**Table 1.** Total Tweet count per city.

| City | Tweet count, 5 mos. | Tweet count, 13 mos. |
|---|---|---|
| San Jose, CA | 49,557 | 129,414 |
| San Francisco, CA | 62,555 | 150,941 |
| Portland, OR | 85,745 | 226,901 |
| San Diego, CA | 115,574 | 264,635 |
| Seattle, WA | 133,955 | 339,886 |

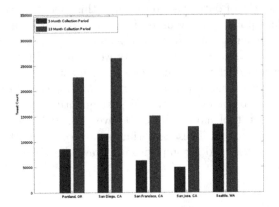

**Fig. 2.** Total Tweet count per city.

note, Tweet collection from downtown San Jose, CA for the investigation [30], shows a parabolic curve from Sunday to Saturday with a mid-week peak. The difference in the curvature for the two datasets can be the result of different social media use-patterns that have developed over the past two years, and/or the result of a non-consistent collection time period. Also of note, is that for Seattle, San Diego and San Francisco, there is a noticeable decrease in the average number of Tweets for the full 13 month time period in comparison to the 5 month time period. The cause of this change in use-patterns is worth investigation for follow-on work.

To begin investigation of Tweet removal, Friday was chosen as an experimentation day. The average tweet count for Friday is not the lowest, nor the highest; but in the median. An average Tweet count per hour can be seen in Fig. 5. All cities show a strong upward trend between 0600 and 0800, and a strong downward trend between 1700 and 1800. The trends correlate precisely with the beginning/end of the work day. As expected, the lowest hours for Tweet generation are from 0000 to 0500, correlating to when users are sleeping. The 13 months of data shows trends commensurate with the 5 month data set.

Normalizing each of the data sets is useful to view the Twitter patterns independent of total quantity of Tweets. Using a basic normalization algorithm [1], such that the length of each data vector is equal to 1, the resulting graph

**Fig. 3.** Twitter query locations and boundary for San Jose, CA. [32]

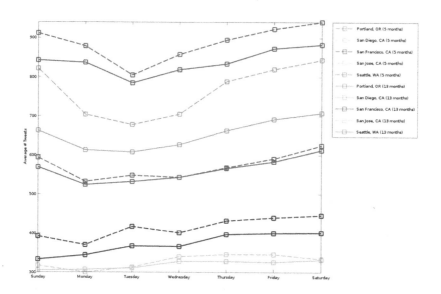

**Fig. 4.** Average Tweet count per day.

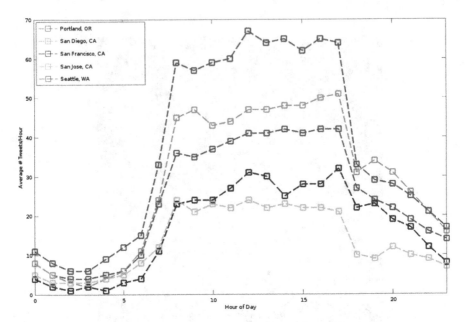

**Fig. 5.** Average Tweet count per hour, fridays, 2016-06-08 to 2017-07-16.

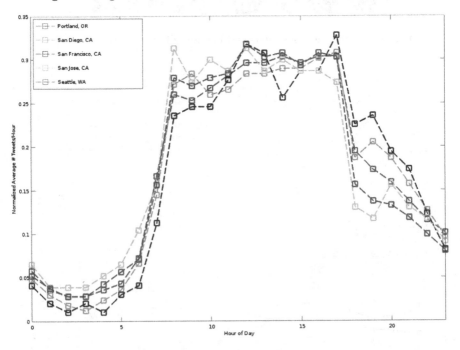

**Fig. 6.** Normalized average Tweet count per hour, fridays, 2016-06-08 to 2017-07-16.

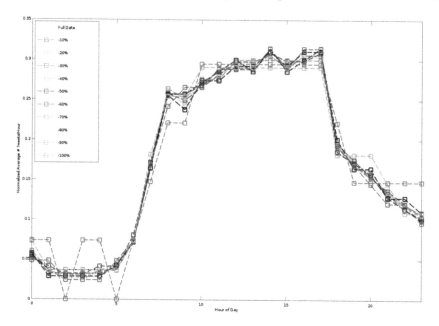

**Fig. 7.** Normalized average Tweet count per hour, fridays for Portland, OR with data removal, 2016-06-08 to 2017-07-16.

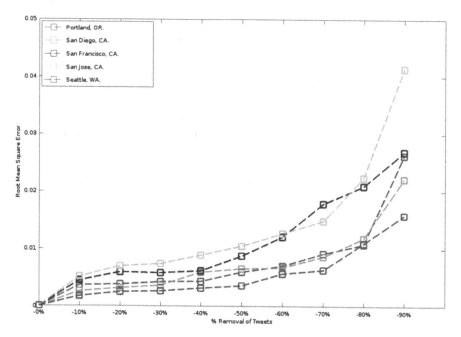

**Fig. 8.** Root mean square error for normalized average Tweet count per hour, on fridays, with data removal, 2016-06-08 to 2017-07-16.

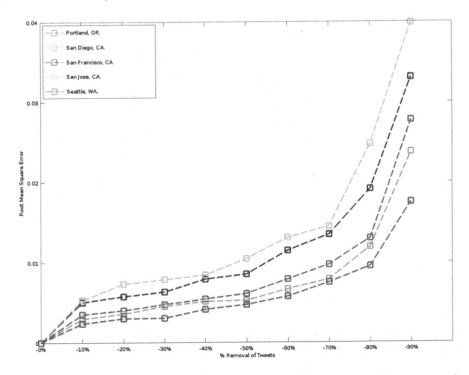

**Fig. 9.** Root mean square error for normalized average Tweet count per hour, averaged from all days of week, with data removal, 2016-06-08 to 2017-07-16.

for normalized average Tweet count per hour for a Friday can be seen in Fig. 6. It is of note that San Francisco, CA gets a slower start to the day, but tends to generate more Tweets, for longer, after the end of the workday. This is perhaps indicative of a strong 'after-work' social culture; a similar pattern is also seen for San Diego, CA.

Under the assumption that the full data is of 100% quantity, Java code is used to randomly remove data in increasing steps of 10%. These tests are performed arbitrarily on Portland, OR, with the city being in the median of the cities for Tweet quantity. Once normalized, the resulting plots are shown in Fig. 7. As each plot has an increasing amount of data removed, it can be seen deviating more from the full data line. 100% removal is not displayed, as there is no data visible. Though coarse, even with 90% of the data removed, the generated plot offers useful insights into the population density throughout the day.

Root mean square error (RMSE) [5,32], is then used to better visualize the effects of decreasing data quantities. RMSE Equation:

$$RMSE = \sqrt{\frac{1}{n}\sum_{i=1}^{n}(y_i - \bar{y}_i)^2} \qquad (1)$$

Each resulting data vector is compared against the full 100% data quantity vector, and the results can be seen in Fig. 8. A full averaging of all the days of the week can be seen in Fig. 9. Of note:

- For each city, a pareto optimal point [18] exists between 50% and 90% loss.
- A reasonable population estimation can still be gleaned with even up to 50% of the data being artificially removed.
- It can be seen that overall data quantity has an impact on the RMSE, with the population estimation of cities with the most overall Tweets being not as adversely affected by loss of data. Seattle, WA shows the lowest RMSE with San Jose, CA showing the highest RMSE. This is seen visibly in Fig. 9, which makes an average from all days of the week.
- Though there is over 100% more data for the 13 month collection period, the averaged RMSEs for both collection periods are commensurate. This is indicative that the 5 months worth of data is more than enough to generate a useful population estimation picture, even with significant percentages of data missing/removed.

## 5   Follow-On Work

This investigation shows the ramifications of data density and collection period for a population estimation using crowd-sourced, geospatially enabled social media data. There are many avenues for further work.

- It has been shown that due to the small amount of Tweets that are actually geotagged, when using the public API an almost complete set of Tweets is available [23]. Obtaining full-stream Twitter data for the geospatial areas in question, and comparing/contrasting with the publicly available data would strengthen previously obtained results.
- Perform experimentation on tighter geographical boundaries. E.g., would these results still hold for a single residential apartment building, a university dormitory or a busy restaurant? What would the impact of reduced data density be on structure occupancy curves [31] for a building throughout days of the week?
- Integration of other social media sources such as Twitter, Facebook, Foursquare, Panaramio, etc.
- Attempt to normalize data acquisition amongst downtown areas. The investigation areas are picked with care, but not with deep knowledge of each urban area. One stadium in one city, or several large office buildings, can skew the total Tweets for an area.
- Experimentation in secondary and/or smaller cities. Each city investigated has a large population of technology adopters; which makes using social media for population estimation possible. Performing this work on cities that don't generate as much data would provide useful for showing limitations of this work.

# 6   Conclusions

This investigation has shown further exploration into the area of population estimation from social media data. Based on previous work showing the implications of data quantity, a comparison of results from a longer data collection period is discussed. While data quantity is critical, it is shown in that the 5 months of data is adequate. Further research would be beneficial, involving similar experiments using shorter collection time spans; knowledge of a minimum-viable collection period would bring greater confidence to population estimation accuracy.

# References

1. Abdi, H., Williams, L.J.: Normalizing Data. Encyclopedia of Research Design, pp. 935–938. Sage, Thousand Oaks (2010)
2. Aubrecht, C., Ungar, J., Freire, S.: Exploring the potential of volunteered geographic information for modeling spatio-temporal characteristics of urban population: a case study for Lisbon Metro using foursquare check-in data. In: 7th International Conference Virtual City and Territory, Lisboa, pp. 57–60 (2011)
3. Aubrecht, C., Özceylan Aubrecht, D., Ungar, J., Freire, S., Steinnocher, K.: VGDI-advancing the concept: volunteered geo-dynamic information and its benefits for population dynamics modeling. Trans. GIS **21**, 253–276 (2016)
4. Boyd, D., Crawford, K.: Critical questions for big data: provocations for a cultural, technological, and scholarly phenomenon. Inf. Commun. Soc. **15**(5), 662–679 (2012)
5. Chai, T., Draxler, R.R.: Root mean square error (RMSE) or mean absolute error (MAE)?-arguments against avoiding RMSE in the literature. Geosci. Model. Dev. **7**(3), 1247–1250 (2014)
6. Coleman, D.J., Georgiadou, Y., Labonte, J., et al.: Volunteered geographic information: the nature and motivation of produsers. Int. J. Spat. Data Infrastruct. Res. **4**(1), 332–358 (2009)
7. FEMA: Cascadia Rising 2016. https://www.fema.gov/cascadia-rising-2016. Accessed 08 Dec 2016
8. Freire, S., Florczyk, A., Ferri, S.: Modeling day-and nighttime population exposure at high resolution: application to volcanic risk assessment in campi flegrei. In: 12th International Conference on Information Systems for Crisis Response and Management (2015)
9. GeoHash grid Aggregation, Elasticsearch Reference 5.0. https://www.elastic.co/guide/en/elasticsearch/reference/current/search-aggregations-bucket-geohashgrid-aggregation.html. Accessed 29 July 2017
10. Goodchild, M.F.: Citizens as sensors: the world of volunteered geography. GeoJournal **69**(4), 211–221 (2007)
11. Goodchild, M.F., Aubrecht, C., Bhaduri, B.: New questions and a changing focus in advanced VGI research. Trans. GIS **21**, 189–190 (2016)
12. GNIP - The World's Largest and Most Trusted Provider of Social Data. https://gnip.com/. Accessed 29 July 2017
13. GNU Octave. https://www.gnu.org/software/octave/. Accessed 29 July 2017
14. Haines, E.: Point in polygon strategies. In: Graphics gems IV, vol. 994, pp. 24–26 (1994)
15. Haklay, M., Weber, P.: Openstreetmap: user-generated street maps. IEEE Pervasive Comput. **7**(4), 12–18 (2008)

16. Haklay, M.: How good is volunteered geographical information? A comparative study of OpenStreetMap and ordnance survey datasets. Environ. Plan. B: Plan. Des. **37**(4), 682–703 (2010)

17. Heaton, T.H., Hartzell, S.H.: Earthquake hazards on the Cascadia subduction zone. Science **236**(4798), 162–168 (1987)

18. Hochman, H.M., Rodgers, J.D.: Pareto optimal redistribution. Am. Econ. Rev. **59**(4), 542–557 (1969)

19. JTS Topology Suite. https://github.com/locationtech/jts. Accessed 29 July 2017

20. Leong, L., Toombs, D., Gill, B.: Magic quadrant for cloud infrastructure as a service, worldwide. Analyst(s) 501, G00265139 (2015)

21. Mennis, J., Hultgren, T.: Intelligent dasymetric mapping and its application to areal interpolation. Cartogr. Geogr. Inf. Sci. **33**(3), 179–194 (2006)

22. Miller, H.J.: The data avalanche is here. Shouldn't we be digging? J. Reg. Sci. **50**(1), 181–201 (2010)

23. Morstatter, F., Pfeffer, J., Liu, H., Carley, K.M.: Is The Sample Good Enough? Comparing Data from Twitter's Streaming API with Twitter's Firehose. arXiv preprint arXiv:1306.5204 (2013)

24. Moussalli, R., Srivatsa, M., Asaad, S.: Fast and flexible conversion of geohash codes to and from latitude/longitude coordinates. In: 2015 IEEE 23rd Annual International Symposium on Field-Programmable Custom Computing Machines (FCCM). IEEE (2015)

25. Oracle Technology Network for Java Developers — Oracle Technology Network — Oracle. http://www.oracle.com/technetwork/java/index.html. Accessed 29 July 2017

26. Overview of Amazon Web Services. https://d0.awsstatic.com/whitepapers/aws-overview.pdf. Accessed 29 July 2017

27. PostGIS - Spatial and Geographic Objects for PostgreSQL. http://www.postgis.net. Accessed 29 July 2017

28. Sagl, G., Resch, B., Hawelka, B., Beinat, E.: From social sensor data to collective human behaviour patterns: analysing and visualising spatio-temporal dynamics in urban environments. In: Proceedings of the GI-Forum, pp. 54–63 (2012)

29. Stewart, R., et al.: Can social media play a role in developing building occupancy curves for small area estimation? In: Proceedings of 13th International Conference GeoComp (2015)

30. Toepke, S.L., Starsman, R.S.: Population distribution estimation of an urban area using crowd sourced data for disaster response. In: 12th International Conference on Information Systems for Crisis Response and Management (2015)

31. Toepke, S.L.: Investigation of geospatially enabled, social media generated structure occupancy curves in commercial structures. In: Grueau, C., Laurini, R., Rocha, J.G. (eds.) GISTAM 2016. CCIS, vol. 741, pp. 49–61. Springer, Cham (2017). https://doi.org/10.1007/978-3-319-62618-5_4

32. Toepke, S.L.: Data density considerations for crowd sourced population estimations from social media. In: Proceedings of the 3rd International Conference on Geographical Information Systems Theory, Applications and Management - GISTAM, vol. 1, pp. 35–42 (2017)

# Bootstrapping the Dynamic Generation of Indoor Maps with Crowdsourced Smartphone Sensor Data

Georgios Pipelidis[✉], Christian Prehofer, and Ilias Gerostathopoulos

Fakultät für Informatik, Technische Universität München, Munich, Germany
{georgios.pipelidis,christian.prehofer,ilias.gerostathopoulos}@in.tum.de

**Abstract.** Although there is a considerable progress in mapping the indoor places, most of the existing techniques are either expensive or difficult to apply. In this paper, we articulate our view on the future of indoor mapping, which is based on customized, crowdsourced and scalable approaches. On the basis of this approach, we discuss the research challenges that we envision to face in this world of customized bootstrapping and diverse techniques and services. We focus our interest in the combination of multiple of indoor mapping generation techniques and discuss challenges and various indoor mapping techniques. We introduce our adaptive method for bootstrapping the procedure of indoor mapping in multiple ways through intermediate services. Those emerged services enable the obtaining of useful data for this procedure, while they increase the quality of those data. We discuss the necessary components for such approach and we give an example of a bootstrapping procedure.

**Keywords:** Indoor mapping · Crowdsourcing · Bootstrapping process

## 1 Introduction

Indoor mapping is an enabler for many applications such as indoor navigation systems, augmented reality or even robotics. This is a useful service even if indoor localization is not available, since it enables people to have a view of the indoor place. Together with indoor localization techniques, which have been an active area of research [1], indoor mapping can help materialize the vision for ubiquitous indoor positioning system on a worldwide scale [2].

There is considerable progress in the mapping of indoor places, and many diverse techniques have been proposed, ranging from vision-based [3] and robot-based [4], up to crowdsourced mapping [2]. However, most of the existing techniques are either expensive or difficult to apply, since sensors and methods are usually prone to error due to a variety of the building structures. It remains a challenge to provide cost-effective, easy-to-apply mapping techniques which can cover the large volume and variety of indoor places with their often unique characteristics and semantics. Furthermore, there is a large volume of indoor places

© Springer Nature Switzerland AG 2019
L. Ragia et al. (Eds.): GISTAM 2017, CCIS 936, pp. 70–84, 2019.
https://doi.org/10.1007/978-3-030-06010-7_5

to be considered. For instance, the building footprints in Open Street Maps (OSM) recently surpassed the amount of the street data—not even considering the indoor maps [5].

In this paper, we articulate our view on the future of indoor mapping, which is based on the fact that (i) mapping techniques differ in terms of complexity, required resources and output and (ii) compared to outdoor maps, indoor mapping is more challenging for several reasons:

- *Indoor places are very diverse* in nature and many of them also change frequently; consider e.g. remodeling of floors or new shops in a shopping mall. This also refers to the semantic description of the objects in the buildings.
- *Indoor mapping techniques are very diverse* and range from manual with ad hoc tuning to crowdsourcing techniques. While manual techniques are often more reliable, the abundance of new personal devices with advanced sensors (e.g., motion sensors, cameras, gyroscopes, pedometers) also enable sophisticated crowdsourcing of indoor maps [6].
- *Services related to indoor mapping are also very diverse* in terms of end-user needs and technical assumptions. For instance, architects have different needs than pedestrians or fire fighters. Also, some services require localization, some only mapping, and some only user traces or landmark identification.

To emphasize the diversity of end-user needs and assumptions in the services related to indoor mapping, consider a hospital: the main service is finding doctors, patients, or equipment, assuming a well administered building with well defined tags for tracing and localization. Here, manually created maps can be used—a costly, yet worthy, investment for the hospital administration. On the other hand, in a shopping mall with diverse shop owners, diverse infrastructure and no central management of tags, users also aim to discover places, find other people and explore the map. Here, users may have time to contribute to crowdsourced map creation in exchange for some useful apps. Finally, in an automated factory, highly accurate indoor maps can be important in guiding robots, augmented reality and help avoiding accidents.

Following the above, in this paper we argue that there will be no single way for mapping indoor places, but rather *a diverse set of techniques and services will be used to build up maps and services for indoor locations in a customized way*. Some services may actually not even require proper maps, as in the case of a "take me to the exit" service for which only user traces can be sufficient. We also posit that we will move towards custom solutions for combining indoor mapping techniques in order to improve accuracy and enable a number of diverse services. On the basis of this approach, we discuss the research challenges that we envision to face in this world of customized bootstrapping and diverse techniques and services.

This paper focuses on the combination of indoor mapping techniques and the services they enable. It presents a research direction that focuses on flexible, customized mapping of buildings. This can integrate existing data, manual techniques as well as crowdsourcing from user data. It specifically targets the

problem of obtaining the critical mass of user data for self-starting crowdsourcing mapping techniques. A main point here is that some services can be offered
earlier in order to collect data for crowdsourcing. This, we also call intermediate
service, as these do not require fully detailed and accurate maps. To illustrate
and exemplify the approach, we show a way to describe such flexible bootstrapping of indoor maps that combines techniques as well as services.

In particular, we contribute by highlighting the need for a bootstrapping
process that can be customized to the available techniques and building characteristics and by providing an example of such a process.

The rest of the paper is structured as follows. Section 1.2 overviews the most
promising indoor mapping techniques. Section 2 provides an overview of our approach, while Sect. 2.3 exemplifies it on a specific bootstrapping process. Section 3
provides a short assessment of the current state of the art, while Sect. 4 puts forward a research roadmap and concludes by summarizing the key points. This
paper is extension of the work already presented by [7]. More specific, in this
paper the approach, the methods and the related work have been extended.

## 1.1   Indoor Mapping and Challenges

An indoor map implies the existence of a model that describes the geometry,
the topology and the semantics of an indoor space [8]. The geometry of an
indoor space indicates the morphology of important places or objects in the
space. For example the shape and the location of a room or a desk. Topological
relationships signify the explicit description of adjacent and connected places in
that space. The semantics indicate the way that places in the space are used. For
example the existence of stairs, elevator, toilet etc. Semantics may also indicate
unique characteristics of locations in that space. For example the Received Signal
Strength Indicator in a place with multiple WiFi Access Points.

Indoor maps are typically created via a manual process that starts off with
obtaining the architecture blueprints of a building, enhancing them with Places
of Interest (POIs), and submitting the result to a floorplan database. The problems of this traditional approach are that (i) it is labor-intensive and slow; (ii)
it is not always economically viable, as many times the cost of creating the
maps can surpass the revenue they create; (iii) it relies on having the building
blueprints in the first place, which is not always true, as e.g., in the case of
developing countries; and (iv) there is a huge effort in keeping the maps up-
to-date, since the manual process has to be repeated to capture changes in the
environment.

Additionally, there is not a well agreed upon model for these procedure.
Beyond the technical challenge of generating the maps, mapping indoor places
is a resource demanding procedure with an expansive cost. Additionally, environment characteristics are never static (i.e. objects displaced etc.). Hence, indoor
maps can often become outdated, while their maintenance effort increase the
overall cost. Legal challenges are often present, since in most cases indoor places
are privately owned. Furthermore, indoor localization cannot use the maps with-

out semantically enhanced and uniquely identified nodes which can be used by an entity for successfully localized.

As a result, there is clearly potential in automating the map creation and update process. In particular, we see a great potential in automated techniques that rely on user data, i.e. crowdsourcing, for creating maps that are cost-effective, semantically-rich and dynamically updated. In this vision, crowd-sourced maps are created based on fusion of data sensed by modern ubiquitous devices such as smart phones.

## 1.2   Mapping Techniques

In this chapter we describe the available technologies for a potential use in a bootstrapping process for indoor maps. We posit that those technologies can be used to provide services, which by their turn can be used as the means for incentivizing users to participate in the envisioned crowdsource-based system. These initial users can provide the critical data mass allowing the creation of more sophisticated services leading to full-blown indoors maps. In this chapter, on top of articulating our generic bootstrapping model, we exemplify how the presented different techniques and technologies for indoor mapping fit within the model.

**Light Detection And Ranging (LiDAR).** LIDAR uses lasers to measure the distance between objects inside a building (i.e., walls, floors, ceilings etc.) like [4]. A LiDAR unit, often mounted on a robot or vehicle, scans the environment. The position of the unit is estimated by vSLAM [9]. A point cloud is generated and by identifying contours (i.e. points of similar distance), a map can be extracted. Semantic annotations are usually manually made by expert surveyors.

**Usage of Existing Architectural Blueprints.** If blueprints are encoded in formats such as Industry Foundation Classes (IFC) [10] or Building Information Modeling (BIM) [11], they contain the geometric information that can be readily used in indoor maps. However, such formats do not include topological nor semantic information. The last is usually added manually by expert surveyors, resulting into mapping data encoded into formats such as IndoorGML [12]. Approaches for automatic derivation of topological relations (e.g., adjacency and connectivity of rooms) from IFC models have also been suggested [13].

**Structure from Motion.** In this technique, a 3D structure of a building can be extracted from a camera [3] by capturing many images of an indoor place and translating them into a single 3D view. To do this, the camera's internal and external parameters, e.g. lens-generated distortion, translation and rotation matrix have to be known or be retrievable from common features of the captured images.

**Depth Sensors.** In this technique, a typical setting is to have an infrared projector that projects a unique pattern. An infrared sensor, whose relative distance to the projector and rotation are known, recognizes this pattern. A depth map is constructed by analyzing the unique pattern of infrared light markers by triangulating the distance between the sensor, projector and the object. Finally, a 3D point cloud is extracted from stereoscopic view algorithms, from which a map can be generated [14].

**Smart Phone 3D Modeling Tools.** In this technique, specialized smart phone apps enable users construct components of a building [15]. After initial versions of the maps have been created, other users can enhance the maps or vote on their accuracy and completeness.

**Activity-Based Map Generation.** An indoor map can be transparently and autonomously generated based on activity recognition of users as it has been suggested by [2]. This technique works as follows: After extracting steps of users by their x and y coordinates or by a series of trajectories, a point cloud can be extracted. A map of the indoor place can be created by fusing data from different users and identifying places with common patterns. For example, places where users performing the same activity (i.e., stairs) can be identified.

From the above, the use of **Structure from motion** or **Depth sensors**, the use of **Smart phone 3D modeling tools** as well as **Activity-based map generation** lend themselves to crowdsourcing, whereas **Lidar** and **Usage of existing architectural blueprints** do not.

## 2   Adaptive Bootstrapping

In this section, we outline our envisioned approach towards indoor mapping, based on the following observations on the present and future research and development in indoor mapping:

- *Techniques Need to be Combined.* There are many indoor mapping techniques which differ in terms of complexity, required resources, and output. For instance, if one wants to use LiDAR, a localization technique has to be in place, and also sophisticated laser equipment has to be available. Activity-based map generation, on the other side, does not make any major assumptions in terms of equipment; however, it assumes a plethora of data. We argue that a combination of different techniques will be used to create or maintain indoor maps that are both cost-effective and accurate.
- *Bootstrapping is Needed for Crowdsourcing.* As discussed, we posit there will be no "single-shot" solution towards indoor mapping; combined solutions, as shown below, will also involve crowdsourcing. Therefore an incremental, stepwise bootstrapping will be needed to obtain user data. This is substantiated by crowdsourcing techniques which not only need user data, but also other inputs like building floorplans or points of interest.
- *No Single Bootstrapping Process.* We believe that the diversity of buildings, mapping techniques, as well as services will lead to individual and custom processes for such bootstrapping. The processes will be adapted to end-user needs, available infrastructure, available budget, and other factors.

## 2.1 Services Related to Indoor Mapping

A number of services with different characteristics, users, and assumptions on crowdsourcing effort can be supported by our approach, e.g.:

**Wellness Monitoring.** This is a family of emerging services that provide feedback to users based on their activities during the day. For example, services that can track the number of steps that a user did during a day can be used for identifying the distance traveled by the user.

**Card Swiping.** This service may substitute the Magnetic stripe cards with smart phone build-in NFC chips. In combination with other sensor data, it can be used to generate a general model for identifying outdoor-indoor transitions and vice versa.

**"Take me to the exit".** This service can work as a digital Ariadne's thread, where users will be able to find their way back to the entrance of indoor places by following their own captured route in reverse. User traces collected from this service can be used for generating a point cloud.

**Instruction-Based Navigation.** This service can provide basic instructions on how to visit an office or a classroom in the form of instructions such as "Enter from the north entrance, walk straight for 10 s, then turn right, walk up the stairs and enter the door on the right".

**Location-Aware Ticketing.** This service can free users of public transportation from the need to purchase tickets in advance, as users can be billed based on the actual distance traveled. In addition, companies that run the transportation services will be able to acquire an accurate view of the usage patterns and optimize their services.

**Elderly Monitoring.** This service can be used to identify accidents involving elderly or people with special needs in real time by detecting problems in mobility or patterns that correspond to sudden falls. Data from such service can be used for semantically enhancing indoor maps, via adding the use of a room.

**Call Forwarding.** This service can use the information of a person's position inside a building (e.g. a specific office) and the position of land lines within the building in order to automatically forward calls to the nearest land line.

**Dynamic Meeting Scheduler.** This service can use the (indoor) user position (or an approximation, e.g. a room) and possibly user calendar data, in order to propose meeting locations that fit the participants' locations. Data from this service can be used for labeling indoor spaces.

It is clear that the services related to indoor mapping are rather diverse, and make different assumptions regarding the maturity and completeness of the supporting indoor mapping systems. For instance, wellness monitoring does not assume any complete mapping or localization system (even though the data captured from such services can actually allow for activity-based mapping techniques). Also, "take me to the exit" does not assume the existence of a complete navigable map, but only of a single well-defined route from a *single* user.

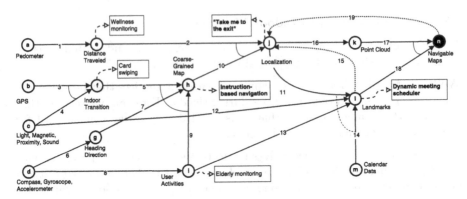

**Fig. 1.** Customized bootstrapping process for a university campus building. Circular nodes are artifacts, arrows are tasks with inputs and outputs, rectangles are intermediate services (services in bold are described in the text) [7].

Even though one might argue that a single indoor mapping techniques will prevail and allow for the creation of different services, including the ones outlined above, we do not believe this will be the case. Instead, we believe that the current fragmented picture of the techniques and services will continue to be the norm. The question then becomes, how can we combine different techniques in a specific indoor setting towards creating innovative applications? The naïve answer is to just use all the available techniques in parallel and pick the best results out of their execution. In reality, though, different techniques have different starting and ending points. Hence, a more realistic view of the composition is as a chain of tasks with inputs and outputs, dependencies between them, even loops, representing that a task receives inputs from other tasks and provides output to them. (As an aside, the simultaneous localization and mapping (SLAM) technique features this exact loop between the localization and mapping module.)

An important observation is that services with rudimentary assumptions in terms of indoor mapping can act as catalysts for gaining the critical mass of user data that can enable services with more advanced mapping needs. For instance, in a hospital building, the target service might be full-blown indoor navigation, whereas intermediate services might be call forwarding for medical personnel, room-based localization of equipment, elderly monitoring, and others. Potential users are the medical personnel, patients, and visitors. In contrast, consider a university campus building: the target service can be the same as in the hospital case, but now intermediate services could be room finders, "take me to the exit", wellness monitoring, etc., whereas potential users are now students and academic employees. Finally, in the case of a subway station, a promising intermediate service is, e.g., location-aware ticketing.

In the following, we are providing a way to model such bootstrapping processes. Our modeling technique is based on the fact that each indoor mapping technique can be broken down to a number of tasks with inputs and outputs.

The input of the initial task indicates the technique's assumptions. As a result, a bootstrapping process can be represented as a graph of tasks. We present an example of this in the next section.

## 2.2 Bootstrapping Components

In this section we discus the number of components needed for initiating the bootstrapping procedure.

**Distance.** An important component of the bootstrapping process, is the one responsible for estimating the traveled distance from the user. The user's travel distance can be estimated from pedometer data. Pedometer applications have become ubiquitous in the today smart-phones, while their accuracy has been dramatically increased [16]. This information is essential for indoor localization, while services can be emerged indicating to the user's distance in a particular time interval.

**Indoor Transition.** A mechanism for detecting the indoor transition is also important, since this will provide an accurate initial location for localization. By fusing GPS and sensor data (i.e. light sensor, wifi RSS etc.), the location of the transition from outdoors to indoors, and vice versa, can be detected [17]. The accurate detection from outdoor to indoor environment will provide with an accurate initial position, which can enhance the localization.

**Heading Direction.** A mechanism for estimating the user direction is equally important for a localization algorithm, since together with the estimated distance traveled can contribute on a pedestrian dead reckoning algorithm. From Inertial Motion Unit IMU data (i.e. accelerometer, gyroscope, compass etc.), the walking or even standing direction of the user can be estimated in various ways [18]. This information can be used for estimating the position of the user.

**User Activity.** A component for recognizing the user's performing activity is needed for more robust localization, for identifying unique landmarks as well as for enhancing the procedure of the semantically annotation of places, by indicating the use of this place. Identifying the activity a user is performing from a given set of activities, using IMU data can be performed accurate enough [19]. Having this information the localization procedure will be improved and the final map can be enhanced with semantic information.

**Localization.** Knowing the orientation, distance traveled and activity a basic pedestrian dead reckoning mechanism can be put in action, since the orientation together with the distance traveled and an initial location (i.e. entrance) can be used for estimating the current user location, while the activity can be used for improving this procedure. For example, the standing activity can be used for re-calibrating the sensors (i.e. gravity direction identification or gather more measurements for restarting the location etc.) or walking can be used for resetting the pedometer error. On this step, applications such as "guide me back to the entrance", or "share my indoor path" can be emerged. Delivery services will have the precise location of the delivery address and will not only be limited on the building location. It can enhance outdoor navigation by suggesting the entrance which is nearest to the destination, or services such as subway transportation suggestions, since the distance from outdoor to the indoor station can be more accurate estimated or even be personalized.

**Landmarks.** After segmenting sensor data based on discrete characteristics, uniquely identified locations will be emerged. For example the activity performed by the user on a specific area, the RSS of the WiFi or the magnetic field intensity, can be used to characterize the area. After mapping these places on a basic map, the localization procedure can be enhanced, thus better localization implies better landmark locations. Similar to a Simultaneous Localization And Mapping (SLAM) algorithm. Services such as "Find an available meeting room" will be emerged. This service can work as follows: It will identify users who are in a meeting room, based on calendar data and similarities in sensor data (i.e. WiFi RSS). Then it will broadcast the name of this room to users who have been delayed and are going to join the meeting, according to their calendar and the room name is either unknown or has been changed.

### 2.3  Bootstrapping Example

This section introduces an example of a bootstrapping process for a university campus building. To illustrate the bootstrapping process, we use a data-flow-like diagram depicted in Fig. 1.

In this diagram, circular nodes correspond to artifacts. Each artifact enables the creation of one or more services. For example, `Distance Traveled` (e) can enable a service such as wellness monitoring, since the walked distance is directly related with exercising. Inputs and outputs of artifacts are visually presented as solid enumerated arrows which indicate data flow. For example, the input of `Indoor Transition` (f) is GPS signal (3) and IMU (4) data (i.e. ambient light, magnetic field, proximity and sound). By reasoning on these input data, similar to [20], the output is the locations of entrances (5). In case of more than one input, a solid line connecting them implies conjunction (e.g. lines 5, 9 and 7); a dashed line implies disjunction (e.g. 11, 12, 13, 14). Finally, dotted connections imply additional inputs which can improve the data quality (e.g. 15).

An artifact can be connected to a number of intermediate services. A service is represented by a rectangle and implies a set of software functionalities which can be a user-facing application. Finally, the target artifact is represented as a filled circular node (e.g. n).

Figure 1 presents a set of possible bootstrapping options. One would start at one or more of the nodes on the left, e.g. assuming devices with GPS (b) or compass/gyroscope and accelerometer (d). Informally speaking, we can then proceed to some of the connected nodes (e.g. f or g), based on user data generated from operating services possible at this point. Based on the new data, we can proceed with further steps in this graph.

As depicted in Fig. 1, the entire bootstrapping process could emerge via existing services, such as wellness monitoring or card swiping. Of course, alternative paths are also available. For example the `Coarse-Grained Map` step could be skipped; similarly, `User activities` might not be needed if semantically-rich calendar data are available.

In our example, the target service is to enable indoor navigation based on dynamically created maps that capture the geometry, topology and semantics of the building. The above information needs to be integrated in a data model, e.g. by using and extending the IndoorGML standard [12]. IndoorGML provides the constructs to denote subdivisions of indoor places (i.e. rooms), spaces that connect two indoor places (e.g., inner doors), spaces that connect indoor places to outdoor ones (e.g., entrance doors), spaces acting as passages between indoor places (e.g., corridors, stairs), and other important properties.

There are a number of intermediate services among the ones described in the beginning of this Section. We describe here the indoor mapping techniques and associated artifacts they rely upon:

**Instruction-Based Navigation.** To provide this service, a `Coarse-Grained Map` is needed. This is a model that includes the elements essential for routing, such as corridors, stairs, doors, and entrances. This is the outcome of merging three other artifacts: `Indoor Transition`, `Heading Direction` and `User Activities` (tasks 5, 7, 9). The first one is derived by using GPS data (task 3) and fusing them with other mobile sensor data such as light, magnetic, and proximity data (task 4). The intuition is that the sensors' behavior changes during the outdoor-indoor transition, where the GPS uncertainty and the WiFi received signal strength are both increasing.

`Heading Direction` can be derived via machine learning algorithms (embodied in task 6) that work on compass, gyroscope and accelerometer data. The intuition is, if a phone's pose is identified, it can be used to extract the user's local direction (i.e. in the phone's coordinate system) via monitoring the acceleration changes due to the gait movement, then relate this direction to a global system using the compass.

Finally, `User Activities` can be derived from the same data using machine learning techniques with high accuracy (task 8), since moving and stationary activities can be detected from disturbances in the acceleration sensor, while movements on the vertical space can be detected from disturbances in the barometric sensor.

**Dynamic Meeting Scheduler.** This service is based on the `Landmarks` artifact. Landmarks are distinctive locations in a building. They are either locations where users consistently perform the same activity (e.g., stairs)—contributed by the `User Activities` (task 13)—or locations with distinct characteristics of a measured quantity (e.g., WiFi RSS, geomagnetism, sound, light)—contributed by the `Light`, `Magnetic`, `Proximity`, `Sound` (task 12). In both cases, landmarks need to be localized in a building—hence the dependence on `Localization` (task 11). Landmarks can also be derived from `Calendar Data` (task 14) via semantics (e.g., meeting room name).

**"Take me to the exit".** In our example, we assume that there is no localization infrastructure in place. As a result, we would need to resort to pedestrian dead reckoning techniques [21]. Pedestrian dead reckoning is based on approximating the position of a user by measuring the distance traveled when walking towards a direction from a known point. This explains why `Localization` depends on the `Distance Traveled` (task 2) and the `Coarse-Grained Map` (task 10). The former is derived directly from pedometer data (task 1). The latter contains information regarding the heading direction (task 7) and the indoor transition points (task 5). These points are the initial *known points* in the dead reckoning algorithm. `Localization` can also depend on `Landmarks` for re-calibrating the algorithm (restarting the error) in distinct locations (task 15).

Finally, `Localization` provides input for the creation of `Point Cloud` (task 16) using existing techniques, and subsequently of `Navigable Maps` (task 17). `Navigable Maps` are also enhanced by the identified `Landmarks` (task 18). In particular, activity-related landmarks can be a rich source of semantic annotation for maps (e.g., places where people sit together for long time can be labeled as meeting rooms). At the same time, `Navigable Maps` can enhance `Localization` by error recalibration on the basis of non-navigable places (task 19). This can be achieved either by relating user traces to sets of possible routes or via uniquely identified locations (e.g. stairs), in which case the context of users (e.g. "climbing stairs") can be used for re-positioning them.

It is important to note that the example bootstrapping process illustrates a cost-effective solution without dedicated equipment and expensive manual work. As an alternative, consider hiring an indoor localization company, for performing tasks 1 and 2 in our example—this would have led to a different customization of the same bootstrapping process.

Being aware of the orientation, distance traveled and activity of the user, a basic pedestrian dead reckoning mechanism—for *Localization*—can be put in action, since the orientation together with the distance traveled and an initial location (i.e. entrance) can be used for estimating the current user location, while the activity can be used for improving this procedure. For example, the standing activity can be used for recalibrating the sensors (i.e. gravity direction identification etc.) or walking can be used for resetting the pedometer error. On this step, applications such as "guide me back to the entrance", or "share my indoor path" can be emerged.

Side-services such as "Find an available meeting room" can provide with labels of the locations, while in combination with a localization technique can provide *Landmark* locations. The side-service can work as follows: It will identify users who are in a meeting room, based on calendar data and similarities in sensor data (i.e. WiFi RSS). Then it will broadcast the name of this room to users who have been delayed and are going to join the meeting, according to their calendar and the room name is either unknown or has been changed. After segmenting sensor data based on discrete characteristics,uniquely identified locations will be emerged. For example the activity performed by the user on a specific area (i.e. door handling events [22]), the RSS of the WiFi or the magnetic field intensity, can be used to characterize the area. After mapping these places on a basic map, the localization procedure can be enhanced, thus better localization implies better landmark locations. Similar to a Simultaneous Localization And Mapping (SLAM) algorithm.

## 3   Related Work

To our understanding, there is no prior work on systematic bootstrapping of indoor maps. There are several works which integrate different intermediate techniques, which we list below. More mapping techniques can be found here [23].

**Heading Direction.** [24] detect the discreate signal vibration when the heel strikes the ground during a gait circle. Then they use this data point as a reference and scan the signal to identify the dominant body's movement partition from the entire signal segment. Finally, they translate the walking direction to the global magnetic system. However, their framework is highly dependent on the terrain as well as on user behavior.

**Indoor-Outdoor Transition.** [20] do not only use the drop of GPS accuracy as an indication of the I/O transition, but also use light censors, cell tower signals, and magnetic field sensors. The acceleration and proximity sensor time series are fused for identifying the I/O transition.

**Activity Recognition.** [25] use a Support Vector Machine classifier to distinguish among moving activities such as walking, running, and ascending and descending stairs and improve existing position systems. Their observation is that the step length varies when a user is walking, running or climbing stairs. Their approach is argued to work in various phone poses. However, their approach uses a large amount of features, which can result in high computational demands.

**Localization.** [26] have developed a ZUPT algorithm for localization. However, they point out the need to identify vertical transitions due to the limitation the vertical displacements cause. To solve this problem they introduce a moving platform detection module. It works by combining accurate sensors, and not those available on a smart-phone, such as accelerometer, barometer and magnetometer. They estimate altitude using the barometric sensor, while they are also using it to identify instance phases.

## 4   Discussion and Outlook

Following the diversity of indoor places, techniques and services, we have outlined our position for an adaptive bootstrapping process. This includes mapping techniques but also intermediate services which enable data collection for improving maps and offering enhanced services. We have illustrated examples of customizations of the process in a visual way and argue that the bootstrapping.

Our view integrates many existing mapping techniques as well as services and also assumes considerable progress in each of these disciplines. As we focus more on how the different processes for mapping can be integrated, our vision is orthogonal to research roadmaps of specific techniques.

Our new bootstrapping approach also gives rise to the several challenges:

**Bootstrapping Processes.** We need research to understand and model bootstrapping processes, similar to our example, in order to obtain a more complete picture of the techniques and services that are available. Also, most of the services described in Section 2.3 are open challenges mainly due to the inherent complexity of indoor localization: existing sensors (both in phones and specialized devices) fail to effectively propagate a discrete signal patterns in indoor space, making simple triangulation-based techniques infeasible. Additionally, robust heading direction identification independent of the phone's pose remains an open challenge [20].

**Intermediate Targets/Artifacts.** We need to understand what can be useful intermediate targets/artifacts, which are both feasible w.r.t mapping techniques and also enable useful services. Moreover, protocols need to be emerged to enable information exchange through APIs between the different services. Importantly, we need to manage the uncertainty inherent to both sensor reading and human users, filter out outliers, and in general work with noisy data. Trust models to manage ambiguous information extracted from multiple users need to be emerged. Existing indoor data models have to be enhanced in order to cope with such incomplete, ambiguous or inaccurate models.

**Process Customization.** We need research to understand when and how to apply different bootstrapping processes to specific buildings. This can also lead to easier or automatic customization of bootstrapping to specific classes of buildings.

## 5    Conclusion

In this paper, we discuss our view on the future of techniques for indoor mapping. We propose customized, crowdsourced and scalable approaches and we discuss the research challenges. We demonstrate methods for the combination of multiple of indoor mapping generation techniques and discuss their challenges. We introduce an adaptive method for bootstrapping the procedure of indoor mapping in multiple ways through a number of intermediate services. Those services enable us to obtain useful data for this procedure, while they increase the quality of those data. Finally, we discuss the necessary components for such approach and we give an example of a bootstrapping procedure.

**Acknowledgments.** This work is part of the TUM Living Lab Connected Mobility project and has been funded by the Bayerisches Staatsministerium für Wirtschaft und Medien, Energie und Technologie.

# References

1. Mautz, R.: Indoor positioning technologies. ETH Zurich, Department of Civil, Environmental and Geomatic Engineering (2012)
2. Alzantot, M., Youssef, M.: CrowdInside: automatic construction of indoor floor-plans. In: SIGSPATIAL 2012, pp. 99–108. ACM (2012)
3. Gao, R., et al.: Jigsaw: indoor floor plan reconstruction via mobile crowdsensing. In: Proceedings of MobiCom 2014, pp. 249–260. ACM (2014)
4. El-Hakim, S.F., Boulanger, P.: Mobile system for indoor 3-d mapping and creating virtual environments. US Patent 6,009,359 (1999)
5. Goetz, M., Zipf, A.: Towards crowdsourcing geographic information about indoor spaces; mapping the indoor world. GIM Int. **26**, 30–34 (2012)
6. Pipelidis, G., Su, X., Prehofer, C.: Generation of indoor navigable maps with crowdsourcing. In: Proceedings of the 15th International Conference on Mobile and Ubiquitous Multimedia, MUM 2016, pp. 385–387. ACM, New York (2016)
7. Pipelidis, G., Prehofer, C., Gerostathopoulos, I.: Adaptive bootstrapping for crowdsourced indoor maps. In: Proceedings of the 3rd International Conference on Geographical Information Systems Theory, Applications and Management: GIS-TAM, INSTICC, vol. 1, pp. 284–289. SciTePress (2017)
8. Chen, J., Clarke, K.C.: Modeling standards and file formats for indoor mapping. In: Proceedings of the 3rd International Conference on Geographical Information Systems Theory, Applications and Management: GISTAM, INSTICC, vol. 1, pp. 268–275. SciTePress (2017)
9. Karlsson, N., Di Bernardo, E., Ostrowski, J., Goncalves, L., Pirjanian, P., Munich, M.E.: The vSLAM algorithm for robust localization and mapping. In: Proceedings of the 2005 IEEE International Conference on Robotics and Automation, ICRA 2005, pp. 24–29. IEEE (2005)
10. ISO 16739:2013 - Industry Foundation Classes (IFC) for data sharing in the construction and facility management industries (2013)
11. ISO/TS 12911:2012 - Framework for building information modelling (BIM) guidance (2012)
12. OGC IndoorGML version 1.0.2 (2016). http://www.opengeospatial.org/standards/indoorgml
13. Liu, H., Shi, R., Zhu, L., Jing, C.: Conversion of model file information from IFC to GML. In: IGARSS 2014, pp. 3133–3136. IEEE (2014)
14. Henry, P., Krainin, M., Herbst, E., Ren, X., Fox, D.: RGB-D mapping: using Kinect-style depth cameras for dense 3D modeling of indoor environments. Int. J. Robot. Res. **31**, 647–663 (2012)
15. Eaglin, T., Subramanian, K., Payton, J.: 3D modeling by the masses: a mobile app for modeling buildings. In: Proceedings of PERCOM 2013 Workshops, pp. 315–317. IEEE (2013)
16. Tomlein, M., Bielik, P., Krátky, P., Mitrík, S., Barla, M., Bieliková, M.: Advanced pedometer for smartphone-based activity tracking. In: HEALTHINF, pp. 401–404. (2012)
17. Pipelidis, G., Rad, O.R.M., Iwaszczuk, D., Prehofer, C., Hugentobler, U.: A novel approach for dynamic vertical indoor mapping through crowd-sourced smartphone sensor data. In: 2017 International Conference on Indoor Positioning and Indoor Navigation (IPIN), pp. 1–8 (2017)
18. Combettes, C., Renaudin, V.: Comparison of misalignment estimation techniques between handheld device and walking directions. In: IPIN 2015, pp. 1–8 (2015)

19. Kwapisz, J.R., Weiss, G.M., Moore, S.A.: Activity recognition using cell phone accelerometers. SIGKDD Explor. Newsl. **12**, 74–82 (2011)
20. Zhou, P., Zheng, Y., Li, Z., Li, M., Shen, G.: IODetector: a generic service for indoor outdoor detection. In: SenSys 2012, pp. 113–126. ACM (2012)
21. Kourogi, M., Kurata, T.: A method of pedestrian dead reckoning for smartphones using frequency domain analysis on patterns of acceleration and angular velocity. In: Proceedings of PLANS 2014, pp. 164–168. IEEE (2014)
22. Wu, M., Pathak, P.H., Mohapatra, P.: Monitoring building door events using barometer sensor in smartphones. In: Proceedings of the 2015 ACM International Joint Conference on Pervasive and Ubiquitous Computing, UbiComp 2015, pp. 319–323. ACM, New York (2015)
23. Pipelidis, G., Prehofer, C.: Models and tools for indoor maps. In: Digital Mobility Platforms and Ecosystems, p. 154 (2016)
24. Roy, N., Wang, H., Roy Choudhury, R.: I am a smartphone and i can tell my user's walking direction, pp. 329–342. ACM Press (2014)
25. Nguyen, P., et al.: User-friendly activity recognition using SVM classifier and informative features. In: IPIN 2015, pp. 1–8 (2015)
26. Kaiser, S., Lang, C.: Detecting elevators and escalators in 3D pedestrian indoor navigation. In: 2016 International Conference on Indoor Positioning and Indoor Navigation (IPIN), pp. 1–6 (2016)

# Soft Image Segmentation: On the Clustering of Irregular, Weighted, Multivariate Marked Networks

Raphaël Ceré[✉] and François Bavaud

Department of Geography and Sustainability, University of Lausanne, Lausanne, Switzerland
{Raphael.Cere,Francois.Bavaud}@unil.ch

**Abstract.** The contribution exposes and illustrates a general, flexible formalism, together with an associated iterative procedure, aimed at determining soft memberships of marked nodes in a weighted network. Gathering together spatial entities which are both spatially close and similar regarding their features is an issue relevant in image segmentation, spatial clustering, and data analysis in general. Unoriented weighted networks are specified by an "exchange matrix", determining the probability to select a pair of neighbors. We present a family of membership-dependent free energies, whose local minimization specifies soft clusterings. The free energy additively combines a mutual information, as well as various energy terms, concave or convex in the memberships: within-group inertia, generalized cuts (extending weighted Ncut and modularity), and membership discontinuities (generalizing Dirichlet forms). The framework is closely related to discrete Markov models, random walks, label propagation and spatial autocorrelation (Moran's I), and can express the Mumford-Shah approach. Four small datasets illustrate the theory.

**Keywords:** Free energy · Image segmentation · Iterative clustering
Soft K-means · Laplacian · Modularity · Moran's $I$
Mumford-shah functional · Multivariate features · Ncut
Soft membership · Spatial autocorrelation · Spatial clustering

## 1 Introduction

Regional data analysis, as performed on geographic information systems, deals with a notion of *"where"* (the spatial disposition of regions), a notion of *"what"* (the regional features), and a notion of *"how much"* (the relative importance of regions, as given by their surface or the population size). The data define a *marked, weighted network*, generally *irregular* (think e.g. of administrative units): weighted vertices represent the regions, weighted edges measure the proximity between regions, on which uni- or multivariate features (the marks) are defined.

Much the same can be said of an image made of pixels, that is a collection of elements embedded in a bidimensional layout. The regularity of the setup

© Springer Nature Switzerland AG 2019
L. Ragia et al. (Eds.): GISTAM 2017, CCIS 936, pp. 85–109, 2019.
https://doi.org/10.1007/978-3-030-06010-7_6

(regular grid, uniform weights, binary regular adjacencies) is exploited in most segmentation algorithms, but the latter may become unadapted, precisely, under irregular situations, such as pixels of various sizes or importance, aggregated pixels, irregular boundaries or connectivities, multi-layered or partially missing data.

The fields of spatial analysis, in particular spatial clustering, on one hand, and image segmentation on the other hand, seem currently to be investigated by distinct, non-overlapping scientific communities. Yet, both communities arguably share the same *what-versus-where-trading* challenge, aimed at obtaining clusters both homogeneous and connected.

This contribution proposes a family of iterative algorithms for unsupervised or semi-supervised image segmentation. It attempts to merge a regularized approach to (non-marked) network clustering with the soft K-means of unconnected, feature-marked observations. The underlying weighted formalism, dubbed "ZED formalism" in short (Sect. 2.1), appears to be relevant for spatial analysis, network clustering, and data analysis in general.

In a nutshell, the network clustering objective is expressed by a *generalized cut* functional, encompassing the *Ncut minimisation* [1,2] and *modularity maximization* [3] as particulary cases (Sect. 2.4). This objective is enriched with a features dissimilarity term, central in the *K-means approach*, and further regularized by an *entropy term*. The three terms are additively combined into a freely parametrized *free energy*, whose minimization provides a principled approach, semi-supervised or unsupervised, to the iterative computation of locally optimal solutions, and the emergence of soft clusters (Sect. 3). The soft nature of clusters induces a membership uncertainty, betraying the inter-cluster boundary (Sect. 5.2). Alternatively, pixels can be finally assigned to the group maximizing their membership, thus defining usual hard clusterings.

Replacing the former generalized cut by a *discontinuity functional* constitutes another meaningful option (Sect. 2.3), and both approaches, although opposite regarding their convexity properties (5.1), are investigated and illustrated on four small datasets (Sect. 4).

The quest for good clusterings makes sense for homogeneous enough images, as attested by the standardized value of Moran's $I$, the canonical measure of spatial autocorrelation, as defined and illustrated in the present multivariate, weighted setting (Sect. 2.2).

Also, the formal connection with the celebrated Mumford-Shah approach in image segmentation is made explicit (Sect. 5.3), culminating in the identification of a non-additive objective involving both the network structure and the pixel features (Eq. (19)).

A discussion (Sect. 6) lists some further research lines, and adresses the connection with some alternative approaches to the clustering of marked networks. The appendix details two constructions (diffusive and Metropolis-Hastings) of the so-called exchange matrix [4], as well as the test of spatial autocorrelation in a weighted, multivariate setting.

The present contribution is an extended version of a paper [5] first published in the GISTAM 2017 proceedings. Additional material includes here the definition and study of *generalized cut functionals*[1], membership uncertainties, Metropolis-Hastings exchange matrices, and new illustrations. It also presents a presumably original *soft Mumford-Shah-like* approach (Sect. 5.3), proposing an adaptation of the original Mumford-Shah image segmentation framework to the "ZED formalism" under investigation (Sect. 2.1).

# 2   Definitions and Formalism

The formalism we consider extends the *spatial autocorrelation formalism* used in Quantitative Geography and Spatial Econometrics to the case of weighted, irregular regions, as well as to multivariate features. It turns out to be extensive enough to provide a flexible framework for unsupervised or semi-supervised *generalized image* segmentation, where the "generalized images" under consideration can be made of irregular pixels, irregularly inter-connected, and endowed with multivariate numerical features.

## 2.1   The *ZED* Framework

In short, the spatial structure of the network (the "where") is specified by a square affinity or *exchange matrix* $E$, interpretable as a joint probability of selecting pairs of pixels; the multi-labelled pixel marks (the "what") are specified by a square *dissimilarity matrix* $D$. A soft network clustering is specified by a rectangular *membership matrix* $Z$, assigning the pixels into groups.

Unsupervised clustering consists in determining a reasonably good $Z$, taking into account both $E$ (strongly connected pixels should belong to the same group) and $D$ (strongly dissimilar pixels should belong to distinct groups).

In the general, irregular setup, the relative weights $f_i > 0$ of the $n$ elementary vertices, regions or pixels are unequal, but fixed. Their feature dissimilarities $D_{ij}$ are also given, while the specification of $E$, reflecting the symmetrical network affinity between vertices, enjoys some flexibility (Sect. 6), yet reflecting in any case the neighborhood structure of the network, and normalized to $e_{i\bullet} = f_i$ (see below). By contrast, the memberships $Z$ are entirely free, and define a soft clustering of the marked network – whose good enough instances constitute the quest of the present paper.

*Space as a Weighted Network: The Exchange Matrix E*
Specifically, consider $n$ regions (generalized pixels) with relative weights $f_i > 0$, normalized to $f_\bullet = \sum_{i=1}^{n} f_i = 1$, together with an $n \times n$ symmetric non-negative *exchange matrix* $E = (e_{ij})$, and *weight-compatible* in the sense $e_{i\bullet} = \sum_{j=1}^{n} e_{ij} = f_i$. Here and in the sequel, "$\bullet$" denotes the sum over all values of the replaced index.

---

[1] Besides the generalized discontinuity functionals, already addressed in the proceedings, but unfortunately referred there to as "cut functionals".

The exchange matrix $E$ interprets as a joint probability $p(i,j) = e_{ij}$ to select the pair of regions $i$ and $j$ (edges), and defines a weighted unoriented network. Its margins interpret as the probability $p(i) = f_i$ to select region $i$ (vertices).

Weight-compatible exchange matrices $E$ define a continuous neighborhood relation between regions. They can be constructed from $f$ and the adjacency matrix $A$, or from another spatial proximity of distance matrix (see the appendix). The row-standardized matrix of spatial weights $W = (w_{ij})$ of spatial autoregressive models obtains as $w_{ij} = e_{ij}/f_i$ and constitutes the transition matrix of a reversible Markov chain with stationary distribution $f$.

*Multivariate Features: The Dissimilarity Matrix D*
Regional features or marks can consist of univariate grey levels, multivariate color or spectral intensities, or (in a geographical context) any regional variable such as the proportions of specific land uses, population density, proportion of retired people, etc. Multivariate characteristics $x_i$ are suitably combined into $n \times n$ squared Euclidean dissimilarities $D_{ij} = \|x_i - x_j\|^2$.

*Soft Clustering: The Membership Matrix Z*
A soft *regional clustering* or *image segmentation* into $m$ groups is described by a non-negative $n \times m$ *membership matrix* $Z = (z_{ig})$ with $z_{ig} = p(g|i) \geq 0$ denotes the probability that region (pixel) $i$ belongs to group $g$, and obeys $z_{i\bullet} = \sum_{g=1}^m z_{ig} = 1$.

The relative weights of the corresponding groups obtain as $\rho_g = \sum_i f_i z_{ig} = p(g) \geq 0$, with $\sum_g \rho_g = 1$. The regional distribution of group $g$ is $f_i^g = p(i|g) = p(g|i)p(i)/p(g) = f_i z_{ig}/\rho_g$, and obeys $f_\bullet^g = 1$.

## 2.2  Spatial Autocorrelation: Moran's *I*

Obtaining a clustering $Z$ both satisfactory regarding the network $E$ and the features $D$ supposes a kind of compatibility between $E$ and $D$, and this precisely constitutes the issue of *spatial autocorrelation*, as measured by the weighted, multivariate generalization (2) of Moran's *I*.

Average multivariate dissimilarities between regions are expressed by *inertias*, generalizing the univariate *variances*. The inertia between randomly selected regions, and the *local inertia* between neighbors, are respectively defined as

$$\Delta = \frac{1}{2} \sum_{i,j=1}^n f_i f_j D_{ij} \qquad \Delta_{\text{loc}} = \frac{1}{2} \sum_{i,j=1}^n e_{ij} D_{ij} \qquad (1)$$

Comparing the global versus local inertias provides a multivariate generalization of *Moran's I*, namely,

$$I \equiv I(E, D) = \frac{\Delta - \Delta_{\text{loc}}}{\Delta} \qquad (2)$$

whose values range in $[-1, 1]$. A large positive $I$ is expected for an image made of large patches characterized with constant features, or at least varying smoothly on average (spatial continuity = positive autocorrelation). A large negative $I$

characterizes an image whose pixel features are contrasted, opposite to their neighbors - such as a chess board with "rook" adjacency. Yet, the value of $I$ in itself is little informative (large values of $I$ are expected whenever diagonal terms $E$ are important), in contrast to its standardized value $z$, which can furthermore be directly tested by the normal procedure, or by the weight-corrected permutation procedure (Sect. 6).

## 2.3  Image Segmentation by Generalized Discontinuity Minimization

The region-group dependency can be measured by the *mutual information*

$$\mathcal{K}[Z] = \sum_{i=1}^{n} \sum_{g=1}^{m} p(i,g) \ln \frac{p(i,g)}{p(i)p(g)} = \sum_{ig} f_i z_{ig} \ln \frac{z_{ig}}{\rho_g} \tag{3}$$

A good clustering should consist of homogeneous groups made of regions not too dissimilar regarding their features, that is insuring a low value of the *within-group inertia* (e.g. [9])

$$\Delta_W[Z] = \sum_{g=1}^{m} \rho_g \Delta_g \quad \text{where} \quad \Delta_g = \frac{1}{2} \sum_{ij} f_i^g f_j^g D_{ij} \tag{4}$$

A good clustering should also avoid to separate a pair of spatially strongly connected pixels, that is to insure a low value of the *generalized discontinuity*

$$\mathcal{G}^\kappa[Z] = \sum_{g=1}^{m} \frac{\varepsilon[z^g]}{\rho_g^\kappa} \quad \text{where} \quad \varepsilon[z^g] = \frac{1}{2} \sum_{ij} e_{ij}(z_{ig} - z_{jg})^2 \quad \text{and} \quad \kappa \in [0,1] \ . \tag{5}$$

The term $\varepsilon[z^g]$ is called Dirichlet form in potential theory, and attains its minimum value zero iff all pixels lying in a connected component of the network possess the same membership in $g$.

We consider a *regularized clustering problem*, aiming at determining, among the set $\mathcal{Z}$ of all memberships matrices, a $n \times m$, non-negative and row-normalized matrix $Z$ minimizing the *free energy* functional

$$\mathcal{F}[Z] = \beta \Delta_W[Z] + \frac{\alpha}{2} \mathcal{G}^\kappa[Z] + \mathcal{K}[Z] \tag{6}$$

where $\alpha, \beta \geq 0$. The terms $\Delta_W$, respectively $\mathcal{G}^\kappa$, behaves as a features dissimilarity energy, respectively a spatial energy, favoring *hard* partitions obeying $z_{ig} = 0$ or $z_{ig} = 1$. By contrast, the regularizing entropy term $\mathcal{K}$ favors the emergence of soft clusterings. Setting $\alpha = 0$ yields the soft $K$-means algorithm based on spherical Gaussian mixtures, where the *inverse temperature* $\beta$ fixes the dissimilarity bandwidth. Canceling the first-order derivative of the free energy with respect to $z_{ig}$ under the constraints $z_{i\bullet} = 1$ yields the minimization condition

$$z_{ig} = \frac{\rho_g \exp(-H_{ig})}{\sum_h \rho_h \exp(-H_{ih})} \tag{7}$$

where

$$\rho_g[Z] = \sum_{i=1}^{n} f_i z_{ig} \qquad\qquad H_{ig}[Z] = \beta D_i^g + \alpha \rho_g^{-\kappa}(\mathcal{L}z^g)_i - \frac{\alpha\kappa}{2}\rho_g^{-\kappa-1}\varepsilon[z^g] \ . \quad (8)$$

Here $D_i^g = \sum_j f_i^g D_{ij} - \Delta_g$ is the squared Euclidean dissimilarity from $i$ to the centroid of group $g$, and $(\mathcal{L}z^g)_i = z_{ig} - \sum_j w_{ij} z_{jg} = z_{ig} - (Wz^g)_i$ is the *Laplacian* of membership $z^g$ at pixel $i$, comparing its value to the average value of its neighbors, and adjusting the former to the latter. For $\kappa > 0$, this adjustment mechanism is downscaled for large groups (factor $\rho_g^{-\kappa}$); in addition, spatially discontinuous small groups are encouraged to grow by the last term in (8), independent of $i$.

## 2.4  Image Segmentation by Generalized Cut Minimization

Another functional whose minimization favors spatially connected clusters is the *generalized cut*

$$C^\kappa[Z] = \sum_{g=1}^{m} \frac{\rho_g^2 - e(g,g)}{\rho_g^\kappa} \quad \text{where} \quad e(g,g) = \sum_{i,j=1}^{n} e_{ij} z_{ig} z_{jg} \quad \text{and} \quad \kappa \in [0,1].$$

$$(9)$$

The choice $\kappa = 1$ amounts to the *N-cut objective* [1], while the choice $\kappa = 0$ is equivalent to the *modularity criterium* [3]. Again, minimizing the corresponding free energy

$$\mathcal{F}[Z] = \beta \Delta_W[Z] + \frac{\gamma}{2} C^\kappa[Z] + \mathcal{K}[Z] \qquad\qquad \beta, \gamma \geq 0 \qquad (10)$$

yields the necessary first-order condition (7), where

$$H_{ig}[Z] = \beta D_i^g + \gamma \rho_g^{-\kappa}[\rho_g - (Wz^g)_i] - \frac{\gamma\kappa}{2}\rho_g^{-\kappa-1}[\rho_g^2 - e(g,g)] \ . \quad (11)$$

For $\kappa = 0$ (modularity clustering), the term $\rho_g - (Wz^g)_i$ compares the average membership of the neighbors of $i$ to the overall average membership (rather than to the membership of $i$ itself, as in (8). The term $(Wz^g)_i$ precisely implements the *label propagation* mechanism acting in some network clustering algorithms (e.g. [6,7]).

For $\kappa > 0$, this adjustment mechanism is downscaled for large groups (factor $\rho_g^{-\kappa}$); in addition, loosely intra-connected small groups are encouraged to grow by the last term in (11), independent of $i$, which prevents the creation of clusters made out of a single pixel – a known defect of the unnormalized cut criterium (e.g. [8]).

## 3  Iterative Procedure: Unsupervised and Semi-supervised

Equation (7) can be solved iteratively from some initial membership $Z^0 \in \mathcal{Z}$, updating at each step $\rho_g$ and the exponent $H_{ig}$ in versions (8) or (11), until convergence to $Z^\infty$, which constitutes a *local minimum* of $\mathcal{F}[Z]$. Matrix $Z^\infty$ constitutes the searched for soft spatial partition or image segmentation of the unsupervised procedure. It can be further hardened by assigning each pixel $i$ to group $g = \arg\max_h z_{ih}^\infty$, breaking possible ties at random.

A semi-supervised implementation of the procedure, imposing the membership of a few pixels (and possibly breaking down the monotonic decrease of $\mathcal{F}[Z]$: see Figs. 3, 4, 5, 6, 7 and 8) goes as follow: first, the set $\Omega$ of the $n$ regions is partitioned into two disjoint, non-empty sets, namely the user-defined *tagged regions* $T$, and the *free regions* $F$, with $\Omega = T \cup F$ and $T \cap F = \emptyset$. The tagged set $T$ itself consists of $m$ non-empty disjoint subregions $T = \cup_{\tau=1}^m T_\tau$ initially tagged with $m$ distinct *strokes* applied on a small number of pixels: they form the *seeds* of the $g = 1, \ldots, m$ figures to be extracted, while the remaining regions will be assigned to the background numbered $g = 0$.

Memberships $Z = (z_{ig})$ consist of $n \times (m+1)$ non-negative matrices obeying $\sum_{g=0}^m z_{ig} = 1$. Their initial value $Z^0$ is set as

$$
z_{ig}^0 \begin{cases} = 1 & \text{if } i \in F \text{ and } g = 0 \\ = 1 & \text{if } i \in T_\tau \text{ and } g = \tau \\ = 0 & \text{otherwise .} \end{cases} \tag{12}
$$

**Table 1.** Variants of the semi-supervised and the unsupervised iterative segmentation algorithm.

---

**Begin**

Fix $\beta > 0$ (the parameter conjugate to the within-clusters inertia) and $\kappa \in [0, 1]$

Compute the weight vector $f$ ($f_i = 1/n$ for regular grids)

Compute the binary adjacency matrix $A$

   ***diffusive exchange matrix :*** For a given $t > 0$, compute $E(f, A, t)$ by (20)

   ***Metropolis-Hastings exchange matrix:*** Compute $E$ by (21)

Compute the matrix of spatial weights as $w_{ij} = e_{ij}/f_i$

Compute the features dissimilarity matrix $D_{ij} = \|x_i - x_j\|^2$

Initialize the $n \times (m+1)$ membership matrix $Z^0$ as:

   $z_{ig}^0 = 1$ if $i \in F$ and $g = 0$

   $z_{ig}^0 = 1$ if $i \in T_\tau$ and $g = \tau$

   $z_{ig}^0 = 0$ otherwise.

---

**Loop :** $Z^{(r+1)}$ for the $r$-th iteration, stop after convergence

Group weight : $\rho_g = \sum_i f_i z_{ig}$

Emission probabilities $f_i^g = \frac{f_i z_{ig}}{\rho_g}$

Dissimilarity to the centroid : $D_i^g = \sum_j f_j^g D_{ij} - \Delta_g$

   ***generalized discontinuity segmentation :*** Fix the parameter $\alpha > 0$ and compute $H_{ig}$ by (8)

   ***generalized cut segmentation :*** Fix the parameter $\gamma > 0$ and compute $H_{ig}$ by (11)

Compute $z_{ig}^{(r+1)}$ by (7)

   ***for the semi-supervised case :*** Re-initialize $z_{ig}^{(r+1)} = \delta_{g\tau}$ for $i \in T_\tau$

   ***for the unsupervised case :*** Do nothing

---

Attribute $i \in F$ to the group $g = \arg\max_{h=0}^m z_{ih}^{(\infty)}$

**End**

Iteration (7) is then performed. At the end of each loop, the tagged regions are reset to their initial values $z_{i_\tau}^0 = 1$ for all $i \in T_\tau$. After convergence, one expects the hardened clusters obtained by assigning $i$ to group $g = \arg\max_{h=0}^m z_{ih}^\infty$ to consist of $m$ connected figures $g = 1, \ldots m$ each containing the tagged set $T_g$, as well as a remaining background supported on $F$.

The iterative image segmentation algorithm summarized below (Table 1) requires

(1) a vector of $n$ weights $f_i > 0$ associated to each pixel or region
(2) a vector of $n$ grey levels or multivariate characteristics $x_i$
(3) a $n \times n$ binary, symmetric, off-diagonal adjacency matrix $A$
(4) a set of disjoint non-empty tagged sets of pixels $\{T_\tau\}_{\tau=1}^m$ .

## 4   Illustrations

### 4.1   Swiss Federal Votes

The irregular network consists on the $n = 309$ communes of canton of Vaud, endowed with their diffusive exchange matrix (20) with $t = 1$, where $A$ is the "queen" adjacency matrix and the non-uniform weights $f$ are the proportion of inhabitants. Features consist, for each commune $i$, of the proportion of "yes" for three Swiss federal initiatives submitted to the citizens on February the 12th 2017, namely (Fig. 1) $x_i$ for the *Corporate Tax Reform Act III* (refused by 40.9% of voting citizens), $y_i$ for the *Federal Decree on the Simplified Naturalisation of Third-Generation Immigrants* (accepted at 60.4%) and $z_i$ for the *Federal Decree on Establishing a Fund for National Roads and Urban Traffic* (accepted at 61.9%). Dissimilarities are simply defined as $D_{ij} = (x_i - x_j)^2 + (y_i - y_j)^2 + (z_i - z_j)^2$, further rescaled in the range $[0, 1]$.

Figures 3, 4, 5, 6, 7 and 8 depict the semi-supervised hard assignment obtained from the initial strokes $T_1 = \{20\}$ (Bière; group 1), and $T_2 = \{3\}$ (Chessel; group 2), after 100 iterations, together with the change of the free energy $\mathcal{F}[Z]$ during the iteration. Generalized cuts and discontinuity variants are both tested for various values of the parameters $\kappa$, $\beta$, $\gamma$ and $\alpha$. In particular, the conditional entropy $H(G|O)$, measuring the softness of the partition (Sect. 5.2), *decreases in $\beta$, decreases in $\gamma$, but increases in $\alpha$*, as expected.

### 4.2   The Portrait

Figure 9 refers to a regular trivariate image (levels of red green blue) of size $n = 100 \times 115$ with uniform weight vector $f_i = 1/n$. Again, the binary adjacency matrix $A$ has been built under the "queen" scheme (8 neighbors for inside pixels), on which the Metropolis-Hastings exchange matrix (21) have been adopted. $D_{ij}$ is the sum of the squared differences between color intensities, rescaled to $[0, 1]$. The corresponding Moran's $I$ (2) is 0.52 for an expectation of $E_0(I) = 0.008$ and variance $\mathrm{Var}_0(I) = 2.201 \times 10^{-05}$ (Sect. 6). Normal test value $z = 108.48$ denotes a massively significant spatial autocorrelation, as it must.

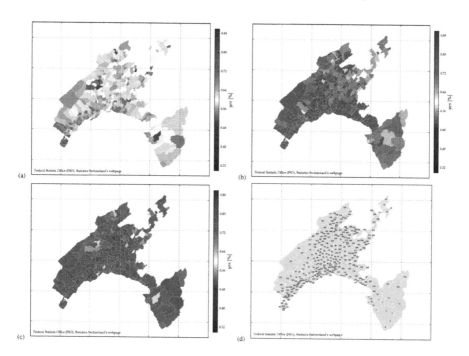

**Fig. 1.** *Swiss federal votes, canton of Vaud*: proportion of "yes" **(a)** $x_i$ for the first votation, **(b)** $y_i$ for the second votation, and **(c)** $z_i$ for the third votation. **(d)** lists the commune numbers used by the cantonal administration.

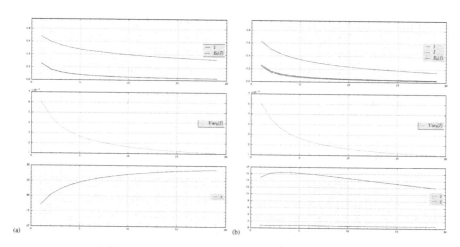

**Fig. 2.** *Swiss federal votes, spatial autocorrelation*: **(a)** Moran's $I$ (top) and standardized $z$ normal test value (bottom), as a function of the free parameter $t \in [1, 20]$ of the diffusive exchange matrix specification (20). **(b)** Moran's $I$ after a plain permutation of the political features $(x, y, z)$ between communes, and Moran's $\hat{I}$ after applying the weight-corrected permutation (22). Note the latter to almost coincide with the expected value $E_0(I)$ under the null hypothesis, as it must.

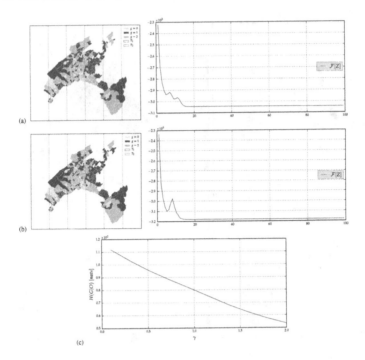

(a)

(b)

(c)

**Fig. 3.** *Swiss federal votes, continued*: **cut minimization** with $\kappa = 0.0$, $\beta = 300$, **(a)** $\gamma = 0.1$ and **(b)** $\gamma = 2.0$. **(c)** decrease of the conditional entropy in $\gamma$.

### 4.3   The Geometer

Figure 10 refers to the levels of grey of a regular image of size $n = 50 \times 50$. The node weights $f$ and univariate dissimilarities $D$ are constructed as above but the diffusive exchange matrix (20) has been adopted. The corresponding Moran's $I$ is 0.848, with an expectation of $E_0(I) = 0.0174$, variance $\mathrm{Var}_0(I) = 0.0001$ and test value $z = 81.88$.

### 4.4   Lausanne

One considers the rectangular network made of $n = 50 \times 60$ hectometers (census blocks) in the region of Lausanne, Switzerland, with regular queen binary adjacency matrix $A$. The features count, for each hectometer, the number of built units possessing a given characteristic, among $p = 63$ criteria in 2014 (source: Swiss Federal Statistical Office). The corresponding squared Euclidean dissimilarities are rescaled to $[0, 1]$.

Figure 11 refers to a uniform weight $f_i = 1/n$, and Fig. 12 to a non-uniform weight $f$ proportional to the number of inhabitants in each hectometer. Note the diffusive scheme (21) to generate two distinct exchange matrices: $A$ is the same, but $f$ differs. One finds $I = 0.404$, $E_0(I) = 0.258$, $\mathrm{Var}_0(I) = 3.019 \times 10^{-5}$

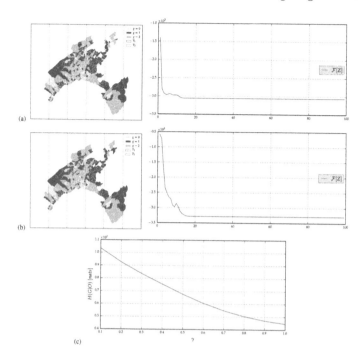

**Fig. 4.** *Swiss federal votes, continued:* **cut minimization** with $\kappa = 1.0$, $\beta = 300$, **(a)** $\gamma = 0.1$ and **(b)** $\gamma = 1.0$. **(c)** decrease of the conditional entropy in $\gamma$.

and $z = 26.550$ for the uniform case; by contrast, $I = 0.877$, $E_0(I) = 0.211$, $\text{Var}_0(I) = 0.0002$ and $z = 52.943$ for the non-uniform case.

## 5   Further Formal Considerations

### 5.1   Convexity, Concavity, and Local Minima

The set $\mathcal{Z}$ of all memberships is convex, and the within-group inertia $\Delta_W[Z]$ is *concave* in $Z$ (e.g. [9]). As a result, the minimum $\arg\min_{Z \in \mathcal{Z}} \Delta_W[Z]$ is attained on the extreme points of $\mathcal{Z}$, that is on *hard memberships*, whose determination is notoriously difficult. By contrast, the mutual information $\mathcal{K}[Z]$ is *convex*, and attains its minimum zero on "independent" soft memberships of the form $z_{ig} = \rho_g$. Mixing the two functionals as in the Gaussian mixture model $\beta \Delta_W[Z] + \mathcal{K}[Z]$ generates, for $\beta$ large enough, a functional possessing many *local minima*, attained after convergence of the iterative procedure of Table 1 (in the unsupervised case, and in absence of spatial terms).

The generalized discontinuity functional $\mathcal{G}^\kappa[Z]$ (5) can be shown to be *convex* in $Z$, for any $\kappa \in [0, 1]$ (proofs are postponed in a forthcoming, more technical note). For a connected network (i.e. whose $E$ exchange matrix is irreducible) the minimizers are again the independent soft memberships $z_{ig} = \rho_g$.

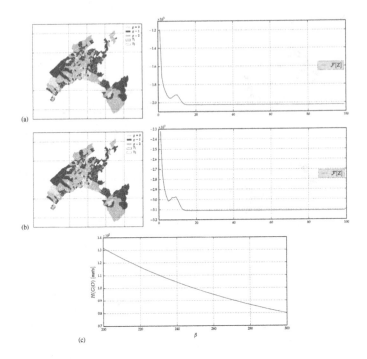

**Fig. 5.** *Swiss federal votes, continued*: **cut minimization** with $\kappa = 0.0$, $\gamma = 1.0$, **(a)** $\beta = 200.0$ and **(b)** $\beta = 300.0$. **(c)** decrease of the conditional entropy in $\beta$.

By contrast, the cut functional $\mathcal{C}^\kappa[Z]$ (9) can be shown to be *concave* for any $\kappa \in [0,1]$, at least for the *positive semi-definite* (p.s.d.) exchange matrices $E$, that is whose eigenvalues are non-negative; such networks are referred to as *diffusive*.

Diffusive exchange matrices (20) define a diffusive network, precisely, by contrast to Metropolis-Hastings exchange matrices (21) which are not p.s.d. in general. Diffusive networks necessarily possess diagonal components (loops), unlike normalized adjacency matrices, or bipartite graphs. Also, exchange matrices of the "radial basis" form $e_{ij} = a_i a_j \exp(-\lambda d_{ij}^2)$, where $d_{ij}$ is a spatial Euclidean distance and $a_i \geq 0$ a calibrating factor ensuring $e_{i\bullet} = f_i$, are diffusive (see e.g. [10]).

For a diffusive network, the membership minimizing $\mathcal{C}^\kappa[Z]$ constitutes a hard partition, difficult to compute, for which various heuristics (such as spectral clustering or label propagation) have been devised. The present regularized approach constitutes another, in line with model-based clustering or simulated annealing (e.g. [11]).

## 5.2   Clustering Softness

The regularizing effect of convex functionals, namely the mutual information $\mathcal{K}[Z]$ and the generalized discontinuity $\mathcal{G}^\kappa[Z]$, are responsible for the softness of

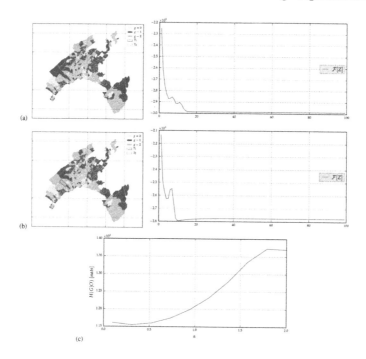

**Fig. 6.** *Swiss federal votes, continued:* **discontinuity minimization** with $\kappa = 0.0$, $\beta = 300$, **(a)** $\alpha = 0.1$ and **(b)** $\alpha = 2.0$. **(c)** increase of the conditional entropy in $\alpha$.

the optimal membership $Z$. Denoting by $G$, resp. $O$, the variables "group", resp. "pixel", the pointwise conditional entropy $H(G|i) = -\sum_g z_{ig} \ln z_{ig}$ measures the membership uncertainty of pixel $i$. The quantity $H(G|i)$ is large for pixels located at the group frontiers, and thus provides a possibly original *boundary detection mechanism* (Fig. 13). Its average $H(G|O) = \sum_i f_i H(G|i) = H(G,O) - H(O)$ constitues a measure of *overall softness* of the clustering, related to the mutual information as

$$\mathcal{K}[Z] = H(G) + H(O) - H(G,O) = H(G) - H(G|O) \tag{13}$$

In soft K-means, increasing $\beta$ increases the influence of the (concave) energy $\Delta_W$ relatively to the (convex) entropy, and hence decreases the softness $H(G|O)$ of the clustering. By the same reasoning, and in view of the remarks of Sect. 5.1, one expects the softness $H(G|O)$ to *decrease* in $\gamma$ (cut minimization), but to *increase* in $\alpha$ (discontinuity minimization), as observed in Figs. 3, 4, 5, 6, 7 and 8.

## 5.3  A Soft Mumford-Shah-like Approach

The influential *Mumford-Shah* approach [12] aims at governing the image segmentation or "morphogenesis" (e.g. [13]) of an image whose support $\Omega \subset \mathbb{R}^2$ and "image intensity" $x(s)$ at $s \in \Omega$ are given.

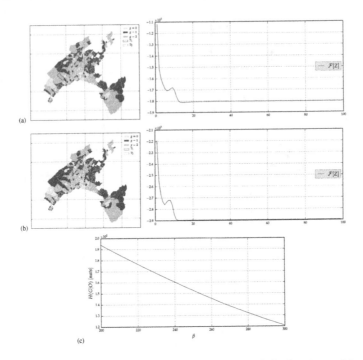

**Fig. 7.** *Swiss federal votes, continued:* **discontinuity minimization** with $\kappa = 0.0$, $\alpha = 1.0$, **(a)** $\beta = 200$ and **(b)** $\beta = 300$. **(c)** decrease of the conditional entropy in $\beta$.

The approach consists in dividing $\Omega$ into $m$ disconnected classes $\Omega_g$ separated by an inter-classes boundary $B \subset \Omega$ (that is $\Omega \setminus B = \cup_{g=1}^{m} \Omega_g$) of size $\mathcal{B} = |B|$, as well as by approximating $x(s)$ within each class by a smooth function $u(s)$. The Mumford-Shah functional, to be minimized over $u$ and $B$, expresses in its original continuous setup as

$$\mathcal{M}(u, B) = \nu \int_{\Omega} (x(s) - u(s))^2 \, ds + \frac{\delta}{2} \sum_{g=1}^{m} \int_{\Omega_g} \|\nabla u(s)\|^2 \, ds + \lambda \mathcal{B} \qquad (14)$$

and its rigorous mathematical treatment is fairly demanding (see e.g. [14]).

In the so-called *cartoon limit* $\delta \to \infty$, minimization of (14) requires $u(s)$ to be a constant $u_g$ within each hard class $\Omega_g$, with solution $u_g = \bar{x}_g = \int_{\Omega_g} x(s) \, ds / |\Omega_g|$: color levels are constant within each cell, which are separated by lines of same thickness, and smooth enough to ensure a low value of $\mathcal{B}$. This definition appears to closely characterize the style of drawing used in Franco-Belgian comics known as *ligne claire* (Fig. 14), epitomized by the series "The Adventures of Tintin" by Hergé [15].

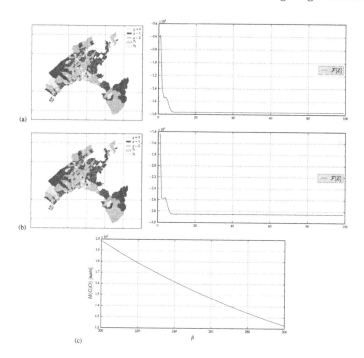

**Fig. 8.** *Swiss federal votes, continued*: **discontinuity minimization** with $\kappa = 1.0$, $\alpha = 0.5$, **(a)** $\beta = 200$ and **(b)** $\beta = 300$. **(c)** decrease of the conditional entropy in $\beta$.

In absence of clustering, that is with a single group ($m = 1$, $B = \emptyset$ and $\mathcal{B} = 0$), the discrete approximation of (14) reads

$$\mathcal{M}(u) = \nu \sum_i f_i(x_i - u_i)^2 + \frac{\delta}{2} \sum_{ij} e_{ij}(u_i - u_j)^2 \qquad (15)$$

with unique minimizer $u = \mu[(1 + \mu)I - W]^{-1}x$, where $\mu = \nu/\delta > 0$.
Soft partitions $Z$ can be introduced by requiring the signal approximation to be of the form $u_i = \sum_g z_{ig} y_g$, that is $u = Zy$ for some freely adjustable vector $y$ with $m$ components. They define a *soft, discrete Mumford-Shah functional* of the form

$$\mathcal{M}(Zy, B) = \nu \, \mathcal{V}[y, Z] + \lambda \, \mathcal{B}[Z]$$

where

$$\mathcal{V}[y, Z] = \sum_i f_i(x_i - (Zy)_i)^2 + \frac{1}{2\mu} \sum_{ij} e_{ij}((Zy)_i - (Zy)_j)^2$$

$$= (Zy - x)'\Pi(Zy - x) + \frac{1}{\mu}(Zy)'(\Pi - E)Zy \qquad (16)$$

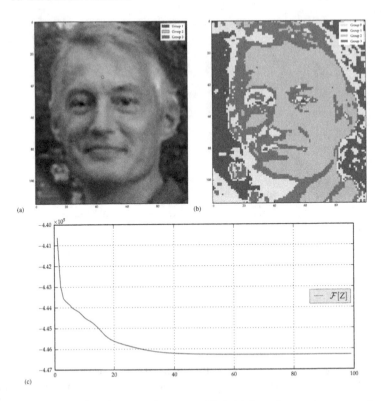

(a)    (b)    (c)

**Fig. 9.** *The Portrait:* **(a–b)** original image with initial strokes and unsupervised hard assignment obtained for background group 0 colored in grey, group 1 in purple, group 2 in green and group 3 in blue, after 100 iterations; (c) decrease of the free energy $\mathcal{F}[Z]$ during the iteration for a **discontinuity minimization** with $\kappa = 0.0$, $\alpha = 0.1$ and $\beta = 950.0$. (Color figure online)

and $\Pi = \mathrm{diag}(f)$ is the diagonal matrix containing the pixel weights. Minimizing (16) over $y$ is an exercise in matrix calculus, and yields the solution

$$y_0 = \Gamma^{-1}\xi \qquad \Gamma = Z'TZ \qquad T = \frac{1}{\mu}[(1+\mu)\Pi - E] \qquad \xi = Z'\Pi x \quad (17)$$

Plugging $y_0$ into (16) yields

$$\mathcal{V}[Z] = \min_{y} \mathcal{V}[y, Z] = \mathcal{V}[y_0, Z] = x'(\Pi - \Pi Z \Gamma^{-1} Z' \Pi)x$$

$$= \frac{1}{2}\mathrm{trace}(\Pi Z\,(Z'TZ)^{-1}Z'\Pi D) \qquad (18)$$

where $D = (D_{ij})$ denotes the matrix of squared Euclidean dissimilarities between pixel intensities $D_{ij} = (x_i - x_j)^2$, and identity $\Gamma 1 = \rho$ has been used in the last expression.

In summary, the original continuous Mumford-Shah functional (14) appears to be *expressible into the present discrete, weighted setting, involving soft partitions $Z$ of marked networks*. Optimal clusterings minimize the functional

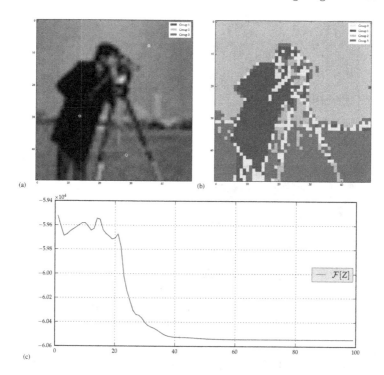

**Fig. 10.** The Geometer: **(a–b)** original image with initial strokes and unsupervised hard assignment obtained for background group 0 colored in grey, group 1 in purple, group 2 in green and in blue, after 100 iterations; (c) decrease of the free energy $\mathcal{F}[Z]$ during the iteration for a **generalized cut minimization** with $\kappa = 0.0$, $\gamma = 4.0$ and $\beta = 350.0$. (Color figure online)

$$\mathcal{M}[Z] = \nu\, \mathcal{V}[Z] + \lambda\, \mathcal{B}[Z] \qquad \nu, \lambda > 0 \qquad (19)$$

where $\mathcal{V}[Z]$, given by (18), both depends on the network structure $E$ (through $T$ in (17)) and on the node dissimilarities $D$, but in a non-additive way, in contrast to proposals (6) and (10). Also, $\mathcal{V}[Z]$ is homogeneous of degree zero (recall that a functional $\mathcal{A}[Z]$ is homogeneous of degree $k$ if, formally, $\mathcal{A}[cZ] = c^k \mathcal{A}[Z]$), while $\mathcal{G}^\kappa[Z]$ and $\mathcal{C}^\kappa[Z]$ are homogeneous of degree $2 - \kappa$, and $\mathcal{K}[Z]$ and $\Delta_W[Z]$ are homogeneous of degree 1.

The inter-cluster boundary length $\mathcal{B}[Z]$ remains to be specified, possibly such as the discontinuity $\mathcal{G}^\kappa[Z]$, or as the generalized cut $\mathcal{C}^\kappa[Z]$, or some other functional. In addition, an entropic regularizing term $\mathcal{K}[Z]$ can be added to (19), hence yielding an alternative, original iterative scheme to be compared to the procedure of Sect. 3.

Expression (18) turns out to hold for multivariate features as well. The issue of the convex versus concave nature of $\mathcal{V}[Z]$, as well as further formal and empirical investigations on soft segmentation based on (19) are postponed for a further work.

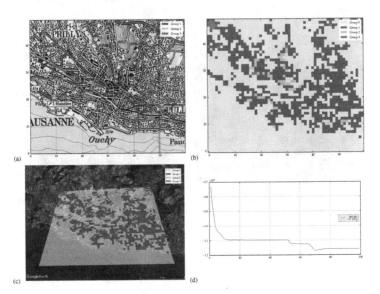

**Fig. 11.** Lausanne, uniform case: **(a–b)** topographic map with initial strokes of the area under study and unsupervised hard assignment obtained for background group 0 colored in grey, group 1 in purple, group 2 in green and group 3 in blue, after 100 iterations; (c) hard assignment projected (d) decrease of the free energy $\mathcal{F}[Z]$ during the iteration for a **generalized cut minimization** with $\kappa = 0.0$, $\gamma = 1.0$ and $\beta = 250.0$. (Color figure online)

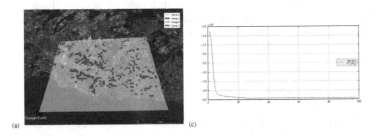

**Fig. 12.** Lausanne, non-uniform case: **(a)** unsupervised hard assignment projected obtained for background group 0 colored in grey, group 1 in purple, group 2 in green and group 3 in blue, after 100 iterations; (c) decrease of the free energy $\mathcal{F}[Z]$ during the iteration for a **generalized cut minimization** with $\kappa = 0.0$, $\gamma = 1.0$ and $\beta = 650.0$. (Color figure online)

In summary, the "ZED formalism" sketched in Sect. 2.1 can express the Mumford-Shah approach within the present framework, whose locally optimal clusters are however bound to differ from the relaxed generalized discontinuity and generalized cut approaches of Sects. 2.3 and 2.4.

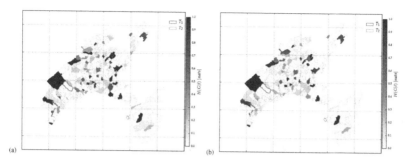

**Fig. 13.** Conditional pointwise entropy $H(G|i)$ for the conditions of Fig. 3 with $\kappa = 0.0$, $\beta = 300$, **(a)** $\gamma = 0.1$ and **(b)** $\gamma = 2.0$. A large value of $H(G|i)$ denotes a large uncertainty in the membership of region $i$, lying at some boundary between groups.

**Fig. 14.** An example of the *ligne claire* style of drawing: comic mural (2000), Rue des Alexiens 49, Brussels: *Le jeune Albert* by Yves Chaland.

## 6  Discussion

The formalism presented here expresses and illustrates a few alternatives defining clustering in two close but little interacting domains, namely image segmentation and regional partitioning. Locally optimal soft clusters $Z$ are both adapted to a given irregular unoriented network $E$ on one hand, and to a given set of node dissimilarities $D$, reflecting the multivariate node features $X$ (marks), on the other hand.

Its basic ingredients have been developed for decades in large, robust scientific communities. In view of the sheer size of the image segmentation domain (including reviews and surveys thereof; see in particular [16,17]), specific claims of originality seem foolish.

Yet, beside the choice of functionals and parameters, let us underline the flexibility of the approach: the determination of a weight-compatible exchange matrix $E$ reflecting the spatial proximity is a vast issue in itself, covering in large part the theory of discrete reversible Markov chains. Considering *probabilities on paths* [18,19] instead of probabilities on nodes or pairs of nodes, permits to extend the formalism to random walks based modularities [20] or multi-target based clustering (e.g. [21,22]). This line of research pursues the "electric interpretation" of reversible Markov chains [23], involving Dirichlet differential equations and computation of the electric potentials, already standard in image segmentation [24]. The possibility, in probabilistic formulations of random walks, to set *independently* the edge *capacities* and the edge *resistances* [17,18,22], seems especially relevant for the clustering of *marked networks*: it is tempting to identify the capacity contribution as a spatial term enabling transitions between neighbors, and the resistance contribution as a barrier preventing transitions between too dissimilar pixels.

The choice of the dissimilarity $D$ is fairly versatile too: the class of squared Euclidean dissimilarities is broader than often presumed, encompassing $L^p$ dissimilarities for $1 \leq p \leq 2$ (in particular the city-block metric), and all positive semi-definite kernel approaches in machine learning, such as radial basis affinities (e.g. [10,25]). $D$ can also express categorical or distributional marks, through chi-square or Hellinger dissimilarities. Covariances between node features (a main theme in Spatial Econometrics; see e.g. [26–30]) can be taken into account by the use of Mahalanobis dissimilarities. Also, recall that any squared Euclidean dissimilarity $D$ generates, through exact multidimensional scaling, a set of multivariate coordinates $X$, unique up to a rotation.

Besides its regularizing virtues, the presence of the entropy term in the free energies (6) or (10) can be be formally justified in the *maximum a priori* approach of Bayesian statistics [31] or [32], the *maximum entropy* approach of Information Theory, or in statistical mechanical models of magnetic materials, where the connection with the Ising or Potts model (in particular regarding the two first "energy" terms of Eq. (14)) has been often noticed.

Other compatible developments, well-known in spatial analysis or machine learning, such as those involving *Moran scatterplots* and *local indicators of spatial autocorrelation* [33], as well as *spectral approaches* for Ncut or modularity clustering [1,8,34,35] have been left aside. Recall that spectral approaches aim at attacking network clustering by means of a matrix eigen-decomposition problem, sacrificing the non-negative nature of $Z$, but producing instead "network factor scores" $\tilde{X}$ on which standard clustering algorithms, such as the K-means, can be performed. The latter can be further mixed with node features to form a generalized set of "where-and-what" features $(\tilde{X}, X)$, on which standard clustering methods can be applied, again; see e.g. [36] and references therein for a recent presentation. In contrast to our approach, which directly confronts $Z$ to the network $E$ (and its marks $X$ or their dissimilarities $D$), the latter strategy is closely related to the search for embedding coordinates $\tilde{X}$ for a network, and the definition of associated squared Euclidean *spatial dissimilarities* $\tilde{D}$ (e.g. [37–39]), for which the question of the positive definite nature of $E$ (Sect. 5.1) plays a prominent role, again.

# Appendix

## Computing the Exchange Matrix $E(A, f)$

Defining an exchange matrix $E$ both weight-compatible (that is obeying $E1 = f$, where the regional weights $f$ are given) and reflecting the spatial structure contained in the binary adjacency matrix $A = (a_{ij})$ is a crucial, necessary step in the "ZED formalism" under consideration. Two constructions, not trivial, nor that difficult either, have been investigated in this paper, namely the *diffusive* specification and the *Metropolis-Hastings* specification.

**The Diffusive Exchange Matrix.** Consider a time-continuous Markov chain $W$ on the $n$ pixels, whose infinitesimal generator or *rate matrix* is proportional to the adjacency matrix $A$, and conveniently normalized so that $f$ constitutes the stationary distribution of $W$. The resulting exchange matrix $E = \Pi W$ turns out to be symmetric and p.s.d., and given by

$$E \equiv E(A, f, t) = \Pi^{1/2} \exp(-t\Psi)\, \Pi^{1/2} \tag{20}$$

where $\Pi = \mathrm{diag}(f)$, and

$$\Psi = \Pi^{-1/2} \frac{LA}{\mathrm{trace}(LA)} \Pi^{-1/2} \qquad (LA)_{ij} = \delta_{ij}\, a_{i\bullet} - a_{ij}$$

$LA$ is the *Laplacian* of matrix $A$, and matrix exponentiation (20) can be carried out by the spectral decomposition of $\Psi$. Specification (20) describes a *diffusive process* at *time* $t > 0$, with limits $\lim_{t \to 0} E(A, f, t) = \Pi$ ("frozen network", consisting of $n$ isolated nodes: spatial autarchy), and $\lim_{t \to \infty} E(A, f, t) = ff'$ ("complete network", with independent selection of the node pairs: complete mobility). Identity $\mathrm{trace}(E(t)) = 1 - t + 0(t^2)$ shows $t$ to measure, for $t \ll 1$, the proportion of *distinct* regional pairs in the joint distribution $E$.

**The Metropolis-Hastings Exchange Matrix.** The natural random walk with Markov transition matrix $a_{ij}/a_{i\bullet}$ correctly describes the spatial structure of the network, but its stationary distribution is $g_i = a_{i\bullet}/a_{\bullet\bullet}$ instead of $f_i$. Applying the Metropolis-Hastings algorithm defines a recalibrated random walk with stationary distribution $f$, ending up in a weight-compatible exchange matrix of the form:

$$E = \Pi - LB \qquad \text{where} \quad B = (b_{ij}), \ b_{ij} = \min(\kappa_i, \kappa_j) \cdot \frac{a_{ij}}{a_{\bullet\bullet}} \ \text{and} \ \kappa_i = \frac{f_i}{g_i} \tag{21}$$

and $(LB)_{ij} = \delta_{ij}\, b_{i\bullet} - b_{ij}$ is the Laplacian of $B$. Expression (21) does not require spectral decomposition, and its computation is much faster than (20) for increasing $n$ (Fig. 15). However, $E$ in (21) is not p.s.d in general, thus threatening the concavity of $\mathcal{C}^\kappa[Z]$ (Sect. 5.1).

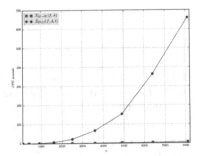

**Fig. 15.** *Deterministic profiling* : CPU time for computing the exchange matrices $E(f, A, t)$ (20) and $E_{M.-H.}(f, A)$ (21), as a function of the number of pixels $n$ in a regular setting and performed with *Python* 2.7.12 on a *CPU Intel Core i7* two Core with a frequency 3.1 GHz (Mac OS X 10.10.5).

## Testing Spatial Autocorrelation

Under the null hypothesis $H_0$ of stationarity and absence of spatial autocorrelation, univariate features are independent, and follow a distribution with common mean and variance *inversely proportional to the size of the region*, namely $E(X_{ik}) = \mu_k$ and $\text{Cov}(X_{ik}, X_{jk}) = \delta_{ij}\sigma_k^2/f_i$ [40]. Under normal approximation, the expected value of the multivariate Moran's $I$ (2) reads

$$E_0(I) = \frac{\text{tr}(W) - 1}{n - 1} \qquad \text{where} \quad w_{ij} = \frac{e_{ij}}{f_i}$$

and its the variance reads

$$\text{Var}_0(I) = \frac{2}{n^2 - 1}\left[\text{trace}(W^2) - 1 - \frac{(\text{trace}(W) - 1)^2}{n - 1}\right]$$

Spatial autocorrelation is thus significant at level $\alpha$ if $z = |I - E_0(I)|/\sqrt{\text{Var}_0}(I) \geq u_{1-\frac{\alpha}{2}}$, where $u_{1-\frac{\alpha}{2}}$ is the $\alpha^{\text{th}}$ quantile of the standard normal distribution.

Alternatively, a permutation test can be performed (e.g. [41]), by generating a series of values $\hat{I}$ of the transformed Moran index, where $\hat{I}$ obtains as (2) with $\Delta_{\text{loc}}$ replaced by $\hat{\Delta}_{\text{loc}} = \frac{1}{2}\sum_{i,j=1}^{n} e_{ij}\hat{D}_{ij}$. The *plain specification*, which consists in replacing the profile $x_{ik}$ of region $i$ by the profile $\hat{x}_{ik} = x_{\pi(i)k}$ of another region $\pi(i)$ (where $\pi$ denotes a permutation), that is in defining $\hat{D}_{ij} = D_{\pi(i),\pi(j)}$, is somehow flawed in the weighted case, in view of the heteroscedasticity of the distribution of $X_{ik}$. Instead, the quantities $\sqrt{f_i}(x_{ik} - \bar{x}_k)$ (with $\bar{x}_k = \sum_i f_i x_{ik}$) for $i = 1, \ldots, n$ are expected to follow the same distribution under $H_0$, thus insuring the validity of the *weight-corrected specification*, with (see Fig. 2)

$$\hat{x}_{ik} = \bar{x}_k + \sqrt{\frac{f_{\pi(i)}}{f_i}}(x_{\pi(i)k} - \bar{x}_k) \qquad \text{and} \qquad \hat{D}_{ij} = \|\hat{x}_i - \hat{x}_j\|^2. \tag{22}$$

# References

1. Shi, J., Malik, J.: Normalized cuts and image segmentation. IEEE Trans. Pattern Anal. Mach. Intell. **22**, 888–905 (2000)
2. Grady, L., Schwartz, E.L.: Isoperimetric graph partitioning for image segmentation. IEEE Trans. Pattern Anal. Mach. Intell. **28**, 469–475 (2006)
3. Newman, M.E.: Modularity and community structure in networks. Proc. Natl. Acad. Sci. **103**, 8577–8582 (2006)
4. Berger, J., Snell, J.L.: On the concept of equal exchange. Syst. Res. Behav. Sci. **2**, 111–118 (1957)
5. Ceré, R., Bavaud, F.: Multi-labelled image segmentation in irregular, weighted networks: a spatial autocorrelation approach. In: Proceedings of the 3rd International Conference on Geographical Information Systems Theory, Applications and Management, Scitepress, pp. 62–69 (2017)
6. Zhu, X., Ghahramani, Z.: Learning from labeled and unlabeled data with label propagation. Technical report CMU-CALD-02-107, Carnegie Mellon University (2002)
7. Raghavan, U.N., Albert, R., Kumara, S.: Near linear time algorithm to detect community structures inlarge-scale networks. Phys. Rev. E **76**, 036106 (2007)
8. von Luxburg, U.: A tutorial on spectral clustering. Stat. Comput. **17**, 395–416 (2007)
9. Bavaud, F.: Aggregation invariance in general clustering approaches. Adv. Data Anal. Classif. **3**, 205–225 (2009)
10. Bavaud, F.: On the Schoenberg transformations in data analysis: theory and illustrations. J. Classif. **28**, 297–314 (2011)
11. Rose, K., Gurewitz, E., Fox, G.: A deterministic annealing approach to clustering. Pattern Recogn. Lett. **11**, 589–594 (1990)
12. Mumford, D., Shah, J.: Optimal approximations by piecewise smooth functions and associated variational problems. Commun. Pure Appl. Math. **42**, 577–685 (1989)
13. Petitot, J.: An introduction to the Mumford-Shah segmentation model. J. Physiol.-Paris **97**, 335–342 (2003)
14. Vitti, A.: The Mumford-Shah variational model for image segmentation: an overview of the theory, implementation and use. ISPRS J. Photogramm. Remote. Sens. **69**, 50–64 (2012)
15. Gaumer, P., Moliterni, C.: Dictionnaire mondial de la bande dessinée. Larousse, Paris (1994)
16. Couprie, C., Grady, L., Najman, L., Talbot, H.: Power watershed: a unifying graph-based optimization framework. IEEE Trans. Pattern Anal. Mach. Intell. **33**, 1384–1399 (2011)
17. Fouss, F., Saerens, M., Shimbo, M.: Algorithms and Models for Network Data and Link Analysis. Cambridge University Press, Cambridge (2016)
18. Bavaud, F., Guex, G.: Interpolating between random walks and shortest paths: a path functional approach. In: Aberer, K., Flache, A., Jager, W., Liu, L., Tang, J., Guéret, C. (eds.) SocInfo 2012. LNCS, vol. 7710, pp. 68–81. Springer, Heidelberg (2012). https://doi.org/10.1007/978-3-642-35386-4_6
19. Françoisse, K., Kivimäki, I., Mantrach, A., Rossi, F., Saerens, M.: A bag-of-paths framework for network data analysis. arXiv preprint arXiv:1302.6766 (2013)
20. Devooght, R., Mantrach, A., Kivimäki, I., Bersini, H., Jaimes, A., Saerens, M.: Random walks based modularity: application to semi-supervised learning. In: Proceedings of the 23rd International Conference on World Wide Web, pp. 213–224. ACM (2014)

21. Sinop, A.K., Grady, L.: A seeded image segmentation framework unifying graph cuts and random walker which yields a new algorithm. In: 2007 IEEE 11th International Conference on Computer Vision. ICCV 2007, pp. 1–8. IEEE (2007)

22. Guex, G.: Interpolating between random walks and optimal transportation routes: flow with multiple sources and targets. Phys. A: Stat. Mech. Appl. **450**, 264–277 (2016)

23. Doyle, P.G., Snell, J.L.: Random Walks and Electric Networks. Mathematical Association of America, Washington D.C. (1984)

24. Grady, L.: Random walks for image segmentation. IEEE Trans. Pattern Anal. Mach. Intell. **28**, 1768–1783 (2006)

25. Critchley, F., Fichet, B.: The partial order by inclusion of the principal classes of dissimilarity on a finite set, and some of their basic properties. In: Van Cutsem, B. (ed.) Classification and Dissimilarity Analysis. LNS, vol. 93, pp. 5–65. Springer, New York (1994). https://doi.org/10.1007/978-1-4612-2686-4_2

26. Bivand, R.S., Pebesma, E.J., Gomez-Rubio, V., Pebesma, E.J.: ApplieD Spatial Data Analysis with R, vol. 747248717. Springer, New York (2008). https://doi.org/10.1007/978-0-387-78171-6

27. LeSage, J.P.: An introduction to spatial econometrics. Revue d'économie industrielle 19–44 (2008). Field number 123

28. Arbia, G.: Spatial Data Configuration in Statistical Analysis of rEgional Economic and Related Problems, vol. 14. Springer, Dordrecht (2012). https://doi.org/10.1007/978-94-009-2395-9

29. Anselin, L.: Spatial Econometrics: Methods and Models, vol. 4. Springer, Dordrech (2013). https://doi.org/10.1007/978-94-015-7799-1

30. Griffith, D.A.: Spatial Autocorrelation and Spatial Filtering: Gaining Understanding Through Theory and Scientific Visualization. Springer, Heidelberg (2013). https://doi.org/10.1007/978-3-540-24806-4

31. Besag, J.: On the statistical analysis of dirty pictures. J. R. Stat. Soc. Ser. B (Methodol.) **48**, 259–302 (1986)

32. Greig, D.M., Porteous, B.T., Seheult, A.H.: Exact maximum a posteriori estimation for binary images. J. R. Stat. Soc. Ser. B (Methodol.) **51**, 271–279 (1989)

33. Anselin, L.: Local indicators of spatial association - LISA. Geogr. Anal. **27**, 93–115 (1995)

34. White, S., Smyth, P.: A spectral clustering approach to finding communities in graphs. In: Proceedings of the 2005 SIAM International Conference on Data Mining, pp. 274–285. SIAM (2005)

35. Ng, A.Y., Jordan, M.I., Weiss, Y.: On spectral clustering: analysis and an algorithm. In: Advances in Neural Information Processing Systems, pp. 849–856 (2002)

36. Lebichot, B., Saerens, M.: An experimental study of graph-based semi-supervised classification with additional node information. arXiv preprint arXiv:1705.08716 (2017)

37. Yen, L., Saerens, M., Mantrach, A., Shimbo, M.: A family of dissimilarity measures between nodes generalizing both the shortest-path and the commute-time distances. In: Proceedings of the 14th ACM SIGKDD International Conference on Knowledge Discovery and Data Mining. KDD 2008, pp. 785–793. ACM, New York (2008)

38. Bavaud, F.: Euclidean distances, soft and spectral clustering on weighted graphs. In: Balcázar, J.L., Bonchi, F., Gionis, A., Sebag, M. (eds.) ECML PKDD 2010. LNCS (LNAI), vol. 6321, pp. 103–118. Springer, Heidelberg (2010). https://doi.org/10.1007/978-3-642-15880-3_13

39. Kivimäki, I., Shimbo, M., Saerens, M.: Developments in the theory of randomized shortest paths with a comparison of graph node distances. Phys. A: Stat. Mech. Appl. **393**, 600–616 (2014)
40. Bavaud, F.: Testing spatial autocorrelation in weighted networks: the modes permutation test. J. Geogr. Syst. **3**, 233–247 (2013)
41. Cliff, A.D., Ord, J.K.: Spatial Processes: Models & Applications. Taylor & Francis, Didcot (1981)

# Goal-Oriented Analysis and Design of Land Administration Systems

Christophe Ponsard[1(✉)] and Mounir Touzani[2]

[1] CETIC Research Center, Charleroi, Belgium
christophe.ponsard@cetic.be
[2] Académie de Toulouse, Toulouse, France
mounir.touzani@ac-toulouse.fr

**Abstract.** Land administration systems involve many complex processes in order to properly manage rights over land, estimate its value, gather related revenues and regulate its use. Reaching those goals generally relies on land registration and cadastre subsystems with many different variants observed across countries. Although elaborated domain models are available and are good at capturing the domain structure, they leave the design rationales quite implicit. This limits the understanding and reasoning capabilities on the systems, e.g. when some process do not correctly reach its goals. This paper proposes a way to extend such domain models with a goal dimension in order to provide a better guidance in the design of new systems and a better understanding of existing systems. Our approach is based on goal-oriented analysis techniques extended with specific spatio-temporal notations, patterns and decomposition rules.

## 1 Introduction

The term Land Administration (LA) was defined by the United Nations Economic Commission for Europe as: *"the process of determining, recording and disseminating information about ownership, value and use of land and its associated resources. These processes include the determination (sometimes called 'adjudication') of land rights and other attributes, their survey and description in a detailed documentation, and the provision of relevant information for supporting land markets"* [1].

The key LA concepts were identified by [2] and are shown in Fig. 1. The owner ("Who") and parcel ("Where"/"How much") concepts are connected by a Right relationship which is often generalised into "triple-R" for Right/Restriction/Responsibilities (for the "How").

Those concepts form the core of reference domain models such as Core Cadastral Domain Model (CCDM), the Land Administration Domain Model (LADM, ISO 19152) and the Social Tenure Domain Model (STDM). Those models are discussed and compared in Sect. 2. The processes managing those concepts are usually split across the following two systems which can be managed by a single or different organisations [2]:

© Springer Nature Switzerland AG 2019
L. Ragia et al. (Eds.): GISTAM 2017, CCIS 936, pp. 110–129, 2019.
https://doi.org/10.1007/978-3-030-06010-7_7

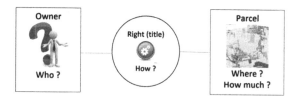

**Fig. 1.** Key domain concepts.

- *Land registration* deals with the official recording of rights on land concerning changes in the legal situation of defined parcel. It can be organised either through deed or title registration, with a progressive transition to the second option observed in many E.U. countries [3]. This covers the "Who" and "How" questions. The land register is the official record of rights on land or of deeds concerning changes in the legal situation of defined parcel.
- *Cadastre* maintains a comprehensive public inventory of data concerning properties of a country or district. It is based on a survey of their boundaries and value. It gives an answer to the questions "Where" (spatial dimension) and "How much" (both for ownership transfer and taxation purposes).

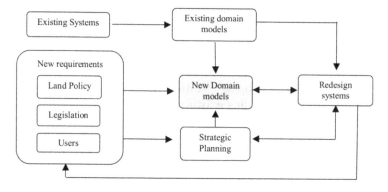

**Fig. 2.** Typical process for (re)designing land administration systems (from [4]).

The above-mentioned domain models essentially provide a reference vocabulary (or ontology) for describing the complex data (rights, geometry of parcels,...) involved LA. Such models support the development and interoperability between LA systems in an efficient way. However, they are less good at driving the design of new systems or at understanding the rationale behind the design of existing systems. Figure 2 shows a typical process for designing or evolving existing LA systems. It strongly relies on a new domain model which is derived from existing ones and needs to cope with new requirements related to land policy, legislation or users [4]. This means that it should also be possible to capture such requirements and more generally the underlying rationales to make sure the design will be globally consistent among all stakeholders. Hence, a LA domain model should be able to explicitly cope with the "Why" which is currently not the case. Typical high level goals and their interactions are however sketched in the classical Land Administration Triangle depicted in Fig. 3 [5,6].

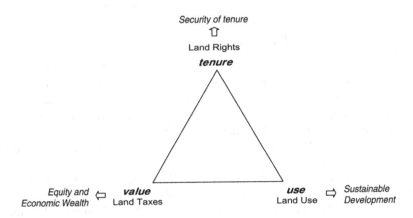

**Fig. 3.** Land administration triangle representation and goals  (adapted from [5]).

Main LA actors (like the FIG and World bank) are also increasingly stressing that LA systems should be "fit-for-purpose" rather than blindly complying with complex technological solutions and rigid regulations, i.e. LA should be designed to meet people's needs and relationship to land in a sustainable way [7] and also according good governance principles which means a good level of transparency [8]. This is especially for developing countries [9].

Our research aims at extending existing domain models to explicitly address the missing goal dimension. In order to achieve this, we apply methods and notations from the goal-oriented requirements engineering field [10].

In our previous work, we have already identified the main existing domain models and motivated the benefit of using goal-oriented analysis methodologies for driving the elaboration of LA systems [11]. This paper is a significant extension that provides a deeper background about the existing modelling approaches for LA systems and about the goal-orientated analysis approach. Based on this, we develop a more extensive application of goal analysis of the high level strategic goals of LA systems, e.g. to capture important non-functional aspects related to the key goals of good governance and transparency [12]. We also explore a larger number of design alternatives and thus provide a better coverage of the design space of LA systems.

This paper is organised as follows. Section 2 presents and compares three main domain models for LA. Section 3 details the goal-oriented framework applied to extend the existing models with explicit goal and responsibility modelling. This extension is detailed in Sect. 4 while Sect. 5 discusses some related work. Finally Sect. 6 draws conclusions and gives some perspectives on our future work.

# 2  Review of Existing Domain Models

## 2.1  Core Cadastral Domain Model

The Core Cadastral Domain Model (CCDM) was initiated by the International Federation of Surveyors in 2002 [13]. It broadly covers land registration and cadastre. It provides an extensible ontology supporting the sound design of a cadastral system using a model-driven architecture that relies on that shared model. CCDM evolved through different intermediary versions to reach version 1.0 in 2006 which is partly depicted in Fig. 4.

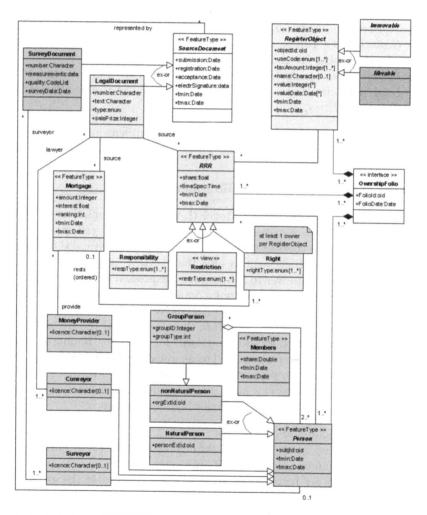

**Fig. 4.** Partial view of CCDM (core and some packages, from [14]). (Color figure online)

CCDM relies on UML class diagram notations. IT is organised in different packages structured around a common core. This core is very close to the abstract model presented in Fig. 1 and is composed of the key concepts of *Person*, *RegisteredObject* and *RRR*. A *RegisteredObject* can either be a *Movable* or *Immovable*. CCDM is composed of many packages with associated colours that details those key concepts and are fully presented in [15].

- the *Parcel Family* package (light blue) is for land (2D) or space (3D). It contains different types of parcels.
- the *Non-land (space)* package (blue) captures *Building*, *Unit*, *NonGeoReal-Estate* and *OtherRegisterObject*.
- the *Surveying* package (pink) captures artefacts related to surveying such as *SurveyPoint* and *SurveyDocument*.
- the *Geometry and Topology* package (purple) provides all the necessary concepts for describing 2D and 3D objects
- the *Person* (green) package gives a classification of the *Person* concept
- the *Legal/Administrative* package details the notions of *Rights*, *Restrictions* and *Responsibilities*.

Note that some CCDM concepts carry explicit identifiers and date attributes for traceability and temporal reasoning. There is however no explicit versioning.

## 2.2 Land Administration Domain Model

The Land Administration Domain Model (LADM) is an evolution of CCDM. In 2006, revision 1.1 was renamed LADM because the term 'cadastral' was not understood by everyone to cover both the legal/administrative and the geometric dimensions. A major achievement is also that LADM has been standardised under ISO 19152 [16] as answer to a strong need expressed since the early 2000s.

LADM is a conceptual model and not a data product specification. It is meant to be a descriptive standard and not a prescriptive one. It provides the domain specific standardisation needed to capture the semantics of the LA domain on top of the agreed foundation of basic standards for geometry, temporal aspects, metadata and also field observations and measurements. The LADM goals are to establish a shared ontology, support development of related software, facilitate the exchange of data and provide support for quality management in LA. More precisely LADM aims at covering the following requirements [17]:

1. Capture a continuum of light rights
2. Capture a continuum of land use right claimants (subjects or parties)
3. Capture a continuum of spatial units (objects)
4. Provide support for basic administrative units, i.e. enable the grouping of spatial units having the same rights
5. Support a range of data acquisition methods (surveying)
6. Support a range of authentic source documents
7. Ensure transparency through tracing the authors of transactions and updates

8. Integrate versioning, might be required for title or deed based systems and also contributing to transparency
9. Facilitate cross-organisation work, e.g. local vs national levels
10. Keep data to the (authentic) source
11. Rely on relevant existing standard, e.g. ISO 191XX series about Geographic Information Systems (GIS)
12. Provide unique identifiers
13. Provide quality assurance on different aspects such as completeness and reliability of information, clarity, simplicity and speed in the registration process.

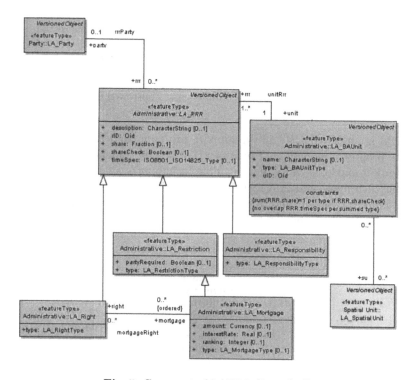

**Fig. 5.** Core part of LADM (from [17]).

LADM has a wider scope than CCDM which mainly focus on the first three requirements of the above list and partially some others like surveying (4) and documents (5). Figure 5 shows the core part of LADM in which the three fundamental objects *LA_Party*, *LA_Spatial_Unit*, *LA_RRR* can be identified but also the extra notion of *LA_BAUnit* (requirement 4) and more specific concepts like *LA_Mortage*. Most objects also inherits from a generic *VersionedObject* which contains quality labels and attributes for history management (requirement 8). This versioning also complies with the ISO 19108 standard. LADM is further refined and structured into packages like CCDM but with some packages substantially more elaborated like *Surveying and Representation* (requirement 4).

## 2.3    Social Tenure Domain Model

The Social Tenure Domain Model (STDM) is a variant of the LADM. It starts from the observation that conventional land administration systems cannot handle customary and informal tenure. Actually there is a whole continuum of land types between informal and formal land rights as described in Fig. 6.

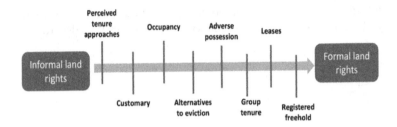

**Fig. 6.** Continuum of land tenure types  (borrowed from [8]).

STDM is an UN-HABITAT to support pro-poor land administration. The aim is to propose a modelling of relations that is independent from their level of formalization and/or legality. For example, it supports all forms of land rights including customary and informal rights shown in Fig. 7. It also supports the recognition, development and maintenance of records in areas where regular or formal registration of land rights has not applied [8].

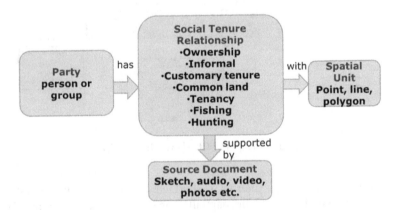

**Fig. 7.** Overview of STDM main principles  (borrowed from [18]).

The STDM approach is to propose a generic and inclusive solution. It was released in 2014 together with Open Source tools with the aim to help in building flexible land administration systems [19]. The transparency dimension present in LADM is enlarged to large principles of good governance, ethics and integrity and sustainability [8, 20].

## 2.4 Domain Model Comparison

Table 1 gives a summary of the comparison of the most important requirements already discussed in the previous sections. LADM and STDM column show extra (+) features w.r.t. the previous column.

**Table 1.** Comparison of main LA domain models.

| Concept | CCDM | LADM | STDM |
|---|---|---|---|
| Owner | Natural person | + Group units<br>+ cooperative | + Company<br>+ municipality<br>+ couple |
| Property | Parcel, building, ways | + Land surveys | + Text description<br>+ unstructured lines<br>+ 3D volume |
| Rights | Formal ownership | + Restriction<br>+ responsibility | + Special rights (e.g. hunting, fishing) |
| Sustainability | No | + Transparency | + Good governance<br>+ ethics, integrity |
| Standardisation | No | Yes | Yes (specialised) |
| Quality assurance | Not specified | + Data and<br>process quality | + Open Source/open<br>data approach |

# 3 Goal-Oriented Analysis Method

Goals capture, at different levels of abstraction, the objectives the system under consideration should achieve. Goal-Oriented Requirements Engineering (GORE) is concerned with the use of goals for eliciting, elaborating, structuring, specifying, analysing, negotiating, documenting, and modifying requirements. To support our research, we focus on KAOS, a specific GORE method [21]. However, the same concepts and methods can be applied in other GORE variants like i* [22] and GRL [23].

A goal is a prescriptive statement of intent about some system (existing or to-be) whose satisfaction in general requires the cooperation of some of the agents. Agents are active components, such as humans, devices, legacy software or software-to-be components that play some role towards goal satisfaction. Some agents thus define the software whereas the others define its environment. Goals may refer to services to be provided (functional goals) or to the way the service is provided (non-functional goals). Unlike goals, domain properties are descriptive statements about the environment, such as physical laws, organisational norms or policies, etc. In LA, a typical high-level functional goal is to *Maintain [Cadastre up-to-date]* and a typical non-functional goal is *Good governance*.

Goals are organized in AND/OR refinement-abstraction hierarchies where higher-level goals are in general strategic, coarse-grained and involve multiple agents whereas lower-level goals are in general technical, fine-grained and involve fewer agents. In such structures, AND-refinement links relate a goal to a set of subgoals (called refinement) possibly conjoined with domain properties; this means that satisfying all subgoals in the refinement is a sufficient condition in the domain for satisfying the goal. OR-refinement links may relate a goal to a set of alternative refinements. Goal refinement ends when every subgoal is realizable by some individual agent assigned to it. A requirement is a leaf goal under responsibility of an agent in the software-to-be; an expectation is a leaf goal under responsibility of an agent in the environment. In LA, a requirement allocated to a *Surveyor* is to *Ensure parcel boundaries precisely measured.*

Obstacles anticipate what could go wrong with the system design [24]. An obstacle is a pre-condition for the violation of a goal. Obstacles is the dual concept to goal and like goal then can be refined into sub-obstacles using a AND-OR refinement tree. An obstacle diagram for a given goal is a tree that shows how a root obstacle is refined into sub-obstacles. Example of obstacles to a registration procedure are long processing times or the presence of frozen titles. Obstacles can be resolved through different tactics like making the obstructed goal less ideal or introducing new mitigation goals.

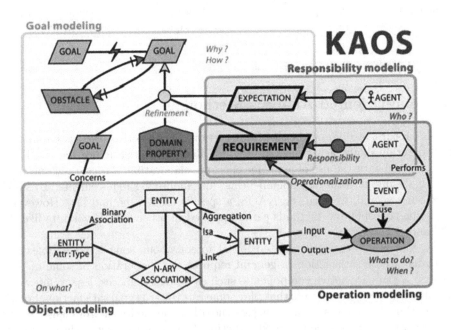

**Fig. 8.** KAOS Meta-model  (from [25]).

In addition the goal model, KAOS is composed of three other models whose content and inter-dependencies are graphically depicted in Fig. 8:

- The **goal model** structures functional and non-functional goals. It also helps to identify related conflicts and reason about their resolution. It is graphically represented as a goal tree which can also capture system design variants.
- The **object model** defines and interrelates all concepts involved in goal specifications. Its representation is aligned with the UML class diagram. Existing LA model are close to this model.
- The **agent model** identifies the agents of both the system and the environment as well as their interfaces and responsibilities. They can be shown as part of goal trees or in more specific diagrams.
- The **operations model** describes how agents functionally cooperate to ensure the fulfilment of their assigned requirements and hence the system goals. Functional flow diagrams are used here.

In the scope of this paper we will mostly focus on the goal, object and responsibility models. Operation model could also be used to study LA workflows in more details but it is out of the scope of this paper. Although the KAOS method supports a formal form of reasoning based on temporal logic, we will only use semi-formal form of reasoning based on graphical UML-like models. However reasoning on both space and time is important in Geographic Information Systems like LA. For this purpose, we will also make use of specific notations depicted in Fig. 9 that have been integrated into the goal and object models together with a set of patterns and heuristics guiding in the discovery and structuring of goals, e.g. spatial and temporal refinement patterns, quantitative reasoning, transposition across domains, etc. [26].

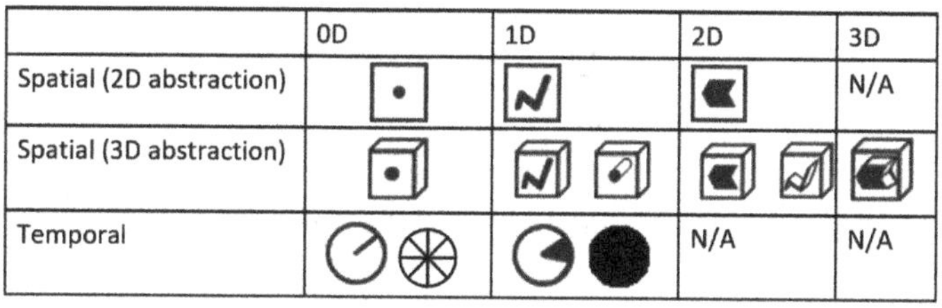

**Fig. 9.** Space-time pictograms from PictograF [27].

The use of these pictograms enables to easily spot concepts or goals that have some temporal or spatial nature and characterise it. For example on the spatial side, a parcel can be marked at 2D spatial concept, an apartment inside a building as 3D spatial concept. A road is a 1D spatial concept. On the temporal side, *Ensuring that cadastral taxes are raised* must be achieved periodically on a yearly basis. The registration process has also different steps with typically specific deadlines and a specific duration sometimes fixed by law. Finally some event can be also recorded like the date of an act. Those can also be explicitly captured in the object model as a date field.

# 4    Goal-Aware Model for Land Administration

This section provides excerpts of the goal-oriented model with the aim to illustrate its global structure and systematic building techniques. The full model is available online with at this digital identifier: doi:10.13140/RG.2.2.21197.84969. It was build using the Objectiver toolset [28].

## 4.1    Capturing the Relevant Vocabulary

In a goal-oriented context, the object model aims at gathering and structuring the vocabulary required for expressing goals. It can be built iteratively together with the goal model. We could validate that the CCDM model fits this purpose. In our modelling, depicted in Fig. 10, identifiers and time intervals during which an entity exists have also been explicitly modelled with more meaningful names (e.g. *dateOfDeath* for a person, *dateOfExpiration* for *RRR*). Concept specialisations were detailed here but are similar to those available in existing domain models. We also used spatio-temporal decorators to tag the dimensions that are present in each concept.

**Fig. 10.** Object Model showing the core concepts [11].

## 4.2    Capturing Strategic Goals

The top goals of our system modelling are of strategic nature and are depicted in Fig. 11. Those goals are also aligned with strategic goals and responsibility assignments published in key literature references such as [29,30]. The diagram should be read vertically with more abstract goals at the top and more operational goals at the bottom and following yellow refinement nodes connecting goals with their sub-goals. So going up/down respectively means asking "Why?"/"How?".

The goal introduced at the top is about sustainability which has three dimensions: financial, social and environmental which can be identified in later subgoals. However, the first refinement is based on the classical functional versus non-functional distinction. The former is called "effectiveness" and covers main functions related to the planning and enforcement of land use. The later is called "efficiency" and is expressed in terms of legal protection and value management, covering both citizen aspects (e.g. for property transfer) and the public authorities (e.g. for collecting taxes).

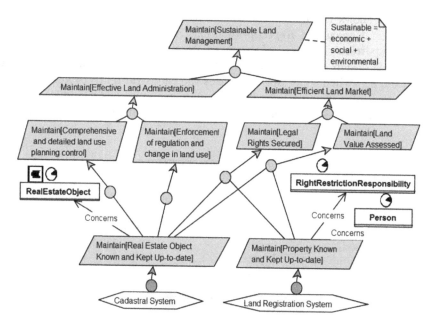

**Fig. 11.** Strategic goals [11].

Further refinements are not fully detailed. However a major observation is that they all rely on two key subsystems: land registration and cadastre. The rationale between this decomposition is based on information control. Looking at the object-model:

- *land registration* is controlling the *Right/Restric-tion/Responsibility* relationship, and consequently many related contractual and legal aspects.
- *cadastre* is controlling the *RealEstateObject*, especially its classification, associated topographic characteristics and the associated value.
- an external system, the *Population Register*, manages the *Person* information.

### 4.3  Robust Design Rationales

High-level goals assigned to sub-systems can be further refined to make explicit all the relevant requirements. Different techniques can be used to provide some assurance of completeness and robustness:

- refinement patterns drive goal decomposition towards completeness with rationales. Some common patterns are temporal milestones and case-based decomposition.
- obstacle analysis enables the identification of undesired behaviours and mitigate them by making existing goals more realistic or by the introduction of goals correcting or anticipating obstacles.

Figure 12 shows the refinement of the main cadastral goal *Maintain [Real Estate Object Known and Kept Up-to-date]*. The left part of the refinement is a milestone pattern composed of three key steps controlled by different agents. However this design does not allow to detect changes that occur outside of a transaction, e.g. when some work increases the cadastral rent. To address this, the right goal introducing a periodic systematic assessment is introduced. However, this goal might suffer from other obstacles, as detailed in the next section.

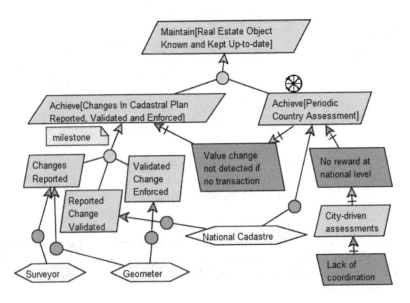

**Fig. 12.** Modelling cadastre updates [11].

## 4.4   Capturing Design Variability

Although systems are developed to fulfil common strategic goals, the fact they where historically designed in different countries implies that there is a large variability in the way those goals are implemented in national systems. We review here the main variability points [31]:

**Deed Registration Versus Title Registration.** Deed registration is based on the transaction document (with rules like: an older document prevails) and thus provide no guarantee of the title. Title registration means the right is really associated to the parcel and can be guaranteed. Both systems are modelled in Fig. 13. Two distinct refinements are used at the top of the diagram. Each alternative is further refined and analysed.

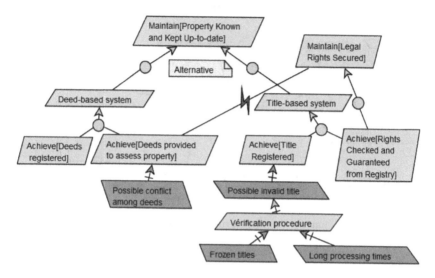

**Fig. 13.** Modelling the titles vs deeds alternatives [11]. (Color figure online)

In the deed-based systems the main obstacle (in red) is that deeds can be questioned and introduce a conflict with the strategic goal of legal protection. In a title-based system, the registration process must be careful and might induce long processing times or even frozen titles. The tendency is to move to title guarantee but could still rely on an underlying "deeds system", thus combining both alternatives. So the distinction is evolving towards positive versus negative systems, given they provide or not a guarantee.

**Land registration and cadastre components separated or integrated** within the same organisation. Given their close interrelation, those components should ideally be integrated. However for historical reasons, they might have been developed independently with some data replication. Different technical designs can cope with this, like synchronisation procedures or a linking database. Long term evolution towards an integrated system is also possible although there is some debate on the pro and cons [32]. The concept of merging was classified in Fully Merged, Merged, and Partly Merged. The merger status covers organizational, legal, and technical aspects [33].

Figure 14 shows a goal model for those three merger alternatives. There are some common requirements on the organisation structure: in all cases a single government agency should be in charge and the management of rights should be centralised. The two other scenarios involve a technical evolution to user interface and then database integration levels and also a legal merger of the operational organisations in charge of land registration and cadastre.

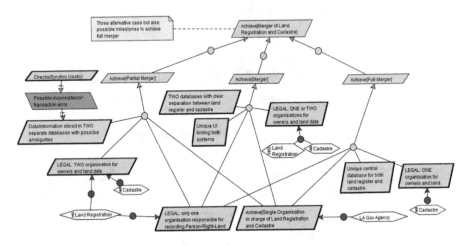

**Fig. 14.** Possible alternatives for integrating land registration and cadastre components.

**Centralized Versus Decentralized Deployment.** Decentralisation can be decided for organisational or political reasons (e.g. in a federal country) but will keep a national authority ensuring consistency, e.g. the global cadastre can be kept at the federal level while tax can be perceived at regional or city level. However, this can induce possible cooperation problems in the organisation, e.g. in Belgium, the cadastral rent is not being systematically updated because the federal level has no revenue out of it and this impacts the funding of cities. Such obstacles were identified in the analysis presented in Fig. 12.

**Fiscal (Tax-Based) Versus Legal Background.** The former is easier to fund and update (only for market value and on a yearly basis) while the later is more complex and expensive because it needs to be accurate and kept up-to-date on a daily basis.

**General Boundaries Versus Fixed Boundaries.** The former relies on visible features of the ground while the later uses exact and marked coordinates. This is already captured by the parcel ontology.

### 4.5  Non-Functional Goals: Good Governance and Sustainability

Good governance is about the processes for making and implementing decisions. It's not about making "correct" decisions, but about the best possible process for making those decisions [34]. Good decision-making processes, and therefore good governance, share several characteristics that are depicted in Fig. 15. This also includes sustainability goals which covers the environmental, social and financial dimensions. The goal refinements are also addressing different obstacles that all contribute to fight corruption, conflict and insecurity.

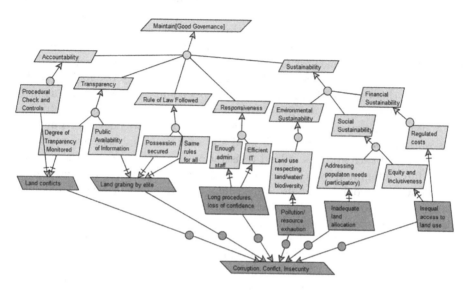

**Fig. 15.** Refining good governance goals to fight corruption, conflict and insecurity.

Such goals and obstacles are quite high level and generic but are meant to serve as a check list of starting point for further refinements to be carried out in the scope of the design or analysis of a specific LA system.

## 5    Discussion and Related Work

UML class diagrams notations are used in CCDM, LADM and STDM which also rely on specific UML profiles and stereotypes enabling to give more domain specific meanings to concepts [35]. The use of profiles also enables to develop specific country profiles. The process to derive such a profile from LADM was described in detail for Portugal [6]. The availability of a UML model enables the use of Model Driven Architecture (MDA) methods and tools and also to specify country specific profile using the Object Constraint Language (OCL). OCL can be used e.g. for specifying specific requirements related to quality and help in better enforcing it.

Besides the use of the class diagram, a wider use of UML model for cadastral system was also proposed by [36]. It shows how different UML diagrams can capture both structural and behavioural dimensions of the system. However UML models have a total lack of goal perspective: the closest diagram is the use case diagram which can only capture functional requirements and performing actors. It is also difficult to capture design variability using pure UML diagrams.

From the ontology point of view, some informal upper ontologies like DOLCE and DnS already provide useful support for general concepts like *person* and *property* and were already successfully experimented in cadastal systems [37]. More formal ontologies like the Basic Formal Ontology (BFO) also capture many interesting spatial and temporal concepts [38]. Interesting specialized ontologies for LA are available such as an GIS ontology including an elaborated axiomatic system [39]. The Sustainable Development Goals Interface Ontology also proposes an interesting framework for capturing more general goals as well as indicators [40]. Our goal framework as well as the key sustainability LA goals could be mapped on this framework. LA domain concepts could also be directly mapped to BFO as alternative to DOLCE so BFO would be the common upper ontology.

A systems approach to land registration and cadastre was developed by [30]. This work focuses on the technical, legal and organisational aspects, and their interrelation of such systems of land registration. The work stresses the need to have a fully integrated system view covering both land registration and cadastre. It covers not only the static dimensions (as described in Sect. 2) but also dynamic dimensions, with a focus on the important adjudication, transfer and subdivision processes. However, it only relies on informal process modelling and is also missing the capture of all the rationales driving the system design.

A KAOS model was build for modelling the Belgian cadastre in 2002 [41]. The goal was to support the development of an unified cadastral database. The object part of the model was not aligned with the still emerging standards but is based on the same key notion of right between a person and a real property. Those concepts are also detailed using a rich inheritance hierarchy. The proposed goal model first details the "as-is" system focusing on the main missions like: maintaining the cadastral map up-to-date, performing value estimation, managing sales, etc. It reveals some duplicated data which were addressed by an improved "to-be" goal model used to drive the system evolution.

At European level, a long term goal is to reach some degree of harmonization of the national LA systems. E.U. member countries have all deployed their own national LA systems that have emerged over a long historical process. Although they share similar principles, they all have their design and implementation specificities. An overview of all European systems has already been carried out as well as some targeted comparative work [3,42]. The goal-model we have developed can help in identifying the difference and defining an evolution path to harmonisation.

## 6    Conclusions

In this paper, we started by surveying and existing the evolution of Land Administration (LA) since their early development (CCDM) to their standardisation (LADM) and the more recent evolution towards sustainability (STDM). Despite those models capture very accurately most aspects of LA, they currently still lack the ability to capture the rationales behind the design of a LA system. To address this, we introduced goal models and related graphical notations and illustrated how they can provide interesting enhancements to LA domain models in order to provide a better understanding and reasoning capabilities on such complex systems. We illustrated the use of key mechanisms to structure goals, analyse obstacles, explore variants and also deal with non-functional requirements like sustainability and good governance.

Our modelling is still being enhanced to cover more features (e.g. for planning tasks) and extra design variants (e.g. adjudication strategies). We also plan to strengthen the link with technical requirements and give better control on how to evolve the deployed systems. A ambitious case study to further validate our approach is to apply our framework to a large scale analysis of European LA systems that will provide a unified view and help in a convergence process. In the long term, our aim is also to propose our extension to be incorporated in future evolution of LA domain models.

# References

1. UNECE: Land Administration Guidelines With Special Reference to Countries in Transition. United Nations Economic Commission for Europe (1996)
2. Henssen, J.: Basic principles of the main cadastral systems in the world. In: Proceedings of Seminar Modern Cadastres and Cadastral Innovations, FIG Commission 7 (1995)
3. Yavuz, A.: A comparative analysis of cadastral systems in the EU countries according to basic selected criteria. In: FIG Working Week (2005)
4. Tuladhar, A.: Reengineering cadastre and land registration systems and business opportunities. In: FIG Working Week and 125th Anniversary, Still on the Frontline, 13–17 April, Paris (2003)
5. Dale, P., McLaughlin, J.: Land Administration. Spatial Information Systems Series. Oxford University Press, Oxford (1999)
6. Hespanha, J., da Fonseca Hespanha de Oliveira, J., van Oosterom, P., Zevenbergen, J.: Development methodology for an integrated legal cadastre: deriving Portugal country profile from the land administration domain model. NCG (2012)
7. Enemark, S., et al.: Fit-For-Purpose Land Administration: Joint FIG. FIG, San Francisco (2014)
8. Asiama, S., et al.: Tools to support transparency in land administration, Training package: Toolkit. UN-HABITAT (2013)
9. Williamson, I.P.: Best practices for land administration systems in developing countries. World Bank Other Operational Studies 16732, The World Bank (2000)
10. van Lamsweerde, A.: Goal-oriented requirements engineering: a guided tour. In: 5th IEEE International Symposium on Requirements Engineering (2001)
11. Ponsard, C., Touzani, M.: Extending land administration domain models with a goal perspective. In: Proceedings of the 3rd International Conference on Geographical Information Systems Theory, Applications and Management (GISTAM), 27–28 April, Porto, Portugal (2017)
12. Zakout, W., Wehrmann, B., Torhonen, M.P.: Good government in land administration principles and good practices. Food and Agriculture Organization of the United Nations (FAO) World Bank, Rome (2009)

13. Van Oosterom, P., Lemmen, C.: Proposal to establish a core cadastral data model. In: 3rd International Workshop 'Towards a Cadastral Core Domain Model' of COST action G9 'Modelling Real Property Transactions', 10–12 October, Delft (2002)
14. Lemmen, C., Oosterom, P.V.: Version 1.0 of the FIG core cadastral domain model. In: Proceedings of XXIII FIG Congress Shaping the Change, Munich, Germany (2006)
15. van Oosterom, P., et al.: The core cadastral domain model. Comput. Environ. Urban Syst. **30**, 627–660 (2006)
16. ISO: 19152 - Geographic information - Land Administration Domain Model (2012). http://www.iso.org
17. Lemmen, C., van Oosterom, P., Bennett, R.: The land administration domain model. Land Use Policy **49**, 535–545 (2015)
18. Christl, A., et al.: Standard open source software for the social tenure domain. In: Annual World Bank Conference on Land and Poverty (2015)
19. GLTN: Social Tenure Domain Model - a pro poor land information tool (2014). http://stdm.gltn.net
20. Williamson, I., Ting, L., Grant, D.: The evolving role of land administration in support of sustainable development. Aust. Surveyor **44**, 126–135 (1999)
21. van Lamsweerde, A.: Requirements Engineering - From System Goals to UML Models to Software Specifications. Wiley, Hoboken (2009)
22. Yu, E.S.K., Mylopoulos, J.: Enterprise modelling for business redesign: the I* framework. SIGGROUP Bull. **18**, 59–63 (1997)
23. ITU: Recommendation Z.151 (10/12), User Requirements Notation (URN) - Language Definition (2012)
24. van Lamsweerde, A., Letier, E.: Handling obstacles in goal-oriented requirements engineering. IEEE Trans. Softw. Eng. **26**, 978–1005 (2000)
25. Respect-IT: KAOS meta-model (2005). http://www.respect-it.com
26. Touzani, M., Ponsard, C.: Towards modelling and analysis of spatial and temporal requirements. In: 24th IEEE International Requirements Engineering Conference (2016)
27. Bédard, Y., Larrivée, S.: Modeling with pictogrammic languages. In: Shekar, S., Xiong, H. (eds.) Encyclopedia of Geographic Information Sciences, pp. 716–725. Springer, Heidelberg (2008). https://doi.org/10.1007/978-0-387-35973-1
28. Respect-IT: The objectiver requirements engineering tool (2005). http://www.respect-it.com
29. Enemark, S.: Land administration infrastructures for sustainable development. Property Manag. **19**, 366–383 (2001)
30. Zevenbergen, J.: A systems approach to land registration and cadastre. Nordic J. Surv. Real Estate Res. **1**(1), 1–10 (2004)
31. Bogaerts, T., Zevenbergen, J.: Cadastral systems - alternatives. Comput. Environ. Urban Syst. **25**, 325–337 (2001)
32. Vries, W.T.D., Wouters, R., Laarakker, P.M.: Land registration and cadastre, one or two agencies? In: Annual World Bank Conference on Land and Poverty, 14–18 March, Washington D.C. (2016)
33. Fetai, B.: Analysing the effects of merging land registration and cadastre. University of Twente Faculty of Geo-Information and Earth Observation (ITC) (2015)
34. UNESCAP: What is good governance? (2009). http://www.unescap.org/sites/default/files/good-governance.pdf
35. OMG: UML - Unified Modelling Language - Version 2.5 (2015). http://www.omg.org/spec/UML

36. Tuladhar, A.M.: Why is unified modeling language (UML) for cadastral systems? M.Sc. University of Twente (2003)
37. Sladic, D., Radulovic, A., Govedarica, M., Jovanovic, D., Przulj, D.: The use of ontologies in cadastral systems. Comput. Sci. Inf. Syst. **12**, 1033–1053 (2015)
38. Arp, R., Smith, B., Spear, A.D.: Building Ontologies with Basic Formal Ontology. The MIT Press, Cambridge (2015)
39. Bittner, T., Donnelly, M., Smith, B.: A spatio-temporal ontology for geographic information integration. Int. J. Geogr. Inf. Sci. **23**, 765–798 (2009)
40. Jensen, M.: Sustainable development goals interface ontology. In: International Conference on Biomedical Ontology and BioCreative (ICBO BioCreative 2016) (2016)
41. Dechesne, B., Delannay, G., Massonet, P.: Agora project: requirements analyse for the creation of an unified cadastral database (2002)
42. EU PCC: Cadastral Information System, a Resource for the E.U. Policies. Overview of the Cadastral Systems of the E.U. Member States - Part I-II-III (2009)

# Data Acquisition and Mapping
# for Geohazard Analysis

D. Lampridou[1], P. Nomikou[1], L. Ragia[2(✉)], M. Alexandri[1],
D. Papanikolaou[1], C. Hübscher[3], Th. Ioannou[1], and P. Sorotou[1]

[1] Department of Geology and Geoenvironment,
National and Kapodistrian University of Athens,
Panepistimioupoli Zografou, 15784 Athens, Greece
dlabgeo@hotmail.com
[2] Natural Hazards, Tsunami and Coastal Engineering Laboratory,
Technical University of Crete, Chania, Greece
lragia@isc.tuc.gr, lemonia.ragia@gmail.com
[3] Institute of Geophysics, Center for Earth System Research and Sustainability,
University of Hamburg, Bundesstraße. 55, 20146 Hamburg, Germany

**Abstract.** The aim of the current work is to introduce bathymetry data into Geographic Information Systems tools for mapping, monitoring and assessing the geohazards in the Greek islands between Crete and Kasos at the Mediterranean sea. The offshore area lying east of Crete is studied on the basis of new bathymetric data. The data was obtained by a multibeam sonar system which allows the imaging of the seafloor. The collected multibeam data have been extensively processed in order to be cleaned of erroneous beams, filtered of noise, processed of navigation data and interpolated of missing beams. The analysis and representation was performed with the ArcGIS software. Resulting maps were analyzed and presented. The analysis of the slope values and the watershed at the eastern part of Crete reflects intense tectonic activity. We have found out that the basin geometry is an elongated rectangular which is divided into seven sub-basins. The multibeam bathymetric data show that the relief is a complex compound of submarine canyons, landslides and a well-defined slump with vertical displacement. These conditions increase substantially the potential of a geohazard in the area.

**Keywords:** Swath bathymetry · Data Acquisition · Mapping
Morphological data · Geohazard analysis

## 1 Introduction

GIS technologies have already been used for geohazards investigation [1, 2]. The challenge of using GIS for oceanographic data has been explicitly discussed in [17]. GIS has been used to process multibeam soundings to reveal information about the topography and geology of the seafloor [7]. In the last years GIS has emerged as a powerful tool for risk assessment for natural hazards such as earthquakes, hurricanes, landslides and flash floods [11]. A GIS system stores, analyzes, manages and represents the data which are associated with spatial location. Spatial relationships can be

L. Ragia et al. (Eds.): GISTAM 2017, CCIS 936, pp. 130–140, 2019.
https://doi.org/10.1007/978-3-030-06010-7_8

recognized and the data with their relationships can be manipulated. Topographic and bathymetric features such as slope geometry and basin or sub-basin characteristics can be visualized and their dynamics through modelling can be described. The 2D and 3D underwater maps provide detailed description and intensive investigation of the examined area.

The importance for improving our understanding of geohazards is evident from global events. Globally, disasters affect millions of people and inflict great damage as documented by various reports [16].

A geohazard in the offshore domain is defined as "local and/or regional site and soil conditions having a potential of developing into failure events causing loss of life or damage to health, environment or field installations" [9]. Examples of such hazards include earthquakes and submarine landslides, iceberg scouring of the seabed, and gas migration that can lead to locally over pressurized sediments and potential terrain instability and/or blowouts. Secondary effects such as tsunamis (either triggered by earthquakes or landslides) also need to be considered, as both their genesis and propagation are strongly controlled by seafloor morphology [3]. Hence, there is an urgent need to determine the development of geohazards and inherent risks associated with them. This need is also accentuated by the increased vulnerability of coastal areas to earthquakes because of rapid growth of urban centers.

The Hellenic subduction zone (HSZ) has historically generated among the most devastating earthquakes, and by far the most damaging tsunamis in the entire Mediterranean region. Historic earthquakes along the HSZ, particularly along the Crete segment, attest to some degree of coupling on the plate interface [4, 15]. The Hellenic subduction zone is the largest, fastest and most seismically active subduction zone in the Mediterranean, where the African slab subducts beneath Crete at a rate of 36 mm yr$^{-1}$ [12, 13]. The subduction rate greatly exceeds the convergence between Africa (Nubia) and Eurasia (5–10 mm yr$^{-1}$) because of the rapid South West motion of the southern Aegean itself, relative to Eurasia [13].

To properly assess geohazards requires an understanding of the broader geologic, sedimentary and tectonic variability. Therefore, multi-disciplinary surveys aimed at detecting and mapping geohazards, are critical.

The advent of multibeam sonar (MBS) technology has allowed imaging of the seafloor with unparalleled resolution, spatial coverage and precision and today offer the most cost effective way to explore the ocean floor [3, 6].

High resolution swath data were obtained during an oceanographic cruise in the framework of FP7 "ASTARTE: Assessment, Strategy and Risk Reduction for Tsunamis in Europe-ASTARTE" project in the South Aegean Sea. The aim of this paper has been the fault recognition by applying morphostructural analysis, which was based on the quantitative interpretation of the seafloor topography, the slope distribution and the drainage pattern development in the offshore area lying between Crete and Kasos. The area is also an extremely important area for geohazards analysis because of the potential routes for underwater cables and gas pipelines.

The offshore area between Crete and Kasos is characterised by the large number of poorly characterized bathymetric scarps that cross the region. Each of these is potentially associated with a fault capable of generating a rare, high-magnitude, earthquake. Unlike the other parts of the Hellenic plate boundary, however, there is no possibility of detecting past earthquakes from on-shore geological evidence. The principal faults lie far enough from the shore that no detectable uplift of shorelines would be expected, making a detailed marine survey essential [5].

Although the Hellenic system represents the most significant seismic and tsunami hazard in the Mediterranean region, its kinematics and associated hazards remain uncertain because available GPS data are not sufficiently precise and spatially distributed to determine the distribution of strain accumulation on the plate boundary faults [4]. Many important details of the kinematics-dynamics of the Hellenic subduction zone remain poorly understood and under debate.

This study aims to map and monitor coastal geohazards using Geographic Information Systems. The aim of the current work is to introduce bathymetry data into GIS tools for mapping, monitoring and assessing the geohazards in the area between Crete and Kasos at the Mediterranean sea. The reduced from error data results in high resolution maps providing a homogeneous and realistic undersea surface. This paper is an extended version of work published in [10].

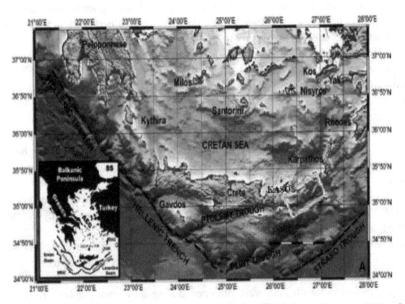

**Fig. 1.** General map of the area [8] the red box corresponds to the study area. (Color figure online)

## 2  Data Acquisition

Data used in this paper have been obtained onboard an R/V Med Surveyor in the area between Crete and Kasos (Fig. 1). Swath bathymetry data were acquired using multibeam echosounder Elac's SeaBeam 3030, which operates in the 30 kHz band and incorporates a multi-ping capability (two swaths per ping). Data were logged with HYPACK software. The SeaBeam 3030 system transmits a sonar signal (ping) from transducers mounted along the ship's keel [14]. The signal, generated in the transmitter subsystem, travels from multiple transducers but forms a single beam projected across a swath under the ship. The sonar signal travels to the sea floor and reflects off the bottom. At the ship, hydrophones mounted across the bottom of the ship (across-ship) listen for the reflection of the sonar signal. They convert the sound to electrical signals and send these signals to the echo processor electronic assembly. The assembly determines the bottom depth, position and other characteristics from echoes received across the swath. Calculations are based on signal intensity and elapsed time in receiving them. The system integrates the sonar data with location information from the ship's navigation system. Each ping cycle, bottom depth and other information about the returned signals are displayed on Operator PC1 (Fig. 2) and can be displayed for real-time viewing of seafloor characteristics. Hydrostar software was used to control the SeaBeam3030 and Hypack was used for navigation, acquisition and storage (Fig. 2).

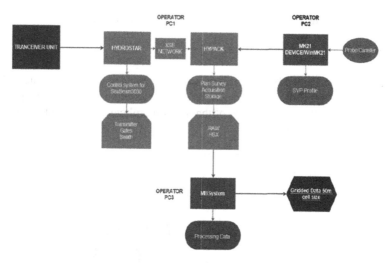

**Fig. 2.** Simplified workflow during the survey.

The collected multibeam data have been extensively processed by means of data editing, cleaning of erroneous beams, filtering of noise, processing of navigation data and interpolation of missing beams, using the open-source software MB-SYSTEM, and then gridded with grid spacing of 50 m. Analyses and representation of bathymetric data were performed with ArcGIS 10.1 software and Global Mapper v.16.

MB-System is an open source software for processing and display of bathymetric data. During "ASTARTE" project, all the processing phases were performed with the latest version of MB-System. The MB-SYSTEM processing steps during this project comprised (Fig. 3):

PROCESSING BATHYMETRIC DATA

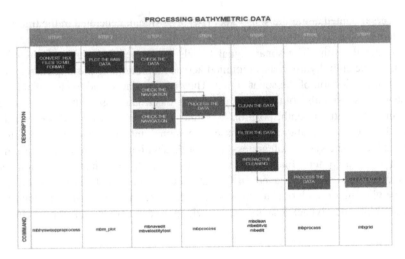

**Fig. 3.** Flow chart representing the processing steps.

## 3 Mapping

The resulting slope-shaded bathymetric map was compiled at 1:300,000 scale and with additional isobaths of 50 m. This map permits a first description of the overall topography of the seafloor as well as the mapping of the major morphotectonic structures (Fig. 4).

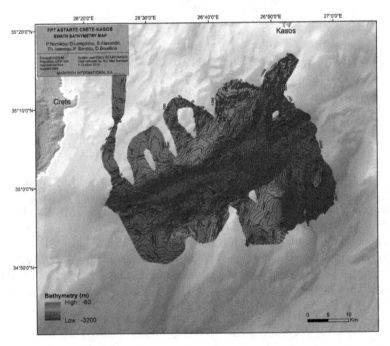

**Fig. 4.** Swath Bathymetry map of Crete-Kasos area. Multi-beam data are plotted above EMODENT bathymetry.

The most interesting is the one comprising the NW flank of the linear channel. It is a typical slump with four distinguishable «steps» at 1500 m, 1600 m, 1700 m 1800 m, meaning that the vertical displacement is approximately 100 m. Noteworthy is that this kind of landslides can trigger tsunamis (Fig. 5).

The bathymetric map of the area was analysed as far as the slope distribution is concerned. The slope distribution map shows the distribution of slope values within the study area distinguished in four categories (a) areas of mean morphological slope 0°– 5°, (b) areas of 5°–20°, (c) areas of 20°–40° (d) and areas of >40°. This classification of the slope magnitude will illustrate the zones where there is an abrupt change of slope, reflecting possible positions of active tectonic zones in contrast with zones with negligible change of slope, which reflect flat-lying areas such as submarine terraces or basinal areas (Fig. 6).

The combined slope- aspect map captures both the direction of the slopes and their steepness, illustrating the overall geometry of the area and changes in the relief orientation which may be attributed to active tectonic structures. The direction of the slope (degrees) is expressed in hue and the steepness of the slope (degrees) is expressed by its saturation (Fig. 7).

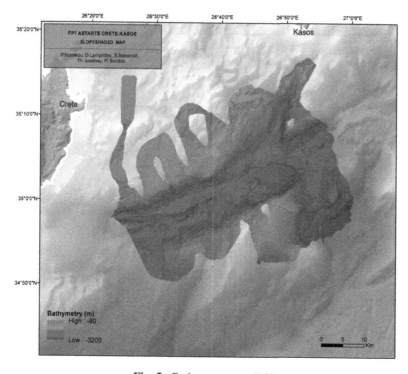

**Fig. 5.** Bathymetry map [10].

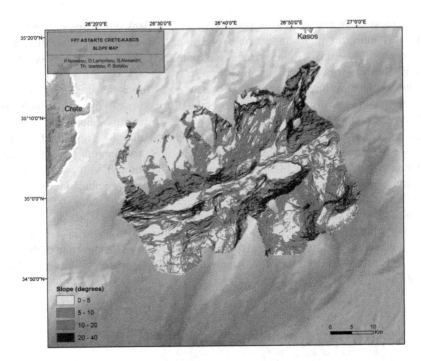

**Fig. 6.** Slope map [10].

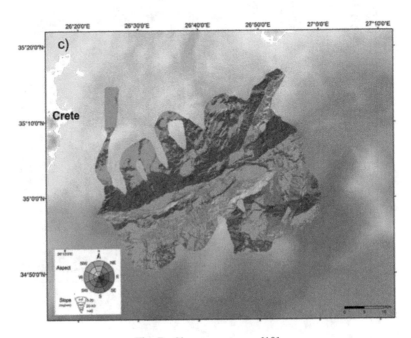

**Fig. 7.** Slope aspect map [10].

Submarine canyons, small gullies and stream network were extracted for the entire area employing the in-built hydrology tools. When extracting the drainage pattern we need to take into account: (a) the flow accumulation output grid that was produced by applying a threshold upstream cell number of 200, (b) multibeam artefacts can result in the interruption of streams or the generation of spurious ones.

The Synthetic Morphotectonic Map of the under study area was carried out by means of the combined use of: (a) Seabed Digital Elevation Model (SDEM), (b) Slope Distribution Map, (c) Slope-aspect Map and (d) Drainage Pattern Map. The composition of the digital modelling in conjunction with the regional geodynamic setting, allows the identification of the main morphological discontinuities.

The bathymetric map reveals a rather rough seafloor topography where flat-lying areas alternate with rough morphology. Two prominent fault zones form the general structure of the area. The first fault zone strikes SW-NE comprising the marginal faults that delineate the central subsided area. The second fault zone, strikes SSW-NNE and crosscuts the first one. The topographic difference along the marginal faults, which apparently correlates with the fault throw, ranges between 1200 m up to 1500 m. The northern marginal fault presents its greater topographic difference at the western and far eastern part, while the southern marginal fault at its eastern part. This is possibly linked to the different structural deformation of the area. The basin area that is bounded by the previous SW-NE identified fault zone, is divided into seven elongated sub-basins, parallel to the alignment of the marginal faults. The sub-basins are lying at 2200 m, 2500 m, 2600 m and 2800 water depths respectively. The eastern basin is a simple geometric basin with a flat-lying sea bottom (2800 m) at the junction of the two major marginal fault zones, and its maximum subsidence is accommodated by the southern marginal fault. The western part of the basin has a very complex topographic regime carved by several sub-basins developed with different geometric shapes at different water depths and separated by distinct intermediate submarine ridge with topographic differences ranging from 150 m of meters.

Numerous gullies that dissect the slopes, trending almost NW-SE, coalesce at several depths ending up at the seven sub-basins. The most prominent submarine canyon is the one bounded by the secondary fault zone that strikes SSW-NNE. It is a U-shaped rather linear feature and its depth ranges between 1300 m and 2800 m water depth. The channel walls are asymmetrical and the axis profile displays a linear morphology (Fig. 8).

Submarine landslides were also identified in the study area by the typical crescent-shape scar. The most interesting is the one comprising the NW flank of the linear channel. It is a typical slump with four distinguishable «steps» at 1500 m, 1600 m, 1700 m 1800 m, meaning that the vertical displacement is approximately 100 m. Noteworthy is that this kind of landslides can trigger tsunamis.

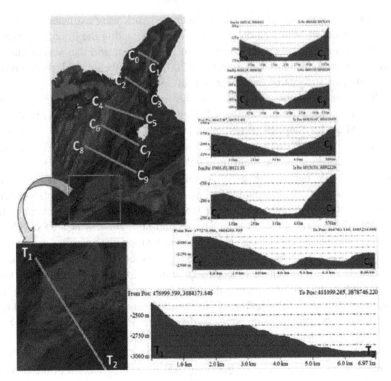

**Fig. 8.** Detailed view of the Kasos canyon with the location of the cross sections. a. C0-C9 vertical topographic sections perpendicular to canyon axis, b. Detailed view and topographic section (T1-T2) at the end of canyon [10].

## 4  Morphotectonic Map

The morphotectonic interpretation, accomplished by the compilation of the previously presented maps in combination with the multichannel seismic profiles acquired during the project, has led to the construction of the Morphotectonic map (Fig. 9).

The Crete – Kasos studied area comprises a more than 50 km long basin in the ENE-WSW direction with an average width of 10 km. This basin forms a tectonic graben bounded by two sub-parallel marginal fault zones, which have produced a relative subsidence of more than 1200 m of the basin area.

The sea bottom of the basin is complicated with seven sub-basins elongated in the ENE-WSW direction separated by intermediate ridges not over 150 m of relative relief. The sea bottom at the eastern larger basin occurs at a depth of 2800 m. Along the shallow slopes of the two marginal fault zones outside the basin a large number of submarine canyons and landslides occur as well as a slumped area of 20 × 30 km at the northern margin, whose overall vertical displacement seems to exceed 400 m. The two ENE-WSW marginal faults form two broad zones of a few km width along their dip towards the subsided zone with topographic differences ranging between 1300 and 1500 m. Several sub-parallel faults are observed within the basin, which form an

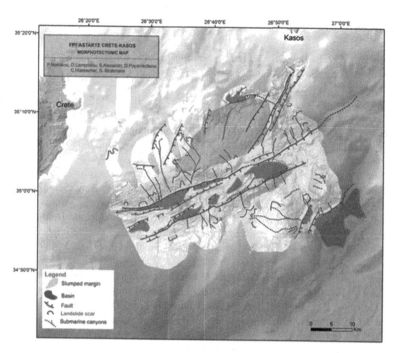

**Fig. 9.** Morphotectonic map [10].

intermediate ridge/horst along the axis of the tectonic graben. The overall tectonic structure resembles a regime with oblique normal faulting combining an opening in the NW-SE direction together with a left-lateral strike slip motion, which is supported also by earthquake mechanisms.

## 5   Conclusions

We have obtained original bathymetry data for an area between Kasos and Crete in the Eastern Mediterranean. The area is known for historic seismic activity and it is difficult to analyze for geohazard risks from shore related data. The data was further cleaned and processed. We introduced the data into a GIS and produced different maps. The maps were combined in a morphotectonic map allowing for study of potential earthquakes and their effect. The resulting qualitative analysis is extremely important for evaluating potential risks from earthquakes and sea floor landslides in the bottom of the sea. The geographical area studied is critical in view of potential routes for underwater cables and gas pipelines.

**Acknowledgements.** This work was supported and funded by the FP7 "ASTARTE: Assessment, Strategy and Risk Reduction for Tsunamis in Europe-ASTARTE". We are grateful to Costas Synolakis and Philip England for their beneficial contribution and comments.

# References

1. Arnous, M., Green, D.: GIS and remote sensing as tools for conducting geo-hazards risk assessment along Gulf of Aqaba coastal zone. Egypt. J. Coast. Conserv. **15**(4), 457–475 (2011)
2. Carrara, A., Guzzetti, F., Cardinali, M., Reichenbach, P.: Use of GIS technology in the prediction and monitoring of landslide hazard. Nat. Hazards **20**(2–3), 117–135 (1999)
3. Chiocci, F.L., Cattaneo, A., Urgeles, R.: Seafloor mapping for geohazard assessment: state of the art. Mar. Geophys. Res. **32**(1–2), 1–11 (2011). https://doi.org/10.1007/s11001-011-9139-8
4. England, P., Howell, A., Jackson, J., Synolakis, C.: Palaeotsunamis and tsunami hazards in the Eastern Mediterranean. Philos. Trans. R. Soc. A: Math. Phys. Eng. Sci. **373**, 20140374 (2015). https://doi.org/10.1098/rsta.2014.037
5. Howell, A., Jackson, J., England, P., Higham, T., Synolakis, C.: Late Holocene uplift of Rhodes, Greece: evidence for a large tsunamigenic earthquake and the implications for the tectonics of the eastern Hellenic Trench System. Geophys. J. Int. **203**, 459–474 (2015). https://doi.org/10.1093/gji/ggv307
6. Hughes Clarke, J.E., Mayer, L.A., Wells, D.E.: Shallow-water imaging multibeam sonars: a new tool for investigating seafloor processes in the coastal zone and on the continental shelf. Mar. Geophys. Res. **18**(6), 607–629 (1996). https://doi.org/10.1007/bf00313877
7. Kearns, T.A., Breman, J.: Bathymetry the art and science of seafloor modeling for modern applications. In: Ocean Globe, pp. 1–36 (2010)
8. Kokinou, E., Tiago, A., Evangelos, K.: Structural decoupling in a convergent forearc setting (southern Crete, Eastern Mediterranean). Geol. Soc. Am. Bull. **124**(7–8), 1352–1364 (2012). https://doi.org/10.1130/B30492.1
9. Kvalstad, T.J.: What is the current "best practice" in offshore Geohazard investigations? A state-of-the-art review (2007). https://doi.org/10.4043/18545-ms
10. Lampridou, D., et al.: Morphotectonic analysis between Crete and Kasos. In: Proceedings of the 3rd International Conference on Geographical Information Systems Theory, Applications and Management, Porto, Portugal, 27–28 April, pp. 142–150 (2017). https://doi.org/10.5220/0006387201420150
11. Lavakare, A.: GIS and risk assessment (2000). http://www.gisdevelopment.net/application/miscellaneous/misc010.htm
12. McClusky, S., et al.: Global positioning system constraints on plate kinematics and dynamics in the eastern Mediterranean and Caucasus. J. Geophys. Res.: Solid Earth **105**(B3), 5695–5719 (2000). https://doi.org/10.1029/1999jb900351
13. Reilinger, R., et al.: GPS constraints on continental deformation in the Africa-Arabia-Eurasia continental collision zone and implications for the dynamics of plate interactions. J. Geophys. Res.: Solid Earth **111**(B5) (2006). https://doi.org/10.1029/2005jb004051
14. SeaBeam 3030: Multibeam Sonar System, GAS II. Technical Specification Doc_No. 52381 (2013)
15. Shaw, B., et al.: Eastern Mediterranean tectonics and tsunami hazard inferred from the AD 365 earthquake. Nat. Geosci. **1**, 268–276 (2008). https://doi.org/10.1038/ngeo151
16. United Nations Office for Disaster Risk Reduction. http://www.unisdr.org/
17. Wright, D.J., Goodchild, M.F.: Data from the deep: implications for the GIS community. Int. J. Geogr. Inf. Sci. **11**(6), 523–528 (1997). https://doi.org/10.1080/136588197242176

# Optimal Evacuation Routing Using LiDAR-Based Flood Models

Zarah Jean Diche[2(✉)], Cinmayii Manliguez[1,2],
Maria Jezebel Jimenez[1], Maureen Agrazamendez[1,2],
and Joseph Acosta[1,2]

[1] Department of Mathematics, Physics, and Computer Science,
University of the Philippines Mindanao, 8022 Davao City, Philippines
[2] Phil-LiDAR 1.B.13 LiDAR Data Processing and Validation in Mindanao:
Davao Region, University of the Philippines Mindanao,
8022 Davao City, Philippines
zarjdiche@gmail.com

**Abstract.** Flooding is one of the most recurring disasters. Evacuation planning is one of the fundamental instruments to mitigate negative impacts of this hazard to the community. Routing is part of evacuation planning that determines the best routes for relocating population. In this study, evacuation routing is focused to the output of the UP Mindanao Phil-LiDAR1. The Light Detection and Ranging (LiDAR) technology is an airborne mapping method that delivers geospatial data in the form of point clouds with high-accuracy elevation values and ground features. Building and road network features extracted from the LiDAR data were used to create network dataset. Flood hazard models were used to identify areas in the network that are at risk of flooding. Capacity Aware Shortest Path Evacuation Routing (CASPER) of the ArcGIS Network Analyst Tool's extension was used to simulate evacuation routes. The tool uses the CASPER algorithm, a heuristic evacuation routing method that takes into account the capacity of the transportation network and the traffic flow in order to minimize traffic congestion. This study and the data it produced can help the local government units in their planning and disaster risk reduction management.

**Keywords:** Flooding · Lidar · Evacuation · Routing · CASPER

## 1 Introduction

Storms, earthquakes and many other natural disasters have been hitting Philippines for centuries. Among the natural calamities that the Filipino community suffered from, flooding is reported as the most recurring [11]. The Philippines experiences an average of 20 typhoons every year making it as one of the most flood-prone countries in the world [9]. One of the most destructive typhoons to have ever been recorded in history, Super Typhoon Yolanda (Haiyan) entered the Philippine archipelago on 08 November 2013 leaving 6,300 people dead, 28,688 injured, and 1,062 missing [8].

Negative impacts of this hazard to the community are mitigated through addressing disaster risk reduction. PHIL-LiDAR1 Project is one of the programs conducted in the country to avoid loss of lives and destruction of properties. Through the resource information generated from the project through the LiDAR output, different studies can be done for planning in preparation to flood. One of which is evacuation planning. Routing is part of the evacuation planning process that determines the best routes to relocate the affected population to the nearest shelters—usually, within the shortest amount of time possible for an individual. However, it is not enough for an evacuation routing problem to generate the optimal paths for each evacuee only since there is a need to consider the whole affected community in such a way that everyone is able to transfer into a safer place considering the road capacity while travelling [7].

The Capacity-Aware Shortest Path Evacuation Routing (ArcCASPER) is a network analyst tool used to generate large scale evacuation routes to the nearest shelter by integrating road capacity and travel times as a means to reduce the global transportation time and minimize traffic congestion [14]. It provides three different evacuation routing methods: shortest path, capacity constrained route planner (CCRP), and CASPER, to investigate the length of their evacuation times and determine the most effective method. The shortest path method is the fastest method of the three but it ignores the road capacities so its accuracy is low [14]. CCRP gives priority to those evacuees who are farthest from their safe zone by allowing them take alternate routes until the roadway has reached its maximum capacity [14]. CASPER initially sorts the evacuees based on their travel times and assigns the evacuees with longest travel time to a shortest path. This process continues until there are no more evacuees left to process. The edge travel costs are constantly updated to ensure that the global evacuation time is at its minimum [15].

### 1.1 Conceptual Framework

The features extracted output from the Digital Surface Model (DSM) and flood hazard model of Padada floodplain are used in this study. The conceptual framework of this study is shown in Fig. 1.

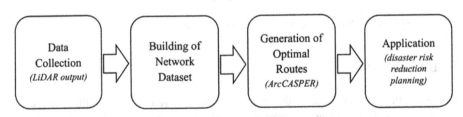

**Fig. 1.** GIS-based optimal evacuation routing using LiDAR-derived features and flood hazard models.

In the Data Collection part, the Lidar data were collected from the project. Building and road network features were used to build a network dataset to generate optimal evacuation routes using ArcCASPER. The output of these steps can now be used by any local government agency located in Padada floodplain for flood hazard risk reduction operations.

## 1.2    Objective

This study aims to create optimal evacuation routes using LiDAR-derived building and road network features and Flood Hazard Models of the Padada Floodplain. The said floodplain covers various barangays from five different municipalities. Road capacity, location and vulnerability status of each building were considered.

# 2    Review of Related Literature

The evacuation execution stage refers to those actions that are taken immediately, once the nature of the disaster becomes known, to reallocate the potentially endangered population to safety. At this stage the location and time of the disaster is the key information [16]. The post-disaster response stage is characterized by emergency personnel caring for the affected population, shelter maintenance, and disaster assessment. For example, Eguchi et al. [2] studied post-disaster damage assessment using integrated GPS sensor network and GIS. Lue et al. [4] studied disaster damage assessment by utilizing geo-tagged videos taken from the affected areas.

Disasters can either be static or dynamic. Dynamic disasters are characterized by their changing behavior, location, or severity. Disasters such as tsunamis and terrorist attacks are considered as static whereas hurricanes, wildfires, and flood are dynamic [16]. These dynamic disasters would evidently add to the complexity in evacuation planning and has to be considered in a realistic evacuation solution.

The evacuation routing problem refers to the process of relocating the potentially affected population towards safe destination points such as shelters and hotels. The objective of this problem is usually to minimize exposure, global evacuation time, average travel time, or traffic congestion. An effective routing solution should consider the characteristics of the transportation network, available transportation vehicles, as well as the capacity of the potential destinations [16]. Other routing optimization problems can also use metaheuristics algorithms to find the best possible route given a minimal cost given the characteristics of the path [6].

## 2.1    Flood Hazard Map

Flood hazard maps are designed to identify the areas that are at a risk of flooding and to increase the awareness of the likelihood of flooding among the public. They also encourage the population residing in flood-prone areas to find out more about the local flood risk and to take the appropriate action [3]. Areas that are marked red indicate a high flood hazard (>1.5 m). Those that are marked orange indicate a moderate flood hazard (0.5 – 1.5 m). Areas that are marked yellow indicate a low flood hazard (<0.5 m) [12].

## 2.2    GIS Application

A geographical information system (GIS) is a computer system that is designed to support the capture, management, manipulation, analysis, and modeling and display of spatially-referenced data suitable for solving complex planning and management problems [1]. All stages of the evacuation planning problem identified by Shahabi [16] can greatly benefit from the application of GIS. Gaining access to the appropriate data is the key [16]. In an emergency, it is critical to have the right data, at the right time, displayed logically, to respond and take the appropriate action. By utilizing GIS, this data can be shared throughout different agencies or departments with the use of spatial databases held in one central location. GIS provides a mechanism to centralize and visually display critical information in the midst of an emergency [1]. With regards to preparation, GIS can be used to provide answers to particular questions such as identifying the safest location for the critical facilities, selecting of evacuation routes based on the anticipated or actual flood, or determining whether the transportation network can handle the sudden increase in traffic flow. Lastly, in the post-disaster response stage, GIS can play a role in the disaster damage assessment and information management. With the use of GPS and telecommunication devices, assessments of the damages can be geo-referenced and transmitted back to the emergency headquarters for realtime update of the recovery [1].

### 2.3    Evacuation Planning

In the face of a natural disaster, evacuation planning refers to the process of relocating the endangered population to safer areas as soon as possible. The study of Shahabi [16] proposed a new taxonomy to the evacuation planning problem in which the problem is divided into three stages: preparation, evacuation execution, and post-disaster response [16]. The evacuation execution stage refers to those actions that are taken immediately, once the nature of the disaster becomes known, to reallocate the potentially endangered population to safety. At this stage the location and time of the disaster is the key information [16]. The post-disaster response stage is characterized by emergency personnel caring for the affected population, shelter maintenance, and disaster assessment. For example, Eguchi et al. [2] studied post-disaster damage assessment using integrated GPS sensor network and GIS. Lue et al. [4] studied disaster damage assessment by utilizing geo-tagged videos taken from the affected areas.

Disasters can either be static or dynamic. Dynamic disasters are characterized by their changing behavior, location, or severity. Disasters such as tsunamis and terrorist attacks are considered as static whereas hurricanes, wildfires, and flood are dynamic [16]. These dynamic disasters would evidently add to the complexity in evacuation planning and has to be considered in a realistic evacuation solution. The evacuation routing problem refers to the process of relocating the potentially affected population towards safe destination points such as shelters and hotels. The objective of this problem is usually to minimize exposure, global evacuation time, average travel time, or traffic congestion. An effective routing solution should consider the characteristics of the transportation network, available transportation vehicles, as well as the capacity of the potential destinations [16].

### 2.4    Evacuation Routing Methods

The existing evacuation routing methods can be divided into the following classifications: simulation, network flow, and heuristic methods [10]. Simulation methods are solutions that visually simulate an emergency situation. It tries to visualize what could possibly happen as realistically as possible. Flow-based modeling, agent-based modeling, and cellular automaton modeling are just some of the methods that would fall into this category [13]. These tend to focus more on the individual evacuees' movements and their interaction with one another [5].

**CASPER Algorithm.** The Capacity Aware Shortest Path Evacuation Routing (CASPER) algorithm is a heuristic evacuation routing method that connects each source node (evacuee) to its nearest destination while taking into account the capacity of the transportation network and the traffic flow in order to minimize traffic congestion and system-wide transportation times [15]. The algorithm first sorts the evacuees based on their distance from the closest destination area. Then, starting from the evacuee with the longest distance, it finds the shortest path and assigns the evacuee to that path. It iteratively continues this process until there are no more evacuees left, indicating that the affected population has successfully been removed from the hazard area. During the analysis, CASPER dynamically updates the edge travel costs based on the number of assigned evacuees and the capacity of the edge [14].

Each source point $s$ is metered ($interval(s)$) so it will generate a different flow on each edge. For example, evacuees leaving from a source point at 20 s intervals have $interval(s) = 20$. Each source point also has only one path $P_s$ assigned to them. A path $P_s$ is an ordered set of edges that will guide all the population from source point $s$ to safety ($t$). From here, the total flow on edge $e$ can be calculated by summing up all flows of all paths that pass through $e$ [15].

*Traffic Model.* The traffic model is defined as a function with two parameters $T(f, c)$. The traffic model predicts the congestion on an edge based on its capacity and total flow. From there, the cost of traversing an edge, and consequently the cost of traversing a path, can be calculated (Eqs. 1 and 2).

$$cost_T(e) = \frac{imp(e)}{T(flow(e), cap(e))} \tag{1}$$

$$cost_T(P_s) = interval(s) \times w(s) + \sum_{e \in p_s} cost_T(e) \tag{2}$$

$$EvcTime = max(cost_T(P_s) | P_s \in P) \tag{3}$$

The *EvcTime* in Eq. 3 denotes the estimated global evacuation time. The main objective here is to minimize the cost of the path with the highest cost.

$$cost_T(e, s) = \frac{imp(e)}{T(flow(s, e) + flow(e), cap(e))} \tag{4}$$

The calculation in Eq. 4 considers both the previously reserved paths and the new population flow (i.e. $flow(s, e)$) so there is a need to record all the reserved paths. Lastly, the costs of all the paths are re-calculated. This step is important since the record of the reserved paths is not complete during the path finding process and therefore the costs are just a lower bound. Once all the paths are reserved, their costs need to be re-calculated to find the most accurate global evacuation time [16].

This algorithm is used in ArcGIS' Network Analyst tool, ArcCasper. The Capacity-Aware Reverse Map Analyzer (CARMA) serves as an extension to the path finding module whose main objective is to improve the overall performance of the CASPER algorithm. This extension has two main features; it sorts the source points according to their predicted evacuation time and it generates heuristic values [15].

## 3    Materials and Methods

In this study, CASPER algorithm was used in evacuation routing using the ArcCASPER to the data network generated from LiDAR-derived features and flood hazard model. The flowchart of methodology is shown in Fig. 2. This study focused on Padada Floodplain which covers several barangays of the municipalities of Hagonoy, Padada, Matanao, Kiblawan and Sulop. Buildings and road networks were extracted from the Data Surface Model (DSM) and were validated to get more specific attributes like building type and number of lanes. There were a total of 17, 365 and 531 verified and attributed buildings and road networks inside the floodplain. The specific barangays covered by the floodplain and the municipality that they belong are presented in Table 1. Figure 3 shows a map of the scope of the floodplain overlaid in the five municipalities' barangay boundaries. The flood hazard model of Padada floodplain was used in this study to identify those areas within the network that are at a risk of flooding. The building features that fall to moderate and high flood risk demarcations are subject for evacuation and exported into point features named "Evacuees" while the rest of the buildings in the floodplain are considered infrastructures that are possible places for evacuation and named as "Safe". The road network features were used as input in the network dataset generation. In the optimal route generation, converted points for Evacuees and Safe were loaded to Evacuees and

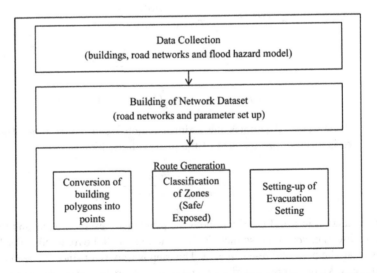

**Fig. 2.** Flowchart methodology of GIS-based optimal evacuation routing using LiDAR derived features and flood hazard models.

**Table 1.** Barangays covered by the Padada Floodplain.

| Hagonoy municipality | Padada municipality | Matanao municipality | Kiblawan municipality | Sulop municipality |
|---|---|---|---|---|
| Paligue | Piape | Buri | Molopolo | Katipunan |
| Guihing | San Isidro | Kauswagan | New Sibonga | Tanwalang |
| Aplaya | Punta Piape | Ceboza | Bagumbayan | |
| Poblacion | Lower Limonzo | Buas | Manual | |
| Hagonoy Crossing | Upper Limonzo | Langaan | Santo Niño | |
| Tologan | NCO District | Bagumbayan | Poblacion | |
| Mahayahay | Almendras | | San Pedro | |
| Lapulabao | Southern Paligue | | | |
| New Quezon | Northern Paligue | | | |
| Maliit | Don Sergio | | | |
| Digos | Osmena | | | |
| La Union | Lower Katipunan | | | |
| Clib | Lower Malinao | | | |
| San Guillermo | Upper Malinao | | | |
| Malabang | | | | |

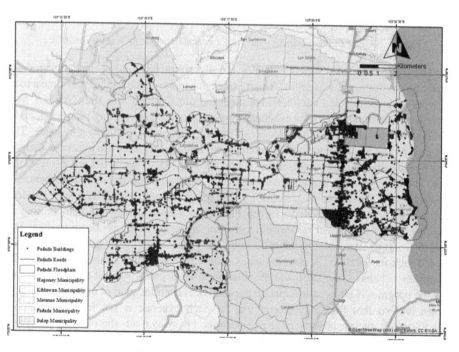

**Fig. 3.** Padada Floodplain coverage.

Zones of the ArcGIS Network Analyst Tool. Necessary set-ups are then considered to ensure optimal routing as shown in Fig. 4.

**Fig. 4.** Snippet of Network Analyst Tool's evacuation routing's set-up interface.

The dynamic mode, which indicates the algorithm for routing in a dynamically changing environment, was set to "Smart" since this mode ensures that every time a road network change, affected cars are identified and are rerouted. For the CARMA Sort Direction, which indicates how evacuees must be sorted before getting processed, "BW Continuous" is selected so that process of routing starts with the farthest evacuee. The Init Delay Cost Per Evacuee which indicates the initial space between evacuees that are sharing the same starting locations was set to "0.0100" which was a default figure of the tool. The Cost per Safe Zone Density helps the program prioritize safe zones hence, it was set to the default value, zero, since enforcing safe zone capacity is not needed. The CARMA Ratio is needed to keep the vertices up-to-date while path finding is ongoing, and setting it near zero would mean that vertices will always be up-to-date. The Selfish Routing Ratio is a number between [0, 1] that determines how each evacuee should pick its location. A zero indicates selfish routing which enables the CASPER algorithm to behave like the usual. Population Split or group was set to "Separate" so that the program is allowed to separate population at each location in order to minimize routes and so that tracking information for each evacuee is not lost. The Export Edge/Street Statistics show the edge reservations, Two way roads share capacity enables CASPER to use each lane in any direction it like while Run CARMA with Dynamic Shortest Path Tree (DSPT) enables newer version of CARMA where heuristic values are updated using DSPT algorithm. The routing options are based on the restricting factors considered in this study which are, the capacity set by lanes, and the length of the road nearest to an evacuee. In the traffic options, traffic model was set to "Power" so that a relative change to one evacuee and road network results to a proportional relative change to the whole data network. The default values were considered for Critical Density per Unit Capacity and the Saturation Density per Unit Capacity.

# 4  Results and Discussion

There were 3,142 building points that were in moderate and high risk of flooding based on the flood hazard model and were input as "Evacuees" and the remaining 14, 223 were input as "Safe" in Zones. A network dataset of 531 polylines representing the roads was generated successfully. Running the ArcCASPER tool, a total of 256 road edges were identified to be used in the event of evacuation. Of the 3,142 evacuees, 517 were not given any road to pass through because the buildings were too near to points under "Safe Zone" or the building is too far from any road. The algorithm was able to assign them to a nearby "Safe" point just like all the other evacuees. Each evacuee was also assigned to which lane of the road to take in terms of vehicles. In Fig. 5, the optimal routes were shown, overlaying the road networks and the flood hazard model of Padada Floodplain. Each evacuee was labeled with specific ID codes and each has been assigned to a specific route to take (see Fig. 6). A complete list of the routes and evacuees' status were recorded. For each route named "RouteID" in Routes' result, evacuee that pass through each route is specified according to "EvcName" which is equivalent to "Name" in the Evacuees' result.

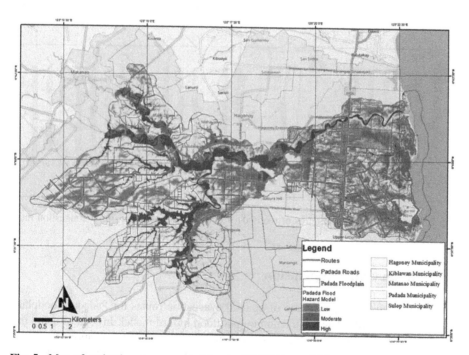

**Fig. 5.** Map of optimal routes generated by ArcCASPER overlaid to flood hazard map, road networks and municipality boundaries.

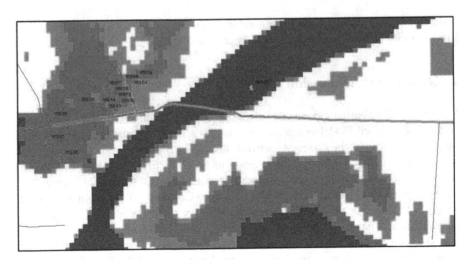

**Fig. 6.** Zoom in view of an evacuee of name 16320 and the path it has to take going to the safe zone.

Congestion among roads has also been observed to be high in most street segments used for evacuation as shown in Fig. 7. Only 26 of the 256 edges did not reach the restricted congestion value set for by the algorithm. The "SourceOID" in the EdgeStat table links the edge to which the evacuation segment taken by each evacuee belongs.

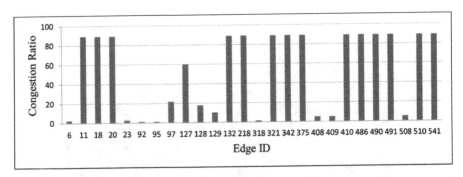

**Fig. 7.** Graph of congestion ratios of road edges that did not reach maximum congestion ratio allowed.

## 5   Summary and Conclusion

This study focused on generation of optimal evacuation routes for Padada Floodplain utilizing the LiDAR feature extraction output flood hazard model. Instead of using the usual shortest path algorithm, the study made use of a heuristic optimization algorithm, Capacity Aware Shortest Path Evacuation Routing (CASPER), through ArcGIS Network Analyst Tool's extension. The result shows that all evacuees were assigned to specific safe zones despite the fact that not all were given a road edge to pass through. The algorithm hence proves to be efficient, being able to lessen global road congestion by assigning evacuees that are very near safe zones to points that do not need a road to pass through.

## 6 Implications and Recommendations

The route generation can be enhanced by embedding processes to the CASPER algorithm especially that the tool does not take into consideration complex restrictions and unexpected behavior. Also, results are better presented if visualized through mobile or web applications. Further studies could be done to improve the results of this research.

**Acknowledgements.** This study is under the Phil-Lidar 1.B.13 research project of the University of the Philippines Mindanao that is funded by the Department of Science and Technology (DOST) and the Philippine Council of Industry, Energy and Emerging Technology Research and Development (PCIEERD) of the Philippines.

## References

1. Cole, J.W., et al.: GIS-Based emergency and evacuation planning for volcanic hazards in New Zealand. Bull. N. Z. Soc. Earthq. Eng. **38**(3), 149–164 (2005)
2. Eguchi, R.T., Huyck, C.K., Ghosh, S., Adams, B.J.: The application of remote sensing technologies for disaster management. In: The 14th World Conference on Earthquake Engineering, Beijing, China (2008)
3. Linham, M.M., Nicholls, R.J.: Flood hazard mapping [WWW Document]. ClimateTechWiki (2010). http://www.climatetechwiki.org/content/flood-hazard-mapping. Accessed 01 Oct 2016
4. Lue, E., Wilson, J.P., Curtis, A.: Conducting disaster damage assessments with spatial video, experts, and citizens. Appl. Geogr. **52**, 46–54 (2014). https://doi.org/10.1016/j.apgeog.2014.04.014
5. Mahmassani, H.S., Sbayti, H., Zhou, X.: DYNASMART-P version 1.0 user's guide. Maryland Transportation Initiative, College Park, Maryland (2004)
6. Manliguez, C., Cuabo, P., Gamot, R., Ligue, K.: Solid waste collection routing optimization using hybridized modified discrete firefly algorithm and simulated annealing - a case study in Davao City, Philippines. In: Proceedings of the 3rd International Conference on Geographical Information Systems Theory, Applications and Management: GISTAM, vol. 1, pp. 50–61 (2017). https://doi.org/10.5220/0006322500500061. ISBN 978-989-758-252-3
7. Manliguez, C., Diche, Z., Jimenez, M., Agrazamendez, M., Acosta, J.: GIS-based evacuation routing using capacity aware shortest path evacuation routing algorithm and analytic hierarchy process for flood prone communities. In: Proceedings of the 3rd International Conference on Geographical Information Systems Theory, Applications and Management: GISTAM, vol. 1, pp. 237–243 (2017). https://doi.org/10.5220/0006327402370243. ISBN 978-989-758-252-3
8. NDRRMC: National Disaster Risk Reduction Management Council, Philippines (2014). www.ndrrmc.gov.ph. Accessed 04 Sept 2016

9. Ortega, A.: Philippines' Country Report 2014 [WWW Document]. Country report, Asian Disaster Reduction Center (ADRC) (2014). http://www.adrc.asia/countryreport/PHL/2014/PHL_CR2014B.pdf. Accessed 31 Oct 2016

10. Shekhar, S., et al.: Experiences with evacuation route planning algorithms. Int. J. Geogr. Inf. Sci. **26**(12), 2253–2265 (2012)

11. Santos, E.I.: CNN Philippines: Philippines among world's most disaster-prone countries (2016). http://cnnphilippines.com/news/2015/11/25/philippines-fourth-most-disasterprone-country.html. Accessed 14 July 2016

12. Project NOAH: DOST - Nationwide Operational Assessment of Hazards (2016). http://noah.dost.gov.ph/. Accessed 04 Sept 2016

13. Santos, G., Aguirre, B.E.: A critical review of emergency evacuation simulation models. In: Building Occupant Movement During Fire Emergencies. Disaster Research Center, University of Delaware (2004)

14. Shahabi, K.: Out of Harm's Way: Enabling Intelligent Location-Based Evacuation Routing [WWW Document]. ArcUSER (2012). http://www.esri.com/news/arcuser/0612/out-ofharms-way.html. Accessed 02 Oct 2016

15. Shahabi, K., Wilson, J.P.: CASPER: intelligent capacity-aware evacuation routing. Comput. Environ. Urban Syst. **46**, 12–24 (2014). https://doi.org/10.1016/j.compenvurbsys.2014.03.004

16. Shahabi, K.: Scalable evacuation routing in dynamic environments. University of Southern California (2015)

# Promoting Citizens' Quality of Life Through Green Urban Planning

Teresa Santos[1](✉), Caio Silva[2], and José António Tenedório[1]

[1] Interdisciplinary Centre of Social Sciences (CICS.NOVA),
Faculty of Social Sciences and Humanities (NOVA FCSH), Lisbon, Portugal
{teresasantos, ja.tenedorio}@fcsh.unl.pt
[2] Faculdade de Arquitetura e Urbanismo, Universidade de Brasília,
Brasília, Brazil
caiosilva@unb.br

**Abstract.** In dense urban areas, the pursuit of outdoor thermal comfort is a development goal included in the city's sustainable plan. The aim of this study is to evaluate the effect of promoting new green areas, at ground and at rooftop levels, in the thermal comfort of the surrounding urban area. The simulation was made based on a recently concluded requalification project in a Lisbon neighborhood. This project was used as a case study to evaluate the effects of the new vegetation areas at ground level on microclimate and urban comfort [43], while the work of [44] was used as a case study to investigate the effect of green roofs.

The ENVI-met software is used to model the past and present (after requalification) scenarios, and a new scenario with green roofs. The simulation results indicate that the presence of new trees and shrubs results in: (i) increased urban comfort in the morning and in the afternoon resulting from the decrease in temperature; (ii) a reduction of up to 3° in the morning (9 h) and up to 3° in the afternoon (15 h); (iii) an increment of 10% in the relative humidity of the air, and (iv) a slight reduction in natural ventilation in both the morning and afternoon periods.

The microclimate simulation results confirm that vegetation is a key element when planning for comfortable public spaces.

**Keywords:** Thermal comfort · Urban planning · Green areas · Green roofs

## 1 Introduction

### 1.1 Sustainable Urbanism

In 2016, the Lisbon City Hall has initiated the requalification of several public spaces within the city. One of these spaces is located in the central business district and foresees the substitution of traffic lanes by new pedestrian zones and green areas. The goal is to provide the citizens with less noise, more pedestrian spaces, comfortable sidewalks and lowered crosswalks for people with reduced mobility, more green areas, places for esplanades and bike lanes.

The role of green areas in urban planning is recognized as a key factor towards urban sustainable development. Green infrastructures promote healthier and safer

© Springer Nature Switzerland AG 2019
L. Ragia et al. (Eds.): GISTAM 2017, CCIS 936, pp. 153–175, 2019.
https://doi.org/10.1007/978-3-030-06010-7_10

environments by regulating the urban temperature, controlling environmental extreme events like floods caused by intense rainwater run-off, regulating air quality or wind speed, reducing noise, or promoting biodiversity within the city. Furthermore, the visual aesthetical quality provided by green landscapes also contributes to the communities' well-being and quality of life. In this context, urban planning constitutes an efficient management tool to promote multi-scale sustainable green development. Local planning may be used to promote street tree plantation, green roofs, green pavements, or to preserve open spaces, natural corridors and parks in the public space. Regional planning, on the other hand, may address the preservation of forest or agriculture areas in the peri-urban fringe through zoning. In this sense, the concept of green infrastructure is generally associated with the concept of ecosystem services [22], i.e. the benefits that humans can obtain from ecosystem functions [14].

The Urban Heat Island (UHI) effect is the characteristic warmth of a settlement compared to its surroundings, and is the best-known climatic response to disruptions caused by urban development [6, 25, 35]. The temperature differential is generally larger at night than during daytime and larger in the winter than in summertime. Many factors contribute to UHI, like the presence of dark sealed surfaces (e.g. asphalt), building material with different thermal properties and albedo (e.g., concrete), or the lack of open green spaces, among others. The urban geometry also contributes to the UHI. Taller buildings implicate higher areas for sunlight reflection and absorption, thus promoting heating. Another urban geometry that affects local temperature is the effect created by having buildings on both sides of the street, also known as the urban canyon effect. The higher the aspect ratio (canyon height/canyon width) the higher is the impact of urban geometry in temperature, wind and air quality of the local. Other sources such as air conditioning, road traffic, or industry, also contribute to the UHI. There are several mitigation strategies like increasing the albedo of buildings and rooftops. Additionally, enhancing ecosystem service provided by the green infrastructures is another strategy to mitigate the heat island effect. In fact, shading and evapotranspiration provided by trees constitute an efficient way of regulating urban temperature [39], also the presence of open green spaces within the city's quartiers helps controlling temperature, relative humidity or wind speed, all key factors contributing to the UHI. Assessing the fine-scale thermal variation due to such changes in land cover within urban environment is a way of quantifying the mitigation impact of green-space planning.

## 1.2    Planning New Green Urban Areas for Lisbon

**The Praça Duque de Saldanha and Avenida da República Requalification Project.** One approach to deal with local urban climate challenges is to requalify typical neighborhoods and squares. Based on this premise, and from a total of 150 squares, 30 were identified by the Lisbon City Hall as priority site intervention. The Praça Duque de Saldanha and the Avenida da República constitute two of these intervention areas.

Several issues were identified in Praça Duque de Saldanha and the Avenida da República, which motivated the urban intervention, namely: (1) the discontinuity of tree alignments; (2) the use of the avenue as an express road generating speed and insecurity in zebra crossings, sometimes resulting in fatal hitches; (3) the avenue's road channel space, with 60 m wide, presented an irregular profile along its axis, mainly as a result of the successive interventions it was subjected to from its initial conception to the present. Furthermore, the road axis presented problems and inadequacies concerning the infrastructures for soft mobility. In fact, the sidewalks had variable widths, sometimes too narrow for walking, with physical obstacles and parking areas. The requalification of the public space was also motivated by insufficiency of cycling lanes and its disconnection with the network in operation and the projected one to the city.

Given these considerations, the requalification project was designed with the intention of enhancing the scenic effect of the square recovering the avenue's initial concept of "boulevard", by eliminating obstacles to pedestrian circulation, improving crossings, providing infrastructure to support cycling and an improved accessibility in individual transport.

Concerning the square's requalification, the project proposed the following actions: (1) to reshape the traffic lanes in the roundabout; (2) to increase the pedestrian space close to the buildings (11.80 m), allowing areas for esplanades; (3) to make a wide green belt (12.50 m) around the roundabout, separating the two urban functions (road and pedestrian); and (4) to eliminate parking spaces and reallocate taxicab stops (Fig. 1).

Regarding the avenue's requalification, the project proposed the maintenance of the main road central axis. Before the intervention, there were four lanes in one way and three in the opposite direction. The project dictated that one of these central lanes was to be eliminated and a new green central separator, 4 m wide was to be planned for the local (Fig. 2). The project predicted the cut of 15 trees, the transplantation of 30, and the plantation of 741 new trees. The selected species include *Fraxinus angustifolia, Tipuana tipu, Jacaranda mimosifolia* and *Plantanus,* among others.

Nevertheless, the project implementation did not occur without some resistance from residents and other people who use this area of the city. The reduction of parking spaces in an area with a high concentration of commercial and tertiary activities, the traffic restrictions as well as the duration of the intervention, raised some reservations. To respond to these concerns, the City Hall promoted five public sessions. The aim was to present and debate the proposals with the local population. Furthermore, citizens were invited to participate with ideas and suggestions through an on-line public participative platform. Consequently, the final proposal emerged with the help of the population and the parish council. To compensate for the loss of parking spaces, the City Hall offered new public parks in the periphery of the city.

**Green Roofing in Lisbon.** Covering roofs with vegetation contributes to mitigate the urban heat island effect by modifying not only the buildings' microclimate but also the local climate of the city [4, 30, 34, 37]. Other public benefits of vegetation on the ground and on roofs include decreasing the indoor cooling load demand and promoting biodiversity [8, 9, 38, 40, 45]. Furthermore, green roofs constitute a valid alternative for increasing green urban areas, when the available space on the ground is generally sparse [7, 18, 21]. Nevertheless, knowing what are the best locations in the city to receive such structures constitutes an essential tool when it comes to green planning.

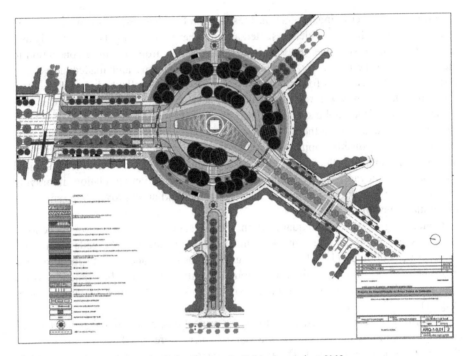

**Fig. 1.** Praça Duque de Saldanha project [11].

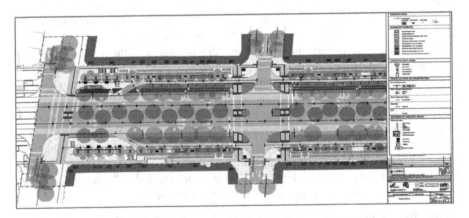

**Fig. 2.** Avenida da República project - two first blocks [11].

In this context, [44] estimated the potential of the city of Lisbon to receive green roofs using 3D data obtained with a LiDAR sensor. The selection of the most suitable rooftops was based on several criteria: roof covering material (tile, non-tile), available area, compatible slope and sunlight for plant development. Using remote sensing data and planimetric information, the city built environment was modelled and several scenarios were considered. In the most conservative scenario – non-tiled roofs, with available area equal or larger than 100 m², and slope less or equal to 11°, and more than 3 h of sunlight per day – 2890 rooftops where identified, representing an overall increase in the city's green area of 6.7% (Fig. 3).

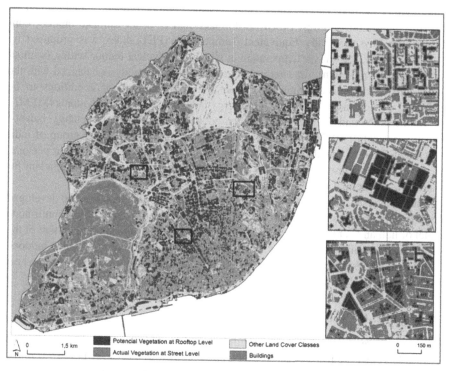

**Fig. 3.** Current vegetation cover at ground level and potential vegetation at rooftops.

## 1.3   Measuring Thermal Comfort

Thermal comfort, according to the ISO 7730 standard (1994), is "the condition of mind which expresses satisfaction with the thermal environment". So, currently to assess outdoor thermal comfort, the human-biometereological methods rely on rational indexes determined by solving the human energy balance equation [5, 31].

Fanger's comfort equation is one of the most used formulas when it comes to the evaluation of thermal comfort conditions. Its input parameters include personal factors such as the metabolic rate estimation and clothing levels, physical factors such as air temperature (Ta), men radiant temperature (MRT), air velocity and humidity. The Fanger's equation is the basis for calculating the Predicted Mean Vote (PMV) model. The PMV is one of the most used models of thermal comfort and it is included in the ISO 7730 standard (1994). Its calculation includes meteorological variables and personal settings. Using a biometeorological reference height of 1.6 m, the required variables include Ta, MRT, vapor pressure and local wind speed. Personal settings include clothing insulation, mechanical energy production of the body and mechanical work factor. The PMV reference person is always 35-year-old, male, with a height of 1.75 m and a weight of 75 kg. It scales from −3 (cold) to +3 (hot), where 0 stands for thermal neutrally, i.e., comfort.

Note that PMV was developed to measure indoor conditions, and its use to outdoor conditions is theoretically possible. Nevertheless, outdoor climatic variables can be diverse from indoor settings. Based on this fact, and to better estimate outdoor conditions, the Physiologically Equivalent Temperature (PET) index was proposed by [31]. It is defined "as the air temperature at which, in a typical indoor setting (without wind and solar radiation), the energy budget of the human body is balanced with the same core and skin temperature as under the complex outdoor conditions to be assessed". PET is based on the Munich energy balance model for individuals (MEMI). So, booth PMV and PET calculus are based on models of human energy balance equation but, while PMV gives a mean vote representative for a large group of individuals, PET can be calculated for specific subjects, which are defined by their personal data [31]. Nevertheless, in most cases using only one of these models is sufficient for characterizing thermal comfort [31].

The Universal Thermal Climate Index (UTCI) [24], the most recent developed index for measuring outdoor thermal conditions, is derived from the Fiala multi-node model of human heat balance. The UTCI it is then defined as the air temperature of the reference environment outdoors, which produces the same strain index value indoors. Its different values are classified in terms of thermal stress, and vary from extreme heat stress to extreme cold stress.

## 1.4  State of the Art

Green areas are known to produce climatic modifications at the micro-scale. This premise has been the focus of researchers, and innumerous works are published in the scientific literature. Many studies address the impact of city morphology (built density and road orientation) and different green scenarios towards outdoor thermal comfort [5, 10, 19, 36, 46–48], others test the impact of different urban green covering scenarios without changing built density [26, 41], while others consider distinct urban densities [15–17, 20, 23, 27, 28, 32, 33, 49].

[49] simulated the impact of urban albedo and urban green covering on the urban microclimate of a planned new residential area in Osaka, Japan. A total of six scenarios were tested and showing that the scenario with low albedo and moderate greenery was the one with the greatest potential for improving urban microclimate. Furthermore, increasing the proportion of greenery is more effective than strategies of increasing the urban albedo for building facades in terms of mitigating Urban Heat Island effect to improve urban microclimate. The cooling effects of greening have already been reported by several authors. [33] in a study conducted in Hong-Kong, concluded that in high-density cities, the amount of tree planting needed to lower pedestrians level air temperature by around 1 °C is approximately 33% of the urban area. [46] also concluded that increasing 10% of urban vegetation could reduce the average temperature (Ta) and the Mean Radiant Temperature (MRT) all through the day and night-time up to 0.8 °C, and that the heat reduction by adding urban vegetation was most observed in

the high-rise area. Among the techniques to mitigate Ta at midday investigated in this paper, adding urban vegetation showed the most significant results.

[41] tested the impact of vegetation and materials with a high albedo in the outdoor thermal comfort, by taking into consideration the PMV model. It was found that the presence of lawn, trees and shrubs leads to an improvement of the outdoor thermal comfort if the facades do not change: in this case, the magnitude of the multiple reflections inside the structure decreases and the reduction of the mean PMV is about 0.5 units. [27] analyzed the micro-climate effect of urban vegetation structures in Dresden, Germany. The cooling effects in air temperature ranged from 1 k to 2.1 K. according to the greenery provision. [36] quantified the cooling effect of a small green space in the surrounding atmospheric environment of a densely urbanized area located in Lisbon, using local measures. The highest difference found was of 6.9 °C in relation to air temperature, between shaded areas inside the garden and sunny areas located on the nearby street.

A different conclusion was found by [23] when investigating the effects of future structural plans on pedestrian thermal comfort in city, by modelling the existing and future scenarios. The study concluded that increasing the tree canopy coverage caused 1–2 °C reduction on PET level and adding a green roof did not show any improvement on PET at pedestrian level. In fact, the success of the increased tree canopy and green roof scenarios in reducing the mean radiant temperature was not as significant as in the increased building height scenario, probably due to the level of shading provided in the last scenario. Also, [16] in a study located in São Paulo, Brazil, found that vegetation had a limited cooling effect on the air temperature, ranging from 0.3 to 1.5 °C. However, when it comes to mean radiant temperature, the differences when comparing a base scenario (without vegetation) with one with street trees, the values are up to 19.5 °C. Also surface temperature is highly affected by the presence of vegetation, which can reduce the temperature by up to 13 to 16 °C.

The aim of this work is to evaluate the effect of promoting new green areas, at ground level and at rooftop level, in the thermal comfort of the surrounding urban area. The simulation is applied in a Lisbon neighborhood that recently went through an urban requalification process. ENVI-met model was used in this study to simulate urban microclimate under three situations: (1) scenario 1, the situation before site intervention; (2) scenario 2, the situation where green cover was increased through an urban requalification project, and (3) scenario 3, where green roofs are proposed.

# 2   Study Area

## 2.1   Urban Context

Lisbon is the capital of Portugal, with an area of 84 km$^2$ and 547 733 inhabitants, according to the latest census (2011). The largest green urban structure is the Monsanto Forest Park (1000 ha), that is linked to other green spaces in the city towards a green corridor. The city has a great diversity of green spaces, from arborized open squares, to tree alignments, public parks, communal gardens and patios. The Lisbon City Council has included in the new Master Plan, through the Biodiversity Strategy, a series of sustainable measures aiming to increase the green structure rates available in the city [13]. The Green Structure Plan predicts an increase of 20% in current areas, achieving 23.6% of the total of Lisbon's area; generally concentrating the new parks and green connections over proposed greenways [12].

The municipality, in its pursuit of a strategy of urban regeneration, has promoted the rehabilitation of vacant buildings and the qualitative improvement of public spaces, by enhancing green spaces and their connectivity. In order to test the implications of this strategy towards urban comfort, an area located in Avenidas Novas neighborhood was selected. The square area has already many trees, being *Tipuana tipu* the most representative species, while *Platanus x hybrida* is the most common tree at Avenida da República.

Two strategies for promoting new green areas in this area will be investigated, considering vegetation at ground level and in rooftops:

- Replacing traffic lanes by green areas and increase tree coverage. This is evaluated based on a requalification project that took place in the study area - the project of Praça Duque de Saldanha and Avenida da República, following a methodology proposed by [43];
- Promoting green roofs in the buildings with known potential. The most suitable buildings are available at [44].

**New Green Areas at the Ground Level.** Although the project covers a larger area (i.e., it requalifies an artery of the city with a total extension of approximately 1.5 km), due to the software constraints, only part of the square and the two first blocks of the avenue will be evaluated, occupying an area of 11.4 ha. This area includes part of the Central Business District of Lisbon, thus concentrating commercial and tertiary activities (Fig. 4). The built environment includes a mix of apartment buildings and multi-storey commercial and mixed-use buildings.

In the study area there are 146 buildings, with a mean of 6 floors. Higher buildings go up to 13 floors and include commercial areas located in the square. In the area, there are approximately 667 residents (value extrapolated from the 2011 Census), but since it is an area with many services and commerce, one can anticipate that the number of people who will potentially benefit from this intervention is much higher.

The project was concluded in early 2017. In Fig. 5 are shown the changes within the square area. On the right side of the picture there used to be a parking area and a taxicab stop. After the requalification, the parking area was eliminated and the taxicabs were reallocated. Furthermore, where there used to be two traffic lanes, nowadays there is only one. The changing effect is now visible in new green areas and cycling lanes, but also in increased pedestrian space close to the buildings, with the possibility of implementing esplanades and other rest zones.

The median divider of Avenida da República suffered a rearrangement: in fact, before intervention this axis was very narrow. So, the median divider was materialized and is now wider, with an alignment of trees and shrub vegetation (Fig. 6). Furthermore, the parallel lanes were also replanted and redesigned, and the parking spaces were reduced. Another important change was to provide the entire extension of the axis with a unidirectional cycle path on each side of the avenue.

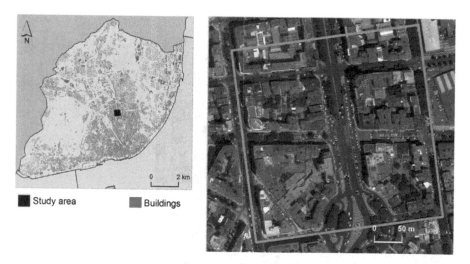

**Fig. 4.** Study area located in Lisbon, Portugal.

**Fig. 5.** Praça Duque de Saldanha after site requalification.

This new road design is expected to discipline the negative impacts of high traffic flows on this axis of the city of Lisbon by reducing the excessive speed of the vehicles, thus decreasing the chances for accidents and, at the same time, improving the quality of the public space.

**Fig. 6.** Avenida da República central separator after requalification.

**Fig. 7.** Rooftops with potential to receive green roofs.

**New Green Areas at the Rooftops.** [44] estimated the city potential to receive green roofs. Through a multi-criteria analysis based on geographic variables, 2890 buildings were identified in the city of Lisbon as suitable locations. From this set, 8 are in the study area, and include 6 offices and 2 residential buildings (Fig. 7). These buildings have from 7 up to 11 floors, and a total roof area of 3264 m$^2$.

Along with the new vegetation at the ground level, planted within the Praça Duque de Saldanha requalification framework, potential new green areas at these rooftops will also be evaluated towards their impact in the urban thermal comfort.

## 2.2    Geographic and Climatic Dataset

The microsimulation of the study area before and after site intervention requires modelling the land cover, elevation and climatology for both situations. The urban requalification project, available at the City Hall, allowed identifying the changes occurring in the area, namely the lanes to be eliminated and replaced by vegetation. Then, using a satellite imagery available at Google Maps, the buildings and street level land cover before and after intervention were modelled.

For modelling the buildings' height, a normalized Digital Surface Model (nDSM), from 2006, with elevation information available with a resolution of 1 m, was selected [42].

To evaluate the cooling effects of the urban requalification project, a climatic characterization of Lisbon city was performed (Fig. 8). Lisbon has a Mediterranean climate, with mild winters and hot and dry summers, classified as Csa according to Köppen system. According to [29], the "strong" UHI (intensity > 4 °C) occurred more often during the summer, with median values of 2 °C by night and 1.8 °C by day. The wind regime is predominantly from the north and northwest all through the year, although western and southwestern winds are also common during the cold season [2]. Based on the climatological normals for the period 1970–2000, August was the hottest month, with an average air temperature of 22.5 °C. For this month, the parameters air temperature, wind speed and direction, and relative humidity 2 m above ground were retrieved from www.portalclima.pt. The value for the roughness length was obtained in [3]. Regarding the specific humidity at model top, the Wyoming University site was consulted (http://weather.uwyo.edu/upperair/sounding.html).

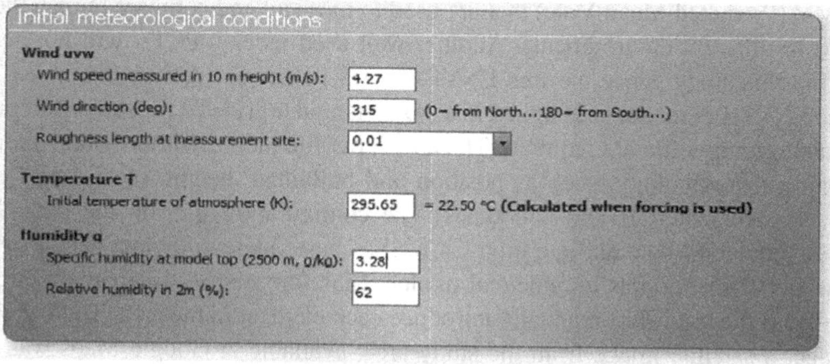

**Initial meteorological conditions**

**Wind uvw**
Wind speed meassured in 10 m height (m/s):    4.27
Wind direction (deg):    315    (0– from North... 180– from South...)
Roughness length at meassurement site:    0.01

**Temperature T**
Initial temperature of atmosphere (K):    295.65    = 22.50 °C (Calculated when forcing is used)

**Humidity q**
Specific humidity at model top (2500 m, g/kg):    3.28
Relative humidity in 2m (%):    62

**Fig. 8.** Meteorological input parameters for summer time of Lisbon, Portugal.

# 3  Methodology

## 3.1  Green Urban Scenarios

Three green scenarios were tested to assess vegetation impact towards thermal comfort:

- Scenario 1 describes the situation, before the site's requalification, with less vegetation;
- Scenario 2 describes the present-day situation, after implementing the requalification project. This scenario represents an increased area of vegetation at ground level, resulting from replacing traffic lanes by shrubs, herbaceous and new tree alignments;
- Scenario 3 foresees the increase in vegetation area though green roofing. In this situation, new green areas are obtained not just by considering the space available at ground level but also the roof areas that have geographic potential to receive green structures.

## 3.2  Microclimatic Simulation

To evaluate the impact of the new green areas implemented within the requalification project as well as new potential ones at rooftops, the ENVI-met software, v3.1 (www. envi-met.com) was selected. The ENVI-met is a 3D microclimate model designed to simulate the surface-plant-air interactions in urban environment, at a microscale level (0.5–10 m in space, and 10 s in time). The main prognostic variables of the software are wind speed and direction, air temperature and humidity, turbulence, radiative fluxes, bioclimatology and gas and particle dispersion. The software considers in the calculations, the radiation flux of short and long waves, and the latent heat of vegetation and water elements. Further details about the equations and architecture of ENVI-met model are presented in [1].

The ENVI-met was chosen due to the simplicity of the modeling process. In addition, the program allows the generation of numerous types of scenarios and the generation of spatialized results. This is a key factor when evaluating the impact of vegetation scenarios towards the pedestrian level of comfort, i.e., for local scale analysis.

Among others, the ENVI-met model includes the calculation of biometrical indices like PMV (Predicted Mean Vote) that are used to measure and compare human thermal comfort in different environments. Another well used index - PET - will not be considered in this study, since the free ENVI-met v.3.1 does not deliver this index.

The ENVI-met model is designed in a 3D rectangular grid. To run, an area input file and a configuration file are required. The area input file includes information about the environment morphology, such as position and buildings' height, plant types' distribution, surface materials and soil types. The configuration file, on the other hand, includes simulation date and duration, as well as basic meteorological data.

The ENVI-met adopts a numerical model. Therefore, the study area is reduced to grid cell and the user must manually introduce each element in the area. To visually aid this stage, a satellite image from the study area, available at Google Maps was used.

The first elements to model are the buildings. For each element in this class, information about the location and the height must be introduced. In this task, the satellite image allowed locating the buildings, while the nDSM indicated the respective height.

After introducing information regarding the built environment, the next element to be modelled is the vegetation cover. ENVI-met has a plant database with several species characterized according to the $CO_2$ fixation, plant type (deciduous, conifers or grass), short wave albedo, plant height, leaf area density, among others.

For Scenario 1 – the past situation – the tree cover was modelled based on the visual interpretation of the image. For Scenario 2 – the present-day situation, after site requalification – the urban requalification map was used to locate the new sidewalks, and new green areas, including trees, and hedges. The species available at ENVI-met plant database that were selected for both scenarios included: (1) trees with 20 m, dense and with a distinct crown layer, (2) trees with 15 m, less dense, (3) grass with 50 cm, and (4) dense hedges. For Scenario3 – considering also green roofs – the layer created by [44] was used to identify the suitable rooftops. The plant species selected from the database for being the one that most resembles those used in Portugal in this type of green infrastructure was Luzerne with 18 cm (Fig. 9).

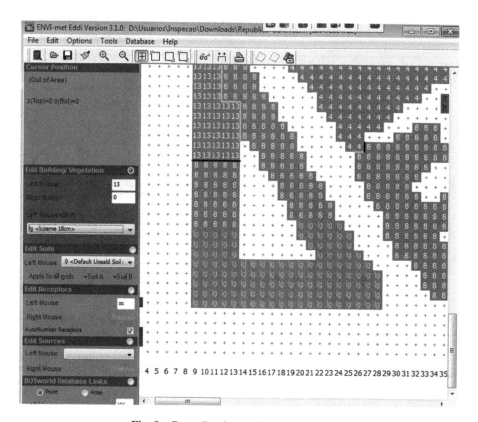

**Fig. 9.** Green Roof modelling in ENVI-met.

The last elements to be modeled are the soil and surface. In the study area, concrete and asphalt are the most common surfaces. This information is available at the satellite image and in the requalification map.

After modelling the land cover of the study area, the basic meteorological framework for simulation must be defined (Fig. 8). The last step is to run the ENVI-met model. The ENVI-met simulations typically cover 24 to 48 h ahead and result in atmospheric outputs for each grid cell in the 3D raster as well as surface and soil variables for the simulated environment. For calculating outdoor thermal comfort and compare it among the three scenarios, three main parameters were selected: air temperature, wind speed, and relative humidity. Additionally, the human thermal comfort index PMV, which is derived from these variables, was also selected. The steps for simulating the human thermal comfort in the study area, considering three distinct green scenarios are present in Fig. 10.

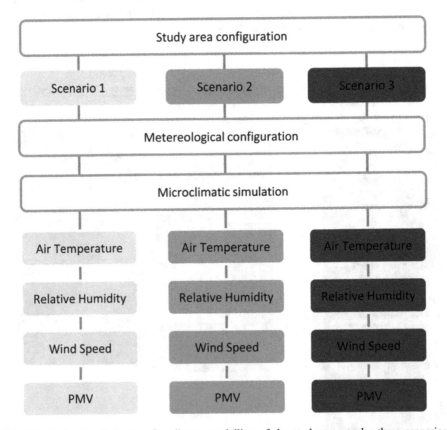

**Fig. 10.** Methodological steps for climate modelling of the study area under three scenarios using ENVI-met.

## 4   Results and Discussion

Three contrasting urban scenarios were modelled to assess the impact of promoting new green areas at ground level and rooftops in the urban thermal comfort. The first scenario (1) represents the situation before requalification, where there was already some vegetation. The second scenario (2) is the present situation, where green areas at ground level where increased through the requalification plan. The third scenario (3) is a theoretical proposal for installing green roofs, based on the findings of [44] (Fig. 11). The three scenarios have different proportions of pervious (vegetation on the ground), semi-pervious (sidewalks – cobblestone) and impervious elements (buildings and asphalt) (Fig. 12).

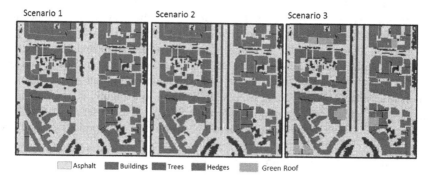

**Fig. 11.** Scenarios 1, 2 and 3 simulated in ENVI-met.

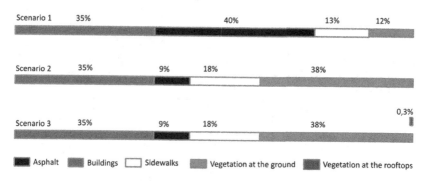

**Fig. 12.** Percentage of each land cover element in the three scenarios.

In every scenario, the same conditions were applied: (1) the area input data was a $135 \times 135 \times 30$ grid, (2) the grid cell size was dx = 2.5, dy = 2.5 and dz = 2 m, and (3) Lisbon geographical position. The simulation duration was 24 h. Each scenario simulation required a total time of 30 h. Table 1 shows the results from the simulation of each scenario.

**Table 1.** Simulation results for scenarios 1 (sc1), 2 (sc2) and 3 (sc3), in Lisbon, Portugal, during summer time.

| Parameter | 9 a.m. | | | 3 p.m. | | |
|---|---|---|---|---|---|---|
| | sc1 | sc2 | sc3 | sc1 | sc2 | sc3 |
| Air temperature | 21°C | 18°C | 18°C | 25°C | 22°C | 22°C |
| Relative humidity | 50% | 60% | 60% | 35% | 45% | 45% |
| Wind speed | 3.0 m/s | 2.5 m/s | 2.5 m/s | 3.0 m/s | 2.5 m/s | 2.5 m/s |
| PMV | +1 (slightly warm) | −1.5 (slightly cold) | −1.0 (slightly cold) | +1.5 (slightly warm) | −1 (slightly cold) | −0.5 (slightly cold) |

The simulation process reveals an improvement in the comfort indexes for the morning and afternoon periods. The PMV summarizes the effects of air temperature, radiation, humidity and wind, on the persons' energy balance in one value weighed with level of influence. In the morning period, the PMV simulated for scenario 1 indicates a slightly warm environment while for the greener scenarios 2 and 3 it indicates a slightly cold environment. In the afternoon period, an inversion of the comfort assessments occurs, going from slightly warm to a slightly cold environment (Fig. 13). The green roof scenario produced a PMV value closer to 0 (comfort), meaning that this type of greening preserves the comfort in both periods of analysis.

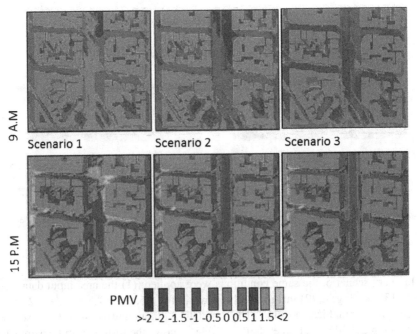

**Fig. 13.** PMV (predicted medium vote) in the three scenarios simulated in ENVI-met at 9a.m and 3p.m.

Considering the different meteorological parameters individually, the comparative results between scenario 1 and scenarios 2 and 3 show a great improvement in the comfort of the area. Observing the air temperature simulation, the results indicate a potential reduction of up to 3° in the morning (9a.m) and in the afternoon (3p.m) (Fig. 14). This condition can be explained by the presence of trees. These contribute to reduce the incoming solar radiation, which consequently reduces the mean radiant temperature. Nevertheless, this effect is more visible on the avenue, rather than on the square. This is due to the fact that, in the current scenario, trees are already present in the square area.

When profiling the green roof influence in the avenue (Fig. 15) a slight modification can be observed near the buildings. In the morning, it is cooler than its surroundings, while in the afternoon, an inversion occurs.

Regarding the relative humidity of the air, the presence of new trees and shrubs in scenario 2, contributes to an increment of 10%. This fact can be attributed to the evaporation of the trees and lower vegetation (Fig. 16). For the green roof scenario 3 the relative humidity is the same as in scenario 2, i.e., it is not modified. Regarding natural ventilation, as expected, there is a slight reduction in natural ventilation in both morning and afternoon periods. In fact, wind speed decreases from 3.0 to 2.5 m/s due to the barrier caused by the treetops, although ventilation is preserved always. Nevertheless, and as anticipated, the green roofs have no influence in this parameter (Fig. 17).

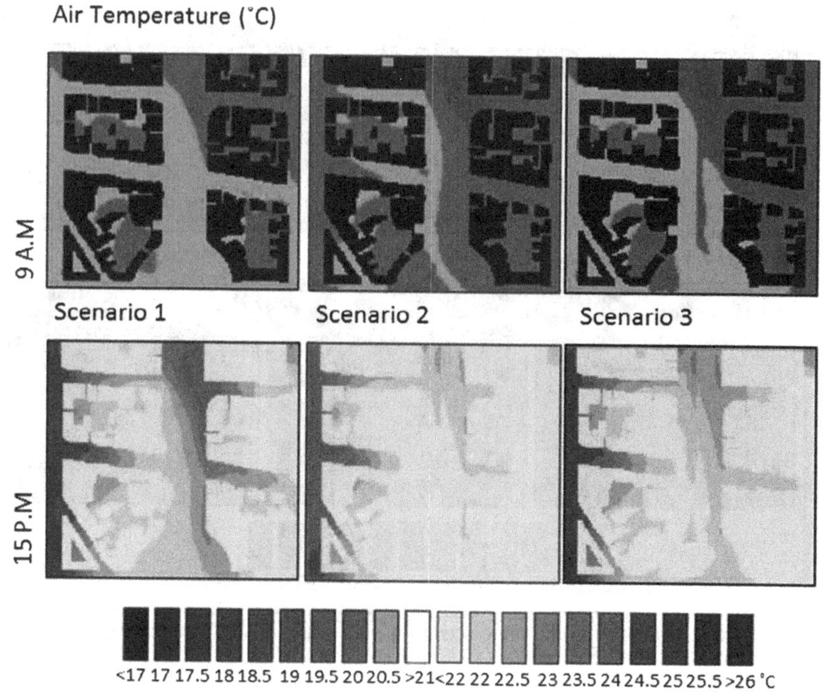

**Fig. 14.** Air temperature in the three scenarios simulated in ENVI-met at 9a.m. and 3p.m.

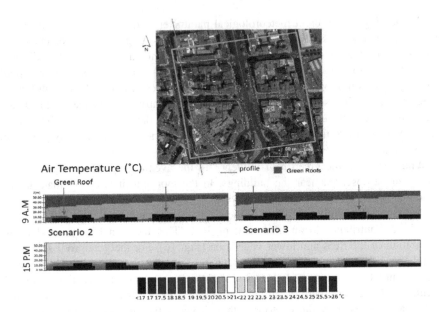

**Fig. 15.** 3D profile of air temperature.

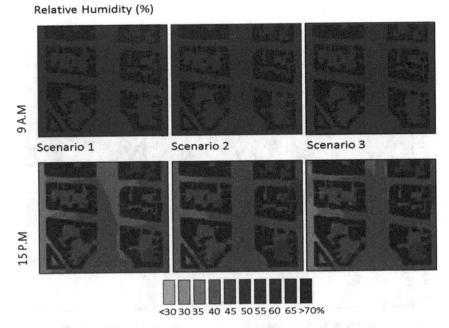

**Fig. 16.** Relative Humidity in the three scenarios simulated in ENVI-met at 9a.m. and 3p.m.

Wind Speed (m/s)

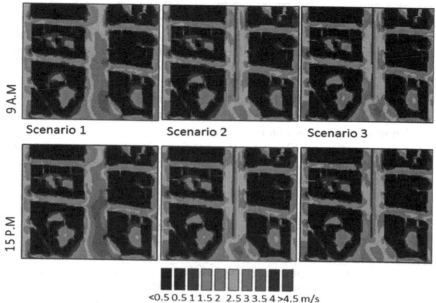

**Fig. 17.** Wind speed in the three scenarios simulated in ENVI-met at 9a.m and 3p.m.

## 5   Conclusions

The microclimate software ENVI-met allowed modelling the improvements towards outdoor thermal comfort of different greening strategies in a public space located in a Lisbon neighbourhood. Two strategies for increasing green areas were investigated: considering vegetation at ground level and in rooftops. The first strategy was based on the urban requalification project implemented in the study area in early 2017. The second strategy was based on the results of [44], where the rooftops with green potential were identified.

The situation before urban requalification included 12% of the area with green cover (trees and shrubs). The present-day situation, after site requalification, is characterized by an increase of 26% of vegetation at the ground level. When considering rooftop level, the proposed increase is 0.3%.

As already indicated in a previous study conducted in the same area [43], the microclimate simulation results confirm that vegetation is a key element when planning for comfort public spaces.

The methodology disregards the details of important urban structures as sidewalks, or urban design. This is due to the model's pixel size. Nevertheless, it is clear that the new urban design, where the road includes more sidewalk area and less area of asphalt, promotes an increase in thermal comfort, and contributes to the reduction of heat island formation.

The role of green roofs in thermal comfort requires further investigation, namely considering the private and public benefits of such structures, based on a multi-temporal analysis, where winter and summer time periods should be investigated. In that context it is also relevant to understand the species of vegetation implanted in green roofs, going beyond the height of the substrates used, as this may interfere with the heat gains of the building.

The area under study is already heavily forested, and the large tree mass might have overshadowed the gains of the green roofs. Consequently, in addition to the climatic seasonality analysis, it is recommended to evaluate the green roofs as one of the mitigation strategies in areas with fewer trees.

A major constraint in ENVI-met is the specified values for vegetation functional types and their form (shape, structure and size). These are broad and generalized and not specific to individual species. A detailed description of the species used in the requalification of the study area would allow refining the results. Nevertheless, the contribution of vegetation as a mitigation factor should be quantified when planning for new urban areas and ENVI-met has demonstrated its efficiency towards that goal.

**Acknowledgements.** The authors would like to thank Logica the opportunity to use the LiDAR data set. This paper presents results partially supported by CICS.NOVA - Interdisciplinary Centre of Social Sciences of the Universidade Nova de Lisboa, UID/SOC/04647/2013, with the financial support of FCT/MCTES through National funds. The first author was funded by the Fundação para a Ciência e Tecnologia, under a post-doctoral grant (Grant SFRH/BPD/76893/2011). The second author was funded by Fundação de Apoio a Pesquisa do Distrito Federal do Brasil (Foundation for Research Support of DF).

# References

1. Ali-Toudert, F.: Dependence of outdoor thermal comfort on street design in hot and dry climate. Ph.D. thesis, Universität Freiburg, Freiburg (2005)
2. Alcoforado, M.J., Andrade, H., Lopes, A., Vasconcelos, J., Vieira, R.: Observational studies on summer winds in Lisbon (Portugal) and. Merhavim **6**, 88–112 (2006)
3. Alcoforado, M.J., Lopes, A.: Windfields and temperature patterns in Lisbon (Portugal) and their modification due to city growth. In: 5th International Conference on Urban Climate (ICUC5), Lodz, Poland, pp. 383–386 (2003). http://www.ceg.ul.pt/climlis/recent_dev_files/alcoforado_lopes.pdf
4. Alexandri, E., Jones, P.: Temperature decreases in an urban canyon due to green walls and green roofs in diverse climates. Build. Environ. Part Spec. Build. Perform. Simul. **43**(4), 480–493 (2008). https://doi.org/10.1016/j.buildenv.2006.10.055
5. Ali-Toudert, F., Mayer, H.: Effects of asymmetry, galleries, overhanging façades and vegetation on thermal comfort in urban street canyons. Sol. Energy **6**, 742–754 (2007). https://doi.org/10.1016/j.solener.2006.10.007
6. Arnfield, A.J.: Two decades of urban climate research: a review of turbulence, exchanges of energy and water, and the urban heat island. Int. J. Climatol. **23**(1), 1–26 (2003). https://doi.org/10.1002/joc.859
7. Bates, A.J., Sadler, J.P., Mackay, R.: Vegetation development over four years on two green roofs in the UK. Urban For. Urban Greening **12**(1), 98–108 (2013). https://doi.org/10.1016/j.ufug.2012.12.003

8. Benvenuti, S.: Wildflower green roofs for urban landscaping, ecological sustainability and biodiversity. Landscape Urban Plan. **124**, 151–161 (2014). https://doi.org/10.1016/j.landurbplan.2014.01.004

9. Berardi, U., GhaffarianHoseini, A., GhaffarianHoseini, A.: State-of-the-art analysis of the environmental benefits of green roofs. Appl. Energy **115**, 411–428 (2014). https://doi.org/10.1016/j.apenergy.2013.10.047

10. Chatzidimitriou, A., Yannas, S.: Street canyon design and improvement potential for urban open spaces; the influence of canyon aspect ratio and orientation on microclimate and outdoor comfort. Sustain. Cities Soc. **33**, 85–101 (2017). https://doi.org/10.1016/j.scs.2017.05.019

11. CML – Câmara Municipal de Lisboa. Eixo Central – Requalificação do espaço público (2017). http://www.cm-lisboa.pt/viver/urbanismo/espaco-publico/uma-praca-em-cada-bairro/eixo-central

12. CML – Câmara Municipal de Lisboa. Corredores Verdes (2017). http://www.cm-lisboa.pt/viver/ambiente/corredores-verdes

13. Cruz, C.S., Alves, F.L.: A Strategy for Biodiversity, The Lisbon Case. Câmara Municipal de Lisboa (2012). https://www.cbd.int/doc/nbsap/sbsap/pt-sbsap-lisbon-en.pdf

14. de Groot, R.S., Wilson, M.A., Boumans, R.M.: A typology for the classification, description and valuation of ecosystem functions, goods and services. Ecol. Econ. **41**(3), 393–408 (2002)

15. D'Souza, U.: The thermal performance of green roofs in a hot. Humid Microclimate 475–86 (2013). https://doi.org/10.2495/sdp130401

16. Duarte, D.H.S., Shinzato, P., dos Santos Gusson, C., Alves, C.A.: The impact of vegetation on urban microclimate to counterbalance built density in a subtropical changing climate. Urban Clim. Cooling Heat Islands **14**(Part 2), 224–239 (2015). https://doi.org/10.1016/j.uclim.2015.09.006

17. Fahmy, M., Sharples, S.: On the development of an urban passive thermal comfort system in cairo. Egypt. Build. Environ. **44**(9), 1907–1916 (2009). https://doi.org/10.1016/j.buildenv.2009.01.010

18. Francis, R.A., Lorimer, J.: Urban reconciliation ecology: the potential of living roofs and walls. J. Environ. Manag. **92**(6), 1429–1437 (2011). https://doi.org/10.1016/j.jenvman.2011.01.012

19. Ghaffarianhoseini, A., Berardi, U., Ghaffarianhoseini, A.: Thermal performance characteristics of unshaded courtyards in hot and humid climates. Build. Environ. **87**, 154–168 (2015). https://doi.org/10.1016/j.buildenv.2015.02.001

20. Goldberg, V., Kurbjuhn, C., Bernhofer, C.: How relevant is urban planning for the thermal comfort of pedestrians? Numerical case studies in two districts of the city of Dresden (Saxony/Germany). Meteorologische Zeitschrift 739–51 (2013). https://doi.org/10.1127/0941-2948/2013/0463

21. Haaland, C., van den Bosch, C.K.: Challenges and strategies for urban green-space planning in cities undergoing densification: a review. Urban For. Urban Greening **14**(4), 760–771 (2015). https://doi.org/10.1016/j.ufug.2015.07.009

22. Hansen, R., Pauleit, S.: From multifunctionality to multiple ecosystem services? A conceptual framework for multifunctionality in green infrastructure planning for urban areas. AMBIO **43**(4), 516–529 (2014). https://doi.org/10.1007/s13280-014-0510-2

23. Jamei, E., Rajagopalan, P.: Urban development and pedestrian thermal comfort in Melbourne. Sol. Energy **144**, 681–698 (2017). https://doi.org/10.1016/j.solener.2017.01.023

24. Jendritzky, G., de Dear, R., Havenith, G.: UTCI—why another thermal index? Int. J. Biometeorol. **56**(3), 421–428 (2012). https://doi.org/10.1007/s00484-011-0513-7

25. Kim, H.H.: Urban heat island. Int. J. Remote Sens. **13**(12), 2319–2336 (1992). https://doi.org/10.1080/01431169208904271
26. Lee, H., Mayer, H., Chen, L.: Contribution of trees and grasslands to the mitigation of human heat stress in a residential district of Freiburg, Southwest Germany. Landscape Urban Plan. **148**, 37–50 (2016). https://doi.org/10.1016/j.landurbplan.2015.12.004
27. Lehmann, I., Mathey, J., Rößler, S., Bräuer, A., Goldberg, V.: Urban vegetation structure types as a methodological approach for identifying ecosystem services – application to the analysis of micro-climatic effects. In: Ecological Indicators, Contemporary Concepts and Novel Methods Fostering Indicator-Based Approach to Urban Complexities, vol. 42, pp. 58–72 (2014). https://doi.org/10.1016/j.ecolind.2014.02.036
28. Lobaccaro, G., Acero, J.A.: Comparative analysis of green actions to improve outdoor thermal comfort inside typical urban street canyons. Urban Clim. Cooling Heat Islands **14** (Part 2), 251–267 (2015). https://doi.org/10.1016/j.uclim.2015.10.002
29. Lopes, A., Alves, E., Alcoforado, M.J., Machete, R.: Lisbon urban heat island updated: new highlights about the relationships between thermal patterns and wind regimes. Adv. Meteorol. **15**, e487695 (2013). https://doi.org/10.1155/2013/487695
30. Luo, H., et al.: Carbon sequestration potential of green roofs using mixed-sewage-sludge substrate in Chengdu world modern garden city. In: Ecological Indicators, vol. 49, pp. 247–259 (2015). https://doi.org/10.1016/j.ecolind.2014.10.016
31. Mayer, H., Höppe, P.: Thermal comfort of man in different urban environments. Theoret. Appl. Climatol. **38**(1), 43–49 (1987)
32. Müller, N., Kuttler, W., Barlag, A.-B.: Counteracting urban climate change: adaptation measures and their effect on thermal comfort. Theoret. Appl. Climatol. **115**(1–2), 243–257 (2013). https://doi.org/10.1007/s00704-013-0890-4
33. Ng, E., Chen, L., Wang, Y., Yuan, C.: A study on the cooling effects of greening in a high-density city: an experience from Hong Kong. In: Building and Environment, International Workshop on Ventilation, Comfort, and Health in Transport Vehicles, vol. 47, pp. 256–271 (2012). https://doi.org/10.1016/j.buildenv.2011.07.014
34. Norton, B.A., Coutts, A.M., Livesley, S.J., Harris, R.J., Hunter, A.M., Williams, N.S.G.: Planning for cooler cities: a framework to prioritise green infrastructure to mitigate high temperatures in urban landscapes. Landscape Urban Plan. **134**, 127–138 (2015). https://doi.org/10.1016/j.landurbplan.2014.10.018
35. Oke, T.R.: City size and the urban heat island. Atmos. Environ. **1967**(7–8), 769–779 (1973). https://doi.org/10.1016/0004-6981(73)90140-6
36. Oliveira, S., Andrade, H., Vaz, T.: The cooling effect of green spaces as a contribution to the mitigation of urban heat: a case study in Lisbon. Build. Environ. **46**(11), 2186–2194 (2011). https://doi.org/10.1016/j.buildenv.2011.04.034
37. Peng, L.L.H., Jim, C.Y.: Economic evaluation of green-roof environmental benefits in the context of climate change: the case of Hong Kong. Urban For. Urban Greening **14**(3), 554–561 (2015). https://doi.org/10.1016/j.ufug.2015.05.006
38. Perini, K., Magliocco, A.: Effects of vegetation, urban density, building height, and atmospheric conditions on local temperatures and thermal comfort. Urban For. Urban Greening **13**(3), 495–506 (2014). https://doi.org/10.1016/j.ufug.2014.03.003
39. Rosheidat, A., Hoffman, D., Bryan, H.: Visualizing Pedestrian Comfort Using Envi-Met, 198–205, Berkeley, California (2008). https://www.academia.edu/8141644/VISUALIZING_PEDESTRIAN_COMFORT_USING_ENVI-MET
40. Rowe, D.B.: Green roofs as a means of pollution abatement. In: Environmental Pollution. Selected Papers from the Conference on Urban Environmental Pollution: Overcoming Obstacles to Sustainability and Quality of Life (UEP2010), Boston, USA, 20–23 June 2010, vol. 159, no. 8–9, pp. 2100–2110 (2011). https://doi.org/10.1016/j.envpol.2010.10.029

41. Salata, F., et al.: Evaluation of different urban microclimate mitigation strategies through a PMV analysis. Sustainability **7**(7), 9012–9030 (2015). https://doi.org/10.3390/su7079012

42. Santos, T.: Producing Geographical Information for Land Planning Using VHR Data: Local Scale Applications. LAP LAMBERT Academic Publishing (2011)

43. Santos, T., Silva, C., Tenedório, J.A.: Modelling urban thermal comfort: evaluating the impact of the urban requalification project of Praça Duque De Saldanha and Avenida da República in Lisbon. In: Proceedings of the 3rd International Conference on Geographical Information Systems Theory, Applications and Management: GISTAM, vol. 1, pp. 70–80 (2017). ISBN 978-989-758-252-3. https://doi.org/10.5220/0006324500700080

44. Santos, T., Tenedório, J.A., Gonçalves, J.A.: Quantifying the city's green area potential gain using remote sensing data. Sustainability **8**(12), 1247 (2016). https://doi.org/10.3390/su8121247

45. Tonietto, R., Fant, J., Ascher, J., Ellis, K., Larkin, D.: A comparison of bee communities of Chicago green roofs, parks and prairies. Landscape Urban Plan. **103**(1), 102–108 (2011). https://doi.org/10.1016/j.landurbplan.2011.07.004

46. Wang, Y., Berardi, U., Akbari, H.: Comparing the effects of urban heat island mitigation strategies for Toronto, Canada. Energy Build. SI: Countermeas. Urban Heat Island **114**, 2–19 (2016). https://doi.org/10.1016/j.enbuild.2015.06.046

47. Yahia, M.W., Johansson, E.: Influence of urban planning regulations on the microclimate in a hot dry climate: the example of Damascus, Syria. J. Housing Built Environ. **28**(1), 51–65 (2012). https://doi.org/10.1007/s10901-012-9280-y

48. Yahia, M.W., Johansson, E.: Landscape interventions in improving thermal comfort in the hot dry city of Damascus, Syria—the example of residential spaces with detached buildings. Landscape and Urban Planning **125**, 1–16 (2014). https://doi.org/10.1016/j.landurbplan.2014.01.014

49. Yuan, J., Emura, K., Farnham, C.: Is urban albedo or urban green covering more effective for urban microclimate improvement?: a simulation for Osaka. Sustain. Cities Soc. **32**, 78–86 (2017). https://doi.org/10.1016/j.scs.2017.03.021

# Developing a Responsive Web Platform for the Systematic Monitoring of Coastal Structures

Alexandre Maia[1], Armanda Rodrigues[1(✉)], Rute Lemos[2], Rui Capitão[2], and Conceição Juana Fortes[2]

[1] NOVA LINCS, Departamento de Informática, FCT-NOVA,
Universidade Nova de Lisboa, 2829-516 Caparica, Portugal
`a.maia@campus.fct.unl.pt`, `a.rodrigues@fct.unl.pt`
[2] Hydraulics and Environment Department (DHA),
National Laboratory for Civil Engineering (LNEC),
Av. do Brasil, 101, 1700-066 Lisbon, Portugal
`{rlemos,rcapitao,jfortes}@lnec.pt`

**Abstract.** Portugal's privileged location and the extension of its coastline has led to the construction and maintenance of a large set of port infrastructures. These structures were built primarily to ensure the tranquillity of the protected areas in the harbour basins, but they also support, among others, the control of sedimentation, as they guide the currents and protect water withdrawn from thermoelectric plants. The rubble-mound breakwater is the most common of these structures and its characteristics impose maintenance and repair works throughout its lifetime. To avoid significant costs or, even worse, the collapse of the structure, the need for these works must be evaluated in advance. This is achieved through the evaluation of the breakwater's Present Condition but also by its comparison with past situations. The Present Condition is periodically checked on-site and all relevant data is systematically gathered. The integration of the data collected during several inspections enables additional comparisons and analyses, supporting the characterisation of the Evolution and Risk conditions. Data collection at periodic inspections of these structures was, until recently, conducted manually, using paper forms and photographs. This was a slow and error prone process. To improve productivity, a monitoring tool, supported by a map-based online geographic information system (WebGIS) was developed. This platform is a device responsive mobile system which adapts to the location of the user's device, enabling the geo-referencing and analysis of the structures concerned. The system includes facilities for the collection of structural information and also supports the association of Media data, such as photos and videos. In this paper, the developed platform is presented in detail focusing on information requirements, architecture, and the functionality available to the user. The resulting platform has been successfully evaluated by involved researchers from the Portuguese National Laboratory for Civil Engineering (the end users of the system) and by non-expert users.

© Springer Nature Switzerland AG 2019
L. Ragia et al. (Eds.): GISTAM 2017, CCIS 936, pp. 176–197, 2019.
https://doi.org/10.1007/978-3-030-06010-7_11

**Keywords:** Geographic information system · Coastal structures
Risk assessment · Adaptation · Georeferencing · Mobile devices

# 1   Introduction

Coastal areas represent a dynamic environment of vital importance for human society. Moreover, a significant part of human settlements are located near the coast. In coastal areas and in ports, the evaluation of wave breaking and overtopping in maritime structures is very important in assessing the risk associated with either the failure of these structures or with the flooding of the protected areas.

In Portugal, the impact of sea agitation on coastal buildings and structures must be taken into account because of the length of the coast line, the concentration of population and economic activity near the sea, and the importance of ports to the national economy. Recent examples of emergency situations in Portugal caused by sea waves hitting the coast are listed below (additional events cited in Sabino *et al.* [19]):

**Estoril.** Frequent overtopping of the seawall, which affects its use and disrupts the nearby railway line;

**Madalena Port in Pico Island.** was affected in February 2017 by a severe storm which damaged several structures of the port;

**Azores.** Alex hurricane reached the archipelago on January 15, 2016 and several events of wave overtopping occurred there on several occasions, causing alert situations and damage. However, no significant consequences occurred due to the mitigation measures adopted by Local Authorities;

**Northeast Atlantic.** Extreme wave conditions in early 2014, led to extensive coastal damage along the western European coast. In Portugal, numerous overtopping events of coastal structures occurred (e.g. Foz do Douro, Espinho, Póvoa de Varzim, Furadouro, Nazaré, Ericeira, Costa da Caparica, Azores Islands, Portimão) and a large number of infrastructures were destroyed. Particularly for the storm of January 6th, estimated damage exceeded 16M Euros and endangered populations close to the sea.

To this date, records of the condition of a maritime structure or of parts of it are mostly generated on paper, a media prone to mistakes. The original paper filling forms will, on the other hand, most likely be passed onto a computer file. This further step means additional delay and constitutes another possible source of errors and inconsistencies. Additionally, the collected information is frequently kept on relational databases, maintained on individual computers. At each inspection of a particular structure, the concerned technician will print the currently existing information and take it to the site, to be able to compare the state of the structure with previous analysis (Fig. 1).

Concerned researchers and inspection teams consider that the digital production and online availability of this information would greatly improve productivity, as well as the quality of structure evaluation results. It was, therefore,

**Fig. 1.** Paper-based visual comparison during inspection.

important to implement an online system to support and facilitate the direct digital gathering of information during visual inspection of coastal structures, which is conducted periodically. Relevant collected information includes structural data as well as media content, such as photos and videos, captured from previously defined locations, physically marked on the ground and considered relevant for the evaluation of state of the structure.

## 2    Developed System

In this paper, a WebGIS system for the on-site collection of information, concerning the current structural condition of coastal structures, is presented. The geographic features associated with each relevant structure can be periodically uploaded into the system, in shapefile format, and consequently overlaid on a map of the region. Information on the general properties of the structures, such as their length, width and other characteristics is also contemplated on the system's database. The locations of Observation points (previously defined locations for analysis and photo capture) are also stored on the database and superimposed on the map as yellow markers. Gathered photos and videos can be accessed thanks to the association of these markers with the files located in a directory of the server.

All of this enables the geographic referencing of the coastal structures and of the media captured. The database also contains all the alphanumeric information collected during visual inspections.

Additionally, the system enables the storing of inspection data and the generation of evaluation measures which will support the work of inspection teams. The coastal structures considered in this system are composed of sections and the availability of this information enables the qualitative and quantitative evaluation of the Present Condition of these sections.

When more than one visual inspection of the same structure are available on the system, collected at different dates, Evolution Conditions can also be calculated. A Risk Condition can be calculated when the Present Condition, as well as the Evolution Condition, are available. These parameters help to define and prioritise the structures' needs for repair.

This system improves on the existing methodology for the evaluation of the condition of coastal structures, adding in productivity and minimising mistakes, by saving the time previously used in inserting, into the computer, all the information that was gathered, on paper, during a visual inspection. It also supports the integration of all the relevant information, in the evaluation of the condition of coastal structures, into a single platform. Finally, the system facilitates the overall process of collecting data during visual inspection as well as accessing and visualising them later on desktop (and other mobile) platforms.

The work presented in this paper results from a collaboration between researchers of the Portuguese National Laboratory for Civil Engineering (LNEC) and the NOVA Laboratory for Computer Science and Informatics (NOVA LINCS) [12,13].

## 3   Concepts

Ports are infrastructures where wave tranquillity is mandatory in order to enable mooring, loading and unloading of ships and also to ensure the safety of people, goods and the ships themselves [5]. Ports were initially installed in naturally sheltered areas such as bays, estuaries and areas protected by islands. However, more recent harbours have been created in less protected regions, which led to the need for protective structures.

Ports can be classified according to type, location, use and size. We can highlight three types of ports:

**Natural:** ports are those where improvement works are not necessary to guarantee the shelter of the port and the access to the berths, since the natural conditions already provide these guarantees;

**Artificial:** ports are those where it is necessary to construct structures to improve the shelter and the conditions of access of ships to the berths;

**Semi-natural:** ports are located in a cove or are protected by promontories on both sides. They ensure an artificial protection at their entrance.

Ports are composed of:

- Protective works (breakwaters, jetties and others);
- Access and navigation channels;
- Docking structures - to moor ships, transfer passengers and move and store goods;
- Earth facilities.

In the context of the platform presented in this paper, one will focus on rubble mound breakwaters (RMBs). A breakwater is an obstacle that reduces the action of waves in the area sheltered by the structure. The action of the waves is reduced by a combination of reflection and dissipation of the energy on the breakwater protective structure. In broad terms, breakwaters can have the following goals:

- To protect port facilities;
- To enable the mooring of ships and their safe loading and unloading;
- To help in the control of sedimentation, in guiding the currents and creating areas with different rates of agitation;
- To protect water outlets from thermoelectric power plants and the coast line against the action of tsunamis.

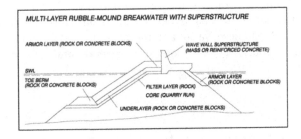

**Fig. 2.** Rubble-mound breakwater structure [13].

These structures may be divided into several types:

**Rubble-mound Breakwaters:** are the most common port protection structures that exist in Portugal [9]. A rubble-mound breakwater (RMB) has a trapezoidal shape (see Fig. 2), with a core of undifferentiated loose materials that is protected by one or more layers of possibly different types of material, also loose. They are easy to build and maintain and efficient in dissipating wave energy;

**Vertical-front Breakwaters:** are another major class of breakwater structures [23]. The basic structure element is usually a sandfilled caisson made of reinforced concrete, but blockwork types made of stacked precast concrete blocks are also used. Caisson breakwaters might be divided into the following types:

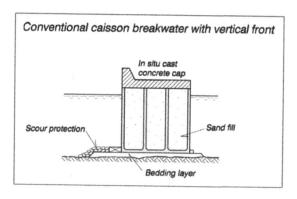

**Fig. 3.** Conventional caisson breakwater with vertical front.

**Conventional:** the caisson is placed on a relatively thin stone bedding layer (Fig. 3);

**Vertical Composite:** the caisson is placed on a high rubble-mound foundation (Fig. 4). This type is economical in deep waters. Concrete caps may be placed on shore-connected caissons;

**Horizontal Composite:** the front of the caisson is covered by armor units or a rubble-mound structure (multilayer or homogeneous) (Fig. 5). This type of breakwater is typically used in shallow water; however, there have been applications in deeper water where impulsive wave pressures are likely to occur. The effects of the mound are reduction of wave reflection, wave impact, and wave overtopping. Depending on bottom conditions, a filter layer may be needed beneath the rubble-mound portion.

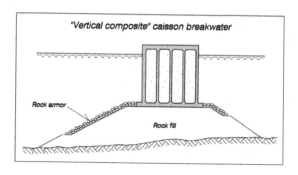

**Fig. 4.** Vertical composite caisson breakwater [13].

Coastal structures, particularly breakwaters, are structures to which a great risk is assumed at the design stage, due to the degree of uncertainty associated with the demands themselves and the characteristics of the materials used in

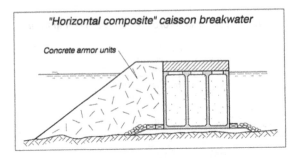

**Fig. 5.** Horizontal composite caisson breakwater [13].

their construction [16]. Although risk is assumed, since a possible collapse is not generally associated with the loss of human life, economic cost is, as a rule, very high.

It is known, therefore, that during the lifetime of the structure, repair works will be necessary, as well as maintenance, due the fatigue of the parts and of the materials involved in the construction. However, in order for these interventions to be effectively carried out in time and at the lowest possible cost, the systematic inspection of the structures is highly recommended.

This is the main reason for the implementation of the software platform presented in this paper.

## 4    Related Work

One of the goals of the work presented in this paper was to develop a mobile WebGIS application to facilitate the task of collecting information during a visual inspection of the monitored structure. Moreover, the system should allow access to the stored information on the evolution of the condition of the structures over the years, enabling the comparison of the Present Condition of one structure with its stored condition, determined at an earlier relevant date (5 years before or at a later date, if repairing works took place). Previous related work has been accomplished with the aim of collecting and storing, in database format (in Microsoft Access), the data collected in previous inspections. This database was called ANOSOM and has been in use, these last years, by LNEC researchers.

The first version of the ANOSOM [18] database was developed in 1995, with the double goal of storing all the information gathered in visual inspection campaigns on coastal structures carried out by LNEC and facilitating the diagnosis of the problems presented by each inspected structure, to identify potential needs for maintenance or repair work. The collection of qualitative information related to the deterioration of the breakwater materials in profile elements, which can only be obtained through visual inspection, is of major importance in the evaluation of the condition of these structures. It was thus decided that the ANOSOM database should contain information collected in the visual inspec-

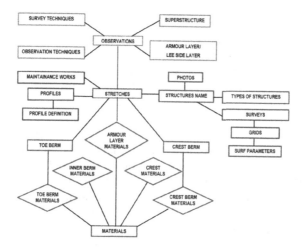

**Fig. 6.** ANOSOM database tables' relationships [13].

tion campaigns, in addition to the general information about the characteristics of the structure [7,8].

Thus, the basic functionality of the 2007 version of ANOSOM application included:

1. Inserting, correcting, and deleting data;
2. Processing the inserted data in order to diagnose the problems of the structure.

Three main categories of data were identified:

1. Structure data, which includes the data relating to the conceptual division of the structure into sections, the characterisation of the profile envelope elements of each of these sections, and the dates of repair/maintenance work performed on those sections;
2. Visual inspection campaign data, including the content filled in inspection forms and the photographs taken during those campaigns;
3. Structure survey data, containing the coordinates of the surveyed points and the envelope surface defined in a regular mesh.

Nevertheless, this original application did not contemplate functionality to handle multimedia data. In fact, the photos taken during inspections were not added to the database, rather they were gathered in folders and the GeoSetter application[1] was used to access the photos metadata, such as position (latitude and longitude) and orientation of photo captures.

The platform presented in this paper reveals some similarities with the work described by Pires et al. [17]. The authors are involved in an interactive monitoring project supported through GIS for the coastal area of Espinho, in Portugal.

---

[1] http://www.geosetter.de/en/.

The system portrays the current state of the shoreline, as well as the degradation state of the protective coastal structures in the area. In this context, a spatial representation of breakwaters and sea walls is provided, enabling the evaluation of the current condition of the structures through photos and additional alphanumeric information. The collected information involves: structure identification, current condition (with hyperlinks for photos), geotechnical evaluation (including observed pathologies and need for future works) and technical specifications and costs. However, the system was not designed for *in situ* inspection (e.g. the user interface is not responsive, meaning that it does not adapt to the mobile device being used) and does not contemplate data structures for collecting inspection data and state evolution analysis. Moreover, the information presented to the user does not consider his current location.

Another related project is the one presented by Marujo *et al.* [15], which contemplates a database with information on coastal structures and a GIS interface which supports the geo-referencing of coastal protection works. Moreover, it enables the generation of inspection forms in printed and digital format. However, this system requires an Android mobile device 4.x version smartphone or tablet. The platform presented below is not restricted to one specific operating system.

Marujo has also compiled a list of similar systems to the one proposed in this paper, both national and international [14]. In this work, the researcher looks at the particular implementation details of these systems and describes their advantages and disadvantages.

Finally, additional relevant work is described by Allsop *et al.* [1], consisting on the development of a database prepared by HR Wallingford and TU Delft with the assistance of the international breakwater community. This database has been made freely available for the benefit of breakwater designers, contractors owners and developers worldwide. Although some technical information is provided here, like some geometrical characteristics and design criteria, as well as the owner, contractor and consultant names, its aim is not the monitoring and diagnosis of the structures, which is the main objective of the application presented in this paper.

On a slightly different note, Li *et al.* [11] developed and improved a coastal decision support system by extending it with a mobile subsystem supported by PDA hardware, GPS, *wireless* and *Web*-based GIS technology. This technology enables the user on the field to precisely locate coastal structures and access remote server coastal data. The authors also present an Internet-based erosion conscious system implemented for Painesville, Ohio. The system supports the local population on certain activities such as buying or selling a house and building erosion protection structures, taking into account coastal changing information. Community leaders can use the system in planning community activities. The GIS-based tool facilitates use of large volumes of data and provides visualisation tools, enabling quick perception of the current state of structures, thus facilitating the decision making process. The application presented in this paper is also supported by WebGIS and GPS technology to enable *in situ* inspections of coastal structures and digital data collection.

## 5   Information Structure

The basis for the implementation of the system is the collected information and how it is made available and used to support and facilitate coastal structures' inspections and evaluations. The relevant information involves user and breakwaters geo-referencing, as well as the breakwaters characteristics (mostly taken from the ANOSOM database) and multimedia breakwater state recordings.

### 5.1   Geo-Referencing

The application is map-centred, based on OpenStreetMap, a free and highly popular map for WebGIS applications. A shapefile layer of breakwater sections (blue polygons) was collected to be overlaid on the base map (see Fig. 8). The set of breakwaters represented in the figure were collected by LNEC and used as a case study in the project, representing shoreline structures throughout Portugal. A simple methodology for the update of this shapefile was put in place for providing scalability to the application. Every time breakwaters are added to the study (and to the shapefile), an updated file is uploaded onto the system, updating the map view of the application.

### 5.2   Breakwater Information

The application database is supported through MySQL. The database model is mainly based on the original ANOSOM database (presented in Fig. 6). It includes the information contained in the tables *Observations*, *Structures Name* and *Stretches* shown in the original database. The structure of the database was maintained with the aim of facilitating interchange between the applications. These tables include the following information:

**Breakwater Sections:** general characteristics of the section such as dimension, geographic coordinates, type, weight, disposition and nature of the used materials, etc;

**Visual Observations:** information on falls, fractures, material degradation, registered observations, etc.

Additional tables were created for managing information associated with observation points, located at breakwater sections, where multimedia data are collected (photos and videos). Observation points are considered of importance for evaluating the state of the breakwater and are visited and photographed (or filmed) during periodic inspections. Information on the users of the system is also maintained on the database, for security reasons.

The connection between the objects presented on the map (breakwater section geometries) and the data stored in the database is achieved through a unique identifier held by each object. This method is also used for observation points.

# 6   Implementation

The developed system follows an architectural structure used in the development
of WebGIS systems. It is described in the next subsection.

## 6.1   Architecture

The general architecture of the developed application is represented in Fig. 7.
It is divided into three layers: the presentation layer, the logic layer and the
database layer. This type of architecture enables a separation of functionality
that facilitates its evolution and maintenance. The tools used for the development of each layer are also described.

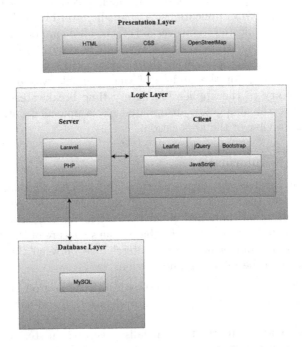

**Fig. 7.** System architecture [13].

The presentation layer is the layer that enables the user to interact with the
system and is developed in HTML, CSS and the base map was OpenStreetMap.
HTML is responsible for displaying the elements that are present in the interface, while CSS is used to provide the style of those elements. The maps that
are shown in the application, both on the home page and on the page corresponding to the photos of a section, are provided by OpenStreetMap. This is
the layer through which the user interacts with the system and it is responsible
for sending the input produced by the user to the logic layer, and consequently

for displaying the data from the logic layer back to the user for feedback. The logic layer is divided into two main components, the client side and the server side. The client side was developed with Leaflet, jQuery and Bootstrap, which rely on JavaScript. Leaflet allows the interaction with the OpenStreetMap map. Bootstrap is used to create a responsive interface in order to adapt to the user's device. Finally, jQuery supports the handling of interface elements. As previously stated, the database layer is made available through the MySQL database management system, which stores all the information regarding the sections of the coastal structures, such as their characteristics, visual inspections' data and the various points of each section and their photographs/videos. The connection to the database is established through PHP.

## 6.2   Functionalities

Due to privacy concerns regarding the information handled by the system, only LNEC researchers can access it. Thus, some security measures were implemented, including password protection. After logging in, the user is redirected to a page where she can access the world map provided by OpenStreetMap. Once she accesses the map, the shapefile features, including all the breakwaters in the database, are loaded into the map (see Fig. 8). The geographic features are displayed in blue and each structure is divided into several sections (see Fig. 9). Each of these sections has a unique code that is stored in the .dbf part of the shapefile. This information allows the connection between the geographic representation of the sections of each structure, on the map interface, with their respective information on the MySQL database, enabling the contextual viewing of a breakwater section's general (as well as inspection) data.

## 6.3   Breakwater and User Location

One of the most important aspects regarding the visual inspections is the user's current location. Data capture is location-based, so the system must be able to associate the captured information with the correct breakwater section. To do this, the user must turn on the location identification of the device that he is using, and the system captures the user's current position, placing a red marker on the map interface (Figs. 8 and 9). The system then tries to associate the user's current position to a particular section of a structure (the one that is nearest) to be inspected. To speed up detection, only the structures that are visible on the map window, at the moment of detection, are considered for inspection. The time taken to detect the section chosen for inspection is important, as the number of structures added to the system is large and the search will be executed on a mobile device. The algorithm used for section selection is an adaptation of the Point In Polygon algorithm [6] by Franklin.

Thus, once the user's location has been detected, as the user walks on a structure, the system will associate the data he collects with one of its sections. In this context, the user can either add observations to existing points on that section or define new points of observation.

**Fig. 8.** *Cluster* of markers. (Color figure online)

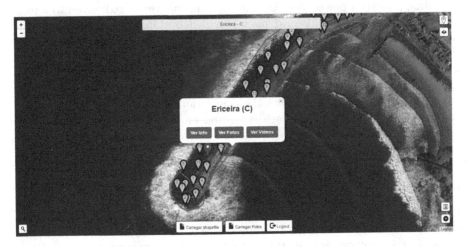

**Fig. 9.** Coastal structure view. (Color figure online)

If, for some reason, it is not possible to detect the user's location (e.g. lack of access permission on the device), it is possible to simulate it but adding a marker on the desired location. This marker's location will become, for the application, the user's position and it will work as if the user was, in fact, working on the nearest breakwater section. This functionality is also useful when using the application on the desktop, as it is possible to simulate a field visit.

**Fig. 10.** Photos from a section of a structure [13].

## 6.4 Observation Points

The user's current location (the red marker) can be used to create new observation points. When need arises, the user requests the creation of an observation point and the system automatically adds a yellow marker on his current location.

Previously defined points of observation are shown on the map as yellow markers, when viewing detail is sufficient for quality observation. However, as the number of observation points is high, some levels of detail may show a large concentration of yellow markers. To account for this difficulty, clustering of observation points was implemented, avoiding overcharging the map and simplifying visualisation. Besides clustering all near points into a green circle, this functionality also shows the number of markers in the cluster (Fig. 8).

## 6.5 Photos and Videos

Media data collection has been contemplated in the platform and, particularly for jpeg photos, it is possible to gather exif metadata from the file and directly add it to the system. Thus, when a jpeg photo is taken near a specific point of observation, the system captures latitude, longitude, altitude and orientation of the photo from the file's metadata and directly creates an association of the photo with the point. Afterwards, a request to view the photos gathered at this point of observation will include the corresponding photo. In fact, all the photos taken and collected on that point are presented to the user for viewing. Moreover, when viewing the photos, the user has the chance to check the photos' metadata, with the help of a map where the orientation of capture is displayed (see Fig. 10). This feature enables the offline upload of photos into the platform, for example, when photos are taken using a particular camera and not using the mobile device.

The user can also capture and associate a video to a point of observation. However, in this case, only the date of upload is stored in the system, no metadata is loaded. The method for uploading videos is similar to the one used for photos. The user clicks on a point of observation, shown on the map, which causes the upload pop-up window to open, then presses the camera button icon (when using a mobile device), takes the photo/video (or chooses a photo/video that has been previously captured) and the file upload starts automatically. After a few moments, the photo/video is stored in a folder on the server, becoming associated with the chosen point of observation. Consequently, the file also becomes part of the observation information belonging to the section of the breakwater that owns the observation point.

### 6.6   Information About a Rubble-Mound Breakwater

Each section in a structure has very specific characteristics, as shown in Fig. 11, such as its size in length and width, information about the superstructure/crown, the armour layer, the outer crest berm, the inner crest berm and so on. This information includes: the slope of the outer armour layer, its width, the values of the maximum and minimum dimensions and their materials (the type of blocks, the weight, the layout, etc). To facilitate information viewing and analysis, the section interface page includes an interactive drawing of a breakwater enabling viewing of a particular part of the information by clicking on the structure's relevant part. The interface has also been structured with several tabs and a navigation bar (at the top of the page) allowing the user to navigate to other pages to see the photos and videos of the section, to access section observations (according to the selected date) and to analyse the characteristics of other sections belonging to the same structure.

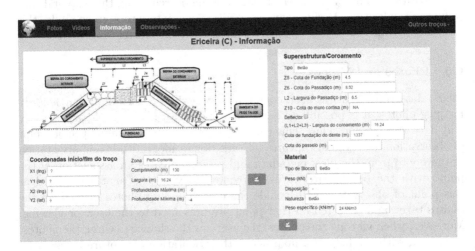

**Fig. 11.** Information about a Rubble-mound Breakwater [13].

## 6.7  Visual Inspections

Periodically, the structures are subjected to visual inspection, performed by LNEC researchers. In general, the structure is inspected yearly but additional inspections may be performed, specially after strong storms. The data collected refer to the current condition of the armour layer, the superstructure and the inner filters. To facilitate data gathering and minimise errors, most of these data are entered into the inspection forms via radio buttons. Predefined, qualitative, value scales have been defined as, for example, in the case of the number of unit displacements (which may have occurred), where values can be 0 (None), 1 (Few), 2 (Some) or 3 (Many). These and other values contribute to calculate the Present Condition of that part of the section of the structure, and these range between 0 and 5. LNEC researchers have developed a methodology that enables the evaluation of the Present Condition of the structure and its evolution [20, 21]. If at least two visual inspections have been performed, it is possible to calculate the Evolution Condition. The Risk Condition associated with the structure can be calculated from existing information on the Present Condition and the Evolution Condition.

## 7  Evaluation of the System

The aim of the evaluation process was to assess the usability of the developed platform as well as its usefulness for LNEC researchers in the data collection and structure evaluation activities. The methodology for the evaluation was designed with the goal of collecting as much qualitative feedback as possible, in order to obtain material for future improvements, as well as to evaluate the result of the developed application, in the final evaluation phase.

During the evaluation process, users were asked to perform various tasks in the developed system. Some tasks were to be performed on a desktop platform, while others were intended to be performed on a mobile device, as in a situation of a field campaign. After each task was completed, each user was asked to complete a questionnaire. The questionnaire was divided into two parts.

The first part consisted of the System Usability Scale (SUS). The second part was composed by specific questions related to specific functionalities of the application. The platform was evaluated by 14 non-expert users and by 4 LNEC researchers, which are its end users. The questionnaire was improved for the latter testers (there were some additional questions and some existing questions were made more specific), given the knowledge they have on the scope of the developed application.

SUS [2,3] was used because, as described by the authors, it provides a robust, reliable and cost-effective method for evaluating the usability of a computational tool. Because it has been widely used, it has become one of the top tools to support this type of evaluation, enabling effective differentiation between usable and unusable systems.

Another advantage of using SUS is that it is a small questionnaire, which leads to greater receptivity on the part of testers to answer its questions. SUS is composed of the following 10 sentences, each evaluated using a five-point scale, ranging from Strongly disagree (the lowest value) to Strongly agree (the highest value):

1. I think that I would like to use this system frequently;
2. I found the system unnecessarily complex;
3. I thought the system was easy to use;
4. I think that I would need the support of a technical person to be able to use this system;
5. I found the various functions in this system were well integrated;
6. I thought there was too much inconsistency in this system;
7. I would imagine that most people would learn to use this system very quickly;
8. I found the system very cumbersome to use;
9. I felt very confident using the system;
10. I needed to learn a lot of things before I could get going with this system.

Although SUS was only designed to measure usability, Lewis and Sauro [10] suggest that two components can be derived from SUS - usability as well as learnability. Therefore, both components were considered to complete the overall value of the SUS, in order to provide a better perception of the total usability of the developed application. Figures 12 and 13 show the results of the SUS questionnaire for regular users and for LNEC researchers. Each vertical line represents a user and in each of those lines there are 3 values calculated based on the user's answers: the value for the overall SUS score, the value for the Usability, and the value for the Learnability. Below those lines, one can see the adjective that the user chose for the user friendliness of the platform. It is a seven-point adjective-anchored Likert scale ranging from Worst Possible to Best Possible. There is a green line placed at value 68 and it represents the mean value for web interfaces according to [22]. A value above that line is thus considered, by the authors, above average, while a value under that line is below average. From these graphics, the average, maximum, minimum and the standard deviation for each of the three components evaluated were calculated, with the resulting values shown in Tables 1 and 2.

Both evaluation results put the platform above the 68 value, the average of the SUS questionnaire being 73.39 for regular users and 84.38 for LNEC researchers. The learnability average for regular users value is quite high (higher than the usability), which leads us to conclude that the platform learning curve is a reduced one, an interesting result for the purposes of the work, as the use of the platform in the field may often be performed by non-expert users. However, some evaluation results were not as good as the rest, which led to an analysis of the requests and suggestions provided by the testers. All the suggestions of the testers were analysed and added to the platform. Those suggestions were related with the usability of the platform. Warning and confirmation messages before deleting data were added. The User Interface also suffered some adjustments in order to become more user friendly. Geocoding was added, enabling a user to request centring of the map by typing the name of a place or city. The possibility to upload videos was also only implemented after the tests. All of these additions led to a successful improvement of the system.

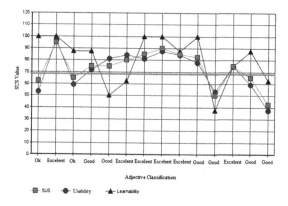

**Fig. 12.** SUS results from regular users [13]. (Color figure online)

**Table 1.** SUS results from regular users [13].

|                    | SUS   | Usab  | Learn |
|--------------------|-------|-------|-------|
| Medium             | 73.39 | 71.65 | 81.25 |
| Maximum            | 95    | 96.88 | 100   |
| Minimum            | 42.5  | 37.5  | 37.5  |
| Standard deviation | 14.41 | 16.65 | 20.66 |

**Table 2.** SUS results from LNEC researchers tests [13].

|                    | SUS   | Usab  | Learn |
|--------------------|-------|-------|-------|
| Medium             | 84.38 | 84.38 | 84.38 |
| Maximum            | 97.5  | 100   | 100   |
| Minimum            | 62.5  | 62.5  | 62.5  |
| Standard deviation | 15.19 | 15.73 | 15.73 |

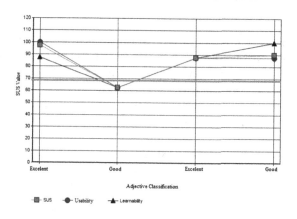

**Fig. 13.** SUS results from LNEC researchers tests [13]. (Color figure online)

## 7.1    Ericeira Rubble-Mound Breakwater Test Case

After the implementation of the functionality which resulted from the evaluation process, the updated system was re-tested during an inspection campaign of a real case scenario on April, 20th, 2017 in Ericeira, Portugal. The test case scenario is completely described in Capitão *et al.* [4].

Figure 14 shows the 4 sections (A, B, C and D, from the root to the head of breakwater) and a total of 17 observation points of the RMB of Ericeira used for the inspection campaign of April 20, 2017. The shown sections were uploaded into the system before the campaign, using a pre-defined shapefile. During the campaign, inspection data and recent photos and videos of observation points were uploaded *in situ*. Observation points are of utmost importance, as the periodically collected data is used to visually compare the damage occurred in each section between consecutive campaigns.

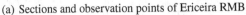

(a) Sections and observation points of Ericeira RMB          (b) Ericeira

**Fig. 14.** Ericeira testing case scenario.

Figure 15 shows examples of screen captures taken during the Ericeira campaign, with a mobile phone (iOS 10.3.1, using Safari browser). Figure 15(a) shows the setup of a new observation point (based on the user's current location, the red marker) in section A of the RMB. In Fig. 15(b), the user is accessing all photos and videos pertaining to section A of the RMB. Note that filenames include a "F" if they refer to the "front" of the RMB and "T" if they present the back, when referring to the direction of the photo.

During this campaign, all captured photos, recorded videos, and other data were successfully uploaded to the server, enabling later viewing on the system's webpage. The tool has clearly increased productivity and efficiency on these structures' periodic inspections.

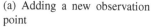

(a) Adding a new observation point

(b) Visualising all photos on section A of Ericeira RMB

**Fig. 15.** Mobile interface tested on the Ericeira 2017 inspection Campaign. (Color figure online)

## 8   Conclusions

The system presented in this paper is an online device responsive platform based on a WebGIS architecture, created to facilitate periodic visual inspections of coastal structures, carried out by LNEC officers. The system facilitates interaction, on desktop and mobile devices, with geographic representations of coastal structures and enables the collection of observational data, when located near a structure. From data collected by the user, such as the type of unit displacement, the state of the armour slope, the degradation of the materials, etc, the system computes the Present Condition of a part of the section of the structure. The user can further define new observation points for the structure, and associate photos or videos to this registered location. These photographic and video recordings, which are considered crucial in these evaluations, can be uploaded to the system during the on-site campaign, but this can also be performed at a later date from specific offline cameras. In any case, the recorded media can always be associated with geo-referenced observation points. The photos metadata is handled by the system and added to the images records, including latitude, longitude, altitude and orientation of capture, thus enabling association of the files to the retrieved locations. The platform handles and displays complete structures as sets of sections, each with several parts. Structural database data is associated with these representations. During periodic inspections, the structures may be analysed in place. Occurrences, such as unit displacements, fracture, and materials' degradation can be considered and dealt with. All these data are stored on the database and geographically associated with the corresponding location on the structure. The collected information is used to calculate the Present Condition of that part of the structure's section. The platform was evaluated by expert and non-expert users with satisfactory results and all the suggestions and requests were added to the platform. The updated system was further tested during a real scenario campaign. The system has been installed at LNEC for production use.

## 8.1    Future Work

As coastal structures largely differ, the authors are working on enabling the back-office configuration of the information viewed on the interface, which would enable LNEC officers to change and improve the structure of the database, as the need arises. Another improvement would be an offline version of the platform, which would enable on-site inspections without an Internet connection.

**Acknowledgements.** This work is partially supported by project NOVA LINCS Ref. UID/CEC/ 04516/2013.

# References

1. Allsop, N.W.H., Cork, R.S., Verhagen, H.J.: A database of major breakwaters around the world. In: Coasts, Marine Structures and Breakwaters 2009 Conference (2009)
2. Brooke, J.: SUS - a quick and dirty usability scale. In: Usability Evaluation in Industry. CRC Press, Reading, June 1996. https://www.crcpress.com/product/isbn/9780748404605
3. Brooke, J.: SUS: a retrospective. J. Usability Stud. **8**(2), 29–40 (2013). http://dl.acm.org/citation.cfm?id=2817912.2817913
4. Capitão, R., Maia, A., Lemos, R., Rodrigues, A., Fortes, C.J.: Towards a mobile monitoring tool for coastal structures inspection: the Ericeira rubble-mound breakwater test case. In: INGEO 2017, Lisbon (2017, submitted)
5. Fortes, C.J.E.M.: Infraestruturas portuárias de proteção. Instituto Politécnico de Leiria, Leiria, Portugal, June 2015
6. Franklin, W.R.: PNPOLY-point inclusion in polygon test (2006). https://wrf.ecse.rpi.edu/Research/Short_Notes/pnpoly.html
7. Lemos, R., Reis, M.T., Silva, L.G.: Observação Sistemática de Obras Marítimas. ANOSOM: Base de Dados de Comportamento de Estruturas. Manual do Utilizador. Relatório 318/02. Technical report, LNEC (2002)
8. Lemos, R., Santos, J.A.: Análise de Observação Sistemática de Obras Marítimas - ANOSOM. Base de dados de Inspecções de Quebra-mares de Taludes. Report 301/07 NPE (2007)
9. Lemos, R., Santos, J.A.: ANOSOM: Análise de Observação Sistemática de Obras Marítimas. 5as Jornadas de Engenharia Costeira e Portuária (2007)
10. Lewis, J.R., Sauro, J.: The factor structure of the system usability scale. In: Kurosu, M. (ed.) HCD 2009. LNCS, vol. 5619, pp. 94–103. Springer, Heidelberg (2009). https://doi.org/10.1007/978-3-642-02806-9_12

11. Li, R., et al.: Digitalization of coastal management and decision making supported by multi-dimensional geospatial information and analysis. In: Delcambre, L.M.L., Giuliano, G. (eds.) ACM International Conference Proceeding Series, vol. 89, pp. 219–220. Digital Government Research Center (2005). http://dblp.uni-trier.de/db/conf/dgo/dgo2005.html#LiBSNZVRZ05
12. Maia, A.: Plataforma para Análise de Estruturas Costeiras. M.Sc. thesis, Faculty of Science and Technolgy, Universidade NOVA de Lisboa (2016)
13. Maia, A., Rodrigues, A., Lemos, R., Capitao, R., Fortes, C.J.: A web platform for the systematic monitoring of coastal structures. In: Proceedings of 3rd International Conference on Geographical Information Systems Theory, Applications and Management - GISTAM 2017. INSTICC, Oporto, April 2017
14. Marujo, N.: Development of a system for life-cycle management of maritime works - SIMOM: the case of rubble-mound breakwaters. Ph.D. thesis, Instituto Superior Técnico, Universidade de Lisboa (2016)
15. Marujo, N., Valle, A., Caldeira, J., Teixeira, A., Araújo, M.: Gestão, monitorização e inspeção de obras marítimas. 8as Jornadas Portuguesas de Engenharia Costeira e Portuária (2013)
16. Oliveira, N., Lemos, R., Simões, J.P., Silva, L.G.: Benefícios associados à observação sistemática de obras marítimas em Portugal continental. In: 4as Jornadas Portuguesas de Engenharia Costeira e Portuária. LNEC, Lisboa, Portugal (2005)
17. Pires, A., Gomes, A., Chaminé, H.: Dynamics of coastal systems using GIS analysis and geomaterials evaluation for groins. Environ. Eng. Geosci. 15(4), 245–260 (2009)
18. Reis, M.T., Silva, L.G.: Observação Sistemática de Obras Marítimas. Manual de Utilização, Base de Dados ANOSOM. Technical report, LNEC, Lisboa, Portugal (1995)
19. Sabino, A., Rodrigues, A., Poseiro, P., Reis, M.T., Fortes, C.J.E.M., Reis, R.: Coastal risk forecast system. In: Grueau, C., Rocha, J.G. (eds.) First International Conference on Geographical Information Systems Theory, Applications and Management, pp. 201–209. INSTICC SciTePress - Science and Technology Publications, Barcelona, April 2015
20. Santos, J.A.: Monitoring of the coastal structures of Macao International Airport. Basic notions of maritime hydraulics. Report 114/00-NPP. Technical report, Portuguese National Laboratory for Civil Engineering, Lisbon, Portugal (2000)
21. Santos, J.A., Neves, M.G., Silva, L.G.: Rubble-mound breakwater inspection in Portugal. In: Melby, J.F. (ed.) Proceedings of Coastal Structures 2003, pp. 249–261. ASCE, Portland, August 2003
22. Sauro, J.: Measuring Usability with the System Usability Scale (SUS) (2011). http://www.measuringu.com/sus.php
23. USACE: CEM: Coastal Engineering Manual. U.S. Army Corps of Engineers (2006)

# Author Index

Printed in the United States
By Bookmasters